DATE DUE

DEMCO 38-297

Testing the Faith

Recent Titles in
Contributions in American Studies

Corporations and Society: Power and Responsibility
Warren J. Samuels and Arthur S. Miller, editors

Abortion, Politics, and the Courts: *Roe v. Wade* and Its Aftermath,
Revised Edition
Eva R. Rubin

The Secret Constitution and the Need for Constitutional Change
Arthur S. Miller

Business and Religion in the American 1920s
Rolf Lundén

Modular America: Cross-Cultural Perspectives
on the Emergence of an American Way
John G. Blair

The Social Christian Novel
Robert Glenn Wright

The Urbanists, 1865–1915
Dana F. White

In the Public Interest: The League of Women Voters, 1920–1970
Louise M. Young

The Rhetoric of War:
Training Day, the Militia, and the Military Sermon
Marie L. Ahearn

Restrained Response:
American Novels of the Cold War and Korea, 1945–1962
Arne Axelsson

In Search of America: Transatlantic Essays, 1951–1990
Marcus Cunliffe

Prophetic Pictures:
Nathaniel Hawthorne's Knowledge and Uses of the Visual Arts
Rita K. Gollin and John L. Idol, Jr.,
with the assistance of Sterling K. Eisiminger

Testing the Faith

The New Catholic Fiction in America

ANITA GANDOLFO

Contributions in American Studies, Number 100
Robert H. Walker, Series Editor

GREENWOOD PRESS
New York • Westport, Connecticut • London

Library of Congress Cataloging-in-Publication Data

Gandolfo, Anita.
   Testing the faith : the new Catholic fiction in America / Anita
Gandolfo.
      p.   cm.—(Contributions in American studies, 0084-9227 ; no.
100)
   Includes bibliographical references and index.
   ISBN 0-313-27843-1 (alk. paper)
   1. American fiction—Catholic authors—History and criticism.
2. American fiction—20th century—History and criticism.
3. Christian fiction, American—History and criticism. 4. Fiction—
Religious aspects—Christianity. 5. Catholic Church in literature.
6. Christianity and literature. 7. Theology in literature.
I. Title. II. Series.
PS153.C3G36   1992
813′.54099222—dc20   91-24836

British Library Cataloguing in Publication Data is available.

Library of Congress Catalog Card Number: 91-24836
ISBN: 0-313-27843-1
ISSN: 0084-9227

First published in 1992

Greenwood Press, 88 Post Road West, Westport, CT 06881
An imprint of Greenwood Publishing Group, Inc.

Printed in the United States of America

The paper used in this book complies with the
Permanent Paper Standard issued by the National
Information Standards Organization (Z39.48-1984).

10 9 8 7 6 5 4 3 2 1

Art lives upon discussion, upon experiment, upon curiosity, upon variety of attempt, upon the exchange of views and the comparison of standpoint.

Henry James
"The Art of Fiction"

Conflict is our actuality. Conversation is our hope.

David Tracy
The Analogical Imagination

May God us keep
From Single vision & Newton's sleep!

William Blake
Letter to Thomas Butts (22 November 1802)

Contents

Preface		xi
1.	Faith and Imagination	1
2.	Visions of Experience	27
3.	Visions of Passionate Intensity	47
4.	Visions of Innocence Restored?	71
5.	Visions of Reconciliation	95
6.	Alternative Visions	119
7.	Visions of Individualism	141
8.	Prophetic Vision: The Spiritual Quest	161
9.	Prophetic Vision: As We Are Now	189
10.	Conclusion: Vision of a Changing Church	205
Bibliography		213
Index		219

Preface

A very spirited conversation is going on these days among Americans of Catholic descent that may presage the future of the Church as much as anything happening in Rome.

Peter Occhiogrosso
Once A Catholic (1987)

When the Second Vatican Council officially ended in 1965, a new era began in Catholicism. After an initial period of adjustment for renewal, the Church entered a more lengthy time of transition, and, as Peter Occhiogrosso indicates, the "future of the Church" is still being debated. What began as renewal is now identified by historians and theologians as a major paradigm shift, a process of change more complex than was imagined little more than a quarter of a century ago when Pope John XXIII expressed a desire to "open the windows" of the Church. In this new age of Catholicism, it is not surprising that a new Catholic fiction has emerged, fiction that is central to the "very spirited conversation" to which Occhiogrosso alludes. That fiction is the subject of this book.

I hesitate to describe this as a study of "the Catholic novel," for that term has long been used to designate a tradition of subliterary parochial publication. As I explain in my first chapter, the classic "Catholic novel" in the United States is a product of the preconciliar Church, which measured the worth of fiction by its literary fidelity to doctrine and dogma and its value as an evangelizing force. Such prose was, ironically, inimical to the genre known as the novel, a form of fiction that emerged from the individualistic reorientation of the Enlightenment. Developing as a representation of a new way of seeing the world, the novel has at its core the depiction of human experience in a pluralistic society. Its form is inherently dialogic, designed to inspire conversation rather than promote rule and law. Thus, it is the ideal literary form for the very spirited conversation characteristic of contemporary Catholic experience.

The fiction in this study is "Catholic" neither because of its fidelity to Church teaching and promotion of institutional values nor because of the religious affiliation of the authors—indeed I ignore the biographical except when the writers themselves have publicly discussed the relationship between life and fiction. This fiction is Catholic insofar as it is informed by a concern for the experience of being a Catholic in the United States. It is clearly a part of that very spirited conversation, Occhiogrosso refers to, and its importance to the Church is often overlooked.

Ironically, despite the demise of the traditional Catholic novel that promoted institutional values, the Catholic experience as a subject for fiction has been increasingly evident in American literature since the Council ended. The experience of Catholicism has been fictionalized by a variety of authors whose sole commonality seems to be a shared tradition that is making claims on their consciousness. Life and art are inextricably joined, and literature reflects the culture in which it is formed. This fiction of Catholic experience is a vital part of the Catholic culture in the United States, and it informs that culture in a way that is not otherwise available. However, this phenomenon of a concern for things Catholic in the American novel has received scant critical attention.

The notorious subliterary quality of the proselytizing prose of the past tends to make literary scholars wary of this significant development. Another problem in addressing Catholic fiction from the literary perspective is the ubiquitous presence of one prolific writer of popular novels and assorted nonfiction. His frequent pronouncements on all aspects of religious life and fiction, combined with his status as a Roman Catholic priest, give him a prominence that suggests this new Catholic fiction remains mired in the tradition of subliterary prose.

But the work of Andrew Greeley is undeniably significant in this study. Contemporary fiction of the Catholic experience is expressive of the unique situation in American Catholicism at this particular historical moment and, while certainly a literary phenomenon, its importance transcends the aesthetic value of individual works. Literary historians would point out that the distinction of Harriet Beecher Stowe's *Uncle Tom's Cabin* is not its aesthetic merit but the fact that it imaged the evils of slavery for white Americans who had no experiential knowledge of that reality, and thus this enormously popular novel aided the cause of emancipation far more than the efforts of antislavery orators relying on fact and rational discourse. Similarly, American fiction of Catholic experience images U.S. Catholicism in a way not otherwise available.

This fiction documents a significant cultural shift among Catholics in the United States, serving as a barometer of that shift, an expression of practical consciousness that is a *sensus fidelium*, as it were. It is from the variety of visions that patterns emerge, and these visions provide the organizing principle of this study. By "vision" I refer to the perspective that informs the text, and, as the citation from William Blake which serves as an epigraph to this study indicates, it is from multiplicity of vision that truth emerges.

Preconciliar Catholicism offered its members a comprehensive philosophical and theological system that informed every aspect of human life. In the United States, Catholicism evolved in a particular social context, a way of life that supplied a social identity as well as a religious affiliation. Thus, I use the term "culture" as a "whole way of life" in referring to Catholicism in the United States. The clear convergence of social and religious factors in this literature impelled me to limit this study to the fiction of the United States. In doing so, I have referred to literature from other countries only tangentially insofar as it illuminates the situation in this country.

My purpose is to highlight the current cultural moment in Catholicism by examining imaginative texts that are important documents of that moment. In seeking to illuminate the patterns of vision in this fiction, I am neither suggesting closure with regard to interpretation of individual texts nor attempting to confer some literary imprimatur. I intend to establish a context for conversation.

The first chapter provides the historical and literary context for this fiction. Subsequent chapters will discuss fiction according to the patterns of vision that emerged from my readings of the texts. Obviously any attempt to identify meaning in a literary text should never be understood as a restriction of that text but as the exploration of meaning within a larger context of other meanings. Nor should one author's vision or one pattern of vision be understood *the* vision for Catholicism. Literature reflects and, ideally, illuminates life for its readers. This fiction is not primarily concerned with pragmatic solutions to ecclesial problems. However, by allowing the literature to illuminate his or her understanding, the reader may be better able to deal with pragmatic concerns.

This book explores the imaginative representations offered by contemporary fiction of the Catholic experience and helps in that process of transmission by which an author's vision is made clear. As a member of the audience addressed by these writers, I am aware that my own limitations will condition this text, and I have tried to compensate for those of which I am aware.

I am indebted to West Virginia University for a sabbatical leave that permitted me to develop this study as a Research Fellow of the Cushwa Center for the Study of American Catholicism at the University of Notre Dame. At Notre Dame, I benefited from the enthusiastic support of the Cushwa Center's Director, Jay Dolan, the Center's staff, and the Notre Dame community, all of whom were exceptionally kind and encouraging. My work was supported at West Virginia University by a Faculty Development Grant, and I received support and encouragement from the Dean of the College of Arts and Sciences, Gerald E. Lang. This work, however, would never have been begun without the encouragement of the English Department Chair, Rudolph P. Almasy, who has been unfailingly supportive of this project since its inception.

I also benefited from the perceptive and encouraging comments of Alden V. Brown and Eugene Lauer, who read early versions of the manuscript, and the enthusiasm of my colleagues Gail and Tim Adams. Jeanette Conner provided editorial assistance for which I am most appreciative. I am especially grateful to my colleague Sandra Woods, who endured my extroversion and listened patiently to endless monologues about Catholicism and its fiction as I grappled with this text. Finally, and perhaps most importantly, I am indebted to all those who taught me about literature, and I dedicate this book to my former teachers Vineta Colby and Robert A. Day.

1

Faith and Imagination

The heart has its reasons of which reason knows nothing.

Pascal

"It was 1968, and I hadn't been paying a bit of attention." Thus speaks the narrator in the opening line of "Before Sewing One Must Cut," a short story by Jeanne Schinto in which the dominant metaphor used to depict an adolescent female's loss of innocence is her relationship to the Catholic Church.[1] Schinto's narrative parallels the effect of the death of the girl's father with the dissolution of American Catholic culture, a significant parallel we shall see in contemporary fiction throughout this study. "I was fifteen years old," announces the narrator in the second line of the story. But whether fifteen or fifty, many Catholics in the United States shared this perception in 1968; while we "hadn't been paying a bit of attention," the world of American Catholicism changed.

Schinto's story is one document of that change, and it is part of a wide range of fiction reflecting the Roman Catholic experience in the United States during the past twenty-five years. All fiction is a product of a particular cultural moment, but this literature is so profoundly influenced by significant changes within the Roman Catholic culture of the United States that critical study must include an examination of those changes.

DAYS OF INNOCENCE

The Catholic Church in the United States during the first half of the twentieth century was still an Immigrant Church, but one that had hitched its wagon to the American dream of prosperity and progress. The monolithic structure of Catholicism, its ties to a foreign power, and the aura of mystery in its worship had made Catholics suspect members of American society (the whore of Babylon seducing the American Adam, as William Halsey succinctly expresses it[2]). But the Irish Jansenist strain that dominated the American Catholic Church actually blended quite nicely with the Calvinist ethic that had guided the United States from colonial times. So the turn of the century found Catholics allied with what intellectual historians term "American innocence," a structure of values in the American culture that corresponded closely with the dominant Roman Catholic *weltanschauung*: belief in a rational cosmos and an objective moral order in nature, confidence in progress, and a preference for didacticism in art forms, especially in literature.[3]

However, the experience of an increasingly complex world and a fragmented culture called nineteenth-century certainties into question, and innocence could not survive long in mainstream America.[4] Within the Catholic culture, though, innocence survived longer than in most other groups of its size in the United States. Supported by a comprehensive system of belief that answered all human questions about the ultimate ends of life, fueled by the energy of a generation determined to succeed in the "new world," and guided by a centralized system of authority unmatched in the modern world in its absoluteness, the American Catholic culture succeeded in preserving its intellectual innocence through the first half of the twentieth century. Despite two World Wars and a major economic Depression, Catholics were able to maintain a sense of optimism and high purpose.

The "rules of the game" were clear. One novelist has described the Catholic world view, as, in fact, not dissimilar to a board game:

Up there was Heaven; down there was Hell. The name of the game was Salvation, the object to get to Heaven and avoid Hell. It was like Snakes and Ladders: sin sent you plummeting down towards the Pit; the sacraments, good deeds, acts of self-mortification, enabled you to climb back toward the light. Everything you did or thought was subject to spiritual accounting. It was either good, bad or indifferent. Those who succeeded in the game eliminated the bad and converted as much of the indifferent as possible into the good.[5]

This analogy is not meant to trivialize a coherent and consistent ethic that satisfactorily guided Catholics for a very long time but to emphasize the simplicity and comprehensiveness of a system of belief and behavior that was inculcated at a very early age. In the United States, the Baltimore Catechism (1884) was the standard rulebook for the Catholic game of Snakes and Ladders, an infallible guide for all questions of ultimate concern. Catholic teaching made it eminently clear that "God was in his heaven and man was in possession of the road map to eternity."[6]

It is hard to overstate the effect of such blithe certitude on a generation of American Catholics who were for the most part undereducated and struggling to "make it" in this land of opportunity. In the spirit of progress, the Immigrant Church of the 1930's and 40's valued pragmatic mission work and church building over intellectualism, and energy was concentrated on the rapidly expanding physical and social structures of the Church. Directed by its hierarchical, often authoritarian, leadership, the American Catholic Church built impressive physical structures and developed its extensive school system rapidly and efficiently. Other Americans may have been struggling with questions about the meaning of life, but within the American Catholic community all such questions were obviated and "innocence was preserved; reality was mapped; the way to salvation was paved, if not with gold, then at least with reinforced concrete."[7]

Catholic optimism and accomplishment during this era eventually seduced the American imagination. Fantasy can both alleviate the suffering of the present and reinforce cultural values that are being eroded. The image of American Catholicism in film during the 1940's reflects the country's infatuation with the fantasy of innocence Catholicism projected. Bing Crosby portrayed Father Chuck O'Malley in *Going My Way* and *The Bells of St. Mary's*, films whose popularity testified to the country's adulation of American Catholic innocence. The central plots of both movies reflected the Church's major investment in buildings during this period. Father O'Malley saves both a church and a parochial school from foreclosure (indeed manages to not simply save the school but to build a new one). And both movies present the Church as able to deal with the perennial concern of every society—its youth. For in addition to his able financial management, Father O'Malley effortlessly transforms a group of potential delinquents into choirboys and charms brash young females into docile womanhood. Fantasy perhaps, but successful fantasy that fulfilled the hopes and dreams of Americans, Catholics and non-Catholics alike, in a world troubled by war and a changing society. It was a fantasy of a "Mother Church" who supplied all the answers and was a safe haven from the social and political tensions of human existence. Father O'Malley was the priest of the popular imagination for America.[8]

This idealization of Catholicism in America through film is satirized by J. F. Powers in his short story "The Presence of Grace" when a rather dim young woman named Velma meets a priest at a dinner party. After a brief conversation during which Velma tries to angle for a date, the priest ironically remarks, "I take it you're not a Catholic," to which Velma replies, "Oh, no, but I see all your movies."[9] The book of short stories in which this incident occurs was published in 1956, a decade of arrival for Catholicism in American culture.

Catholicism's seduction of American society is also illustrated by the enormous popularity of Fulton J. Sheen in the 1950's with his aptly titled television program, "Life is Worth Living." That Bishop Sheen was able to overcome Protestant repugnance for the full ecclesiastical regalia in which he conducted his weekly program is an indication of American hunger for his Catholic message of security and hope. The success of the 1950's for American Catholicism was capped by the election of the first Catholic as President of the United States in 1960. And in 1963, Powers, a writer whose fiction is typically located in Roman Catholic rectories, won the National Book Award for *Morte D'Urban*, his first novel.

Ironically, as has been frequently observed, at the very moment when American Catholics had clearly "made it" in American society, the Church seemed to self-destruct.[10] So intense were those years of innocence, so tightly organized was the American Catholic culture, that few people recognized the dark side to all that prosperity, a dark side implicit in the assumptions underlying that very attractive and seemingly satisfying Catholic system.

THE CLASSICAL PARADIGM

For innocence to survive in the United States, Catholicism had to entrench itself against chance, and resistance to change was the heritage from the First Vatican Council in 1870. The Church met the nineteenth-century's crisis of faith by bolstering centralized authority. The doctrine of Papal infallibility not only affirmed the authority of the Bishop of Rome but it recreated the "Great Chain of Being" (that coherent concept of order and purpose that sustained Western thinking prior to the Enlightenment) as a "Great Chain of Ecclesiastical Hierarchy." Just as the hierarchical Great Chain of Being had ordered all existence and provided a coherent explanation of reality, Catholicism's allegiance to medieval Scholastic philosophy, combined with Vatican I's reiteration of the importance of authority, created a similar coherent chain for American Catholics. The Baltimore Catechism's succinct summaries of all issues of faith and morals, supplemented by the authority of Pope and Bishop which was conveyed to the average Catholic through the opinions and decisions of the local pastor, effectively preserved U.S. Catholics in an enclave of intellectual innocence.

The strong authority of pastors and Bishops resulting from the First Vatican Council was especially significant in American Catholicism, facilitating the formation of a unified Church from among the various nationalities that immigrated to the United States in the late nineteenth and early twentieth centuries. Any culture predicated on strong authority will foster submission and docility among its people, so Catholicism came to be described in relation to its various strictures. Catholics spoke of a Sunday Mass *obligation*, observed the *laws* of fast and abstinence, and annually made their Easter *duty*. Like the Great Chain of Being, the Great Chain of Hierarchy was maintained through a clearly defined system of rules and obligations.

Catholics talked less about faith than about The Faith, that body of dogma and doctrine, allegiance to which would guarantee salvation. This reflected the classical paradigm of a fixed and static reality in which Catholicism had remained when the rest of Western civilization responded to a more modern paradigm informed by the Renaissance, the Enlightenment, and the Age of Romanticism.

It is important to note the specialized meaning of the term paradigm as developed by Thomas Kuhn in his landmark study *The Structure of Scientific Revolutions* (1970). Kuhn's work has become especially helpful to historians and theologians in the post-Vatican II Church because, as Kuhn himself notes, his concept of paradigm shift is as applicable to social change as to change in science. When he uses the term paradigm, it stands for "the entire constellation of beliefs, values, techniques, and so on shared by members of a given community."[11] The culture of American Catholicism, as it existed during the first six decades of the twentieth century, is a clearly identifiable paradigm, but its lineaments correspond most closely to the premodern (i.e., pre-Enlightenment) paradigm of Western society. According to Kuhn's analysis, a new paradigm develops after a crisis with the older paradigm, a crisis that is significant as an indication that "an occasion for retooling has arrived."[12]

In the 1950's there was a slight tremor in American Catholicism, which seemed to indicate that such a crisis might be imminent. The social movements of the 50's reflected the increasing distance between the world of Snakes and Ladders and the world of human experience in which its members actually lived their lives. But there was insufficient unrest to actually identify the central problem as the fact that Catholics were living in the modern world according to a religion located in a premodern paradigm. The seismic indicators of the 1950's gave little warning of the cataclysm that was to follow.

Social historians term the 50's a period of "anti-ghettoism,"[13] or, as Wilfred Sheed characterizes it, a time of "finding new ways to be a Catholic."[14] Following World War II, the upward mobility of the second generation of immigrants and the increased opportunities for education in American society resulted in a more economically secure and better educated Catholic population. Many lay Catholics began to look for outlets for their faith experience beyond the confines of the typical parish where religious privatism was still the norm, and significant social movements prospered in postwar America.

The Catholic Worker movement, begun in the 1930's but in decline during the war years because of its radical pacifist stance, experienced a renewal in the 1950's, becoming a focus for the Catholic peace movement.[15] Friendship House, an urban ministry among the poor, also prospered as did the Grail, with its goal of converting the world from secularism to Christian humanism. Other social movements, the Young Christian Students (YCS), the Young Christian Workers (YCW), and the Christian Family Movement (CFM) were also led by the now more socially conscious, economically secure, and better educated American Catholic laity.

It is important to note that none of these movements reflected any dissatisfaction with official Catholic teaching. All the groups stressed loyalty to the Church and promoted the personal spiritual development of their members as well as social consciousness. Clergy involvement in an advisory capacity insured adherence to orthodoxy. But it is equally important to note that these were movements led by the laity and were outside the local parish structure. They represented an impulse to bridge the gap between Church and world and served as indicators of the deficiency in Catholicism's premodern paradigm.

This social action was complemented by an interest in the intellectual life—or the absence of the intellectual life—among Catholics. The Catholic publishing firm of Sheed & Ward, imported to America at the beginning of World War II, had brought with it the lively Catholic intellectual life of England and France, which Frank Sheed disseminated to American Catholics as he toured parishes and schools to prepare a readership for his product.[16] He found a striking absence of intellectual activity among Catholics in the United States, a development resulting from the Church's origins among immigrants and its resulting clericalism. To Sheed, "the land of the free was predominantly the land of Sister Says—except, of course, for Sister, for whom it was the land of Father Says."[17]

In a 1955 essay, the historian John Tracy Ellis criticized the lack of intellectual life among American Catholics and sought to account for this failing. Among his criticisms was the complaint of eschatological bias in theology and an overemphasis on morality in Catholic religious education.[18] Ellis' criticisms point to the negative effects of the premodern paradigm in Catholic education. When relationship with Transcendence is viewed as a static reality, the lineaments of which can be codified, religion is reduced to obedience to laws and precepts and becomes increasingly separated from human experience. We keep the laws not to be better persons in this world but to guarantee our place in the next, hence the "eschatological bias" and "overemphasis on morality."

In spite of the social movements of the 1950's, at the end of that decade privatism still predominated and triumphed as the essential form of the American Catholic experience; the game of "Snakes and Ladders" was as prevalent as ever.[19] As Max Weber pointed out in his classic study of the sociology of religion, any form of worship that limits the individual to a spectator role (as in the Tridentine Mass) inspires a strong personal piety, and one of the hallmarks of the Immigrant Church in the United States was the strong devotional life among its members, a devotional life that represented an entire religious heritage.[20]

DEVOTIONAL CATHOLICISM

Members of the Immigrant Church in the United States sustained their faith by developing a rich devotional life centered on the Mass and the sacraments but embroidered with an array of public devotions and private observances—from Benediction of the Blessed Sacrament, Forty Hours, May crownings, and weekly novenas through "making" the nine First Fridays, consecrating the home to the Sacred Heart, and seeking the intercession of a particular saint. This devotional life was, as Dolan has pointed out, "the popular working theology of both priests and people."[21] It was also an outlet for the more aesthetic, nonrational side of human nature that was marginalized by the official rational and legalistic theology derived from Scholasticism and central to the premodern paradigm that Catholicism preserved.

A strong Catholic culture developed that was a vital part of Catholic identity in the United States. It was, in fact, essential to the sense of belonging and self-identification of many Catholics who were second- and third-generation Americans. Wishing to be assimilated into American society, they sacrificed the foreign language and culture of their immigrant ancestors, and, as Will Herberg commented in 1960, "Religious association now became the primary context for self-identification and social location for the third generation, as well as for the second generation, of America's immigrants."[22] Thus one contemporary writer, relating the experience of growing up Catholic in New York City in the 40's and 50's, mentions neither social action nor profound ideas but the memory of the ordinary details of Catholic parish life:

> I was an altar boy aware of the incense, benediction, surplices, novenas, plenary indulgences, confessions on Saturday afternoon and Monsignor Scully's sermon at the nine o'clock Mass on Sunday morning about holy mother church and the pain of eternal damnation.[23]

The title of this essay, " 'Wonder Years' as Metaphor of Lost Innocence" refers less to the contemporary television show, which provides the specific occasion for reflection, than to the decades preceding 1960 that serve as the embodiment of innocence for American Catholics. Given the fact that most Catholics lived their faith through ritual and popular devotions, it is hardly surprising that the most vociferous complaints about Vatican II stem from liturgical changes mandated by the Council. This nostalgia for a lost culture is a prevailing theme among Catholics today, and it is often (and erroneously) dismissed as a reactionary response to change.

Such a dismissal fails to appreciate the fact that formative experiences have a primacy in our lives and that for most Catholics who grew to adulthood in the 40's and 50's the various pious practices of Catholic culture are an indelible part of their personal heritage. As Herberg's analysis makes clear, ritual and devotions supplied an important psychological and sociological need for Catholics in American society. Thus, the purification of the liturgy, rationally intended as a renewal, was, as evidence indicates, a dislocation for most Catholics to whom the liturgy is never a rational experience. As the novelist Mary Gordon has commented,

> Whatever religious instincts I have bring their messages to me through the senses—the images of my religious life, its sounds, its odors, the kind of kinesthetic sense I have of prayerfulness. These are much more important to me than anything that takes place in the life of the mind.[24]

At the end of the 1950's there was a new Pope, one who would begin the process of change. But the indications were that while there might be a few individuals with the ability to perceive the Church's situation in the modern world, the institution had so effectively marginalized the imaginative that the attempt at change would produce a crisis in Catholicism.

IMAGINATION IN THE CLASSICAL PARADIGM

The marginalization of imagination is another aspect of the premodern paradigm, and understanding the ramifications of this is essential to an appreciation of the difficulties ushered in with Vatican II. The concept of imagination is overlaid with centuries of pejorative associations and must be explored in some detail before its importance to the present discussion can be fully appreciated.

One measure of this problem is illustrated in James Fowler's 1981 study of human development and the search for meaning, *Stages of Faith*. His important fourth chapter, "Faith and Imagination" begins on page twenty-four, but only after six pages of explanation does Fowler remark, "By now I hope it is clear that imagination is not to be equated with fantasy or make-believe. Rather, imagination is a powerful force underlying all knowing."[25] Fowler is speaking of imagination from a particular historical vantage point, one that is central to an understanding of the difficulties Catholicism experienced in attempting renewal in the 1960's.

In the history of Western thought, the human ability to "image" or "imagine" something has been understood according to two aspects: (1) as a representational or mimetic faculty that *mirrors* some reality, or (2) as a creative faculty that *illuminates* reality through the production of original images. The history of the concept of imagination is, interestingly, paradigmatic; that is, although both aspects of imagination have always been known, each paradigm privileges some metaphor that characterizes its primary understanding of imagination.[26] Hence, imagination is expressed as both a mirror (the premodern metaphor that emphasizes its mimetic aspect) and a lamp (the modern metaphor that privileges its illuminative power). What is especially significant is the fact that the premodern concept of imagination, which developed from both the Bible and Greek thought, significantly marginalized imagination, and that is the concept of the imaginative which informed Catholicism until the 1960's.

In the classical paradigm, the simple mimetic aspect of imagination (comparable to "fantasy" or "daydreaming") is emphasized because the creative faculty has a distinct ethical dimension. In fact, there is a strong association with the creative aspect of imagination and the Original Sin in

Genesis. The Hebrew word for imagination, *yetser*, derives from the same root as creator, creation, and the verb "to create."[27] Hence, the serpent's temptation in Genesis 3:5, "as soon as you eat this fruit your eyes shall be open and you shall be like gods knowing good and evil," is an assurance that the human pair can share the creative powers of the deity by tapping into their latent imaginative faculty. (All citations from Scripture are taken from The New American Bible [1970] with the Revised New Testament [1986].)

Hence, in Judaic thought, *yetser* is associated with the story of the Fall. Eve imagines that she and Adam can be like gods, and chooses to eat the forbidden fruit. With the Genesis tale as a model, the human imagination's dark side was emphasized. It can enhance the desirability of choices that are essentially evil. Imagination was thus conceived as a faculty in need of a strong governor, and Hellenic thought emphasized that governor in privileging human reason.

For Plato, knowledge is bifurcated into the faculties of reason and imagination. However, only reason provides direct access to the transcendental world of Ideas, the Platonic ultimate reality. The capacity to image things simply provides a copy of real things, which are themselves only copies of Ideas. Imagination, then, is a weak faculty for Plato, a faculty that is principally mimetic. And in spite of the fact that Aristotle does not share Plato's idealist epistemology, he similarly views imagination as a reproductive, rather than productive, faculty and insists on its subordination to reason.

The medieval view of imagination derived both from the Bible and Hellenic thought is doubly negative. Associated with the Fall, imagination is envisioned as an ethical disorder, a faculty that can lead the human person astray. And from the metaphysical perspective of Plato and Aristotle, imagination is of lesser importance epistemologically; it must always be subordinate to the faculty of reason in the human person. Hence Scholastic philosophy, drawing on this dual heritage, privileged reason and marginalized imagination. This premodern view of imagination existed until the paradigm shift into modern thinking.

The creative power of imagination was officially reclaimed with Kant's *Critique of Pure Reason* in 1781. Rescuing imagination from its subservient role as the handmaiden of reason, Kant identified imagination as a vital way of knowing, a power of synthesis without which our knowledge would have no coherence. The rehabilitation of imagination would be the great work of Romanticism, and in the modern paradigm the locus of meaning for the concept of imagination remains the famous passage that begins Chapter XIII of Samuel Taylor Coleridge's *Biographia Literaria*

(1817) in which the poet claims primacy for the creative power of the imaginative faculty, carefully distinguishing it from its related but lesser mimetic faculty he terms "fancy." To emphasize the creative imagination's synthesizing power, Coleridge coined the word "esemplastic," meaning "molding into unity."

However, the rehabilitation of imagination as an important faculty of knowing was a part of the secularizing of values and thought inherent in the shift to the modern paradigm, so the Biblical heritage, which associated the power of human imagination with sin, continued to exert a claim. This underlying fear of the dangers of the imagination is expressed most vividly in Mary Shelley's *Frankenstein* (1818), a text that reifies the potential evil of the human imagination.

Victor Frankenstein's imagination inspires his decision to reanimate a human corpse, as is clear from his thoughts following the discovery of the ability to animate lifeless matter:

> I doubted at first whether I should attempt the creation of a being like myself, or one of simpler organization; but my imagination was too much exalted by my first success to permit me to doubt of my ability to give life to an animal as complex and wonderful as man.[28]

His relation to Eve is apparent as his imagination continues to consider this feat:

> Life and death appeared to me ideal bounds, which I should first break through and pour a torrent of light into our dark world. A new species would bless me as its creator and source; many happy and excellent natures would owe their being to me. (pp. 38–39)

In the imagery of bringing light into darkness combined with the scientist's image of himself as a creator of life, Shelley unmistakably associates Frankenstein's actions with the original sin of Eve who imagined it possible to challenge the Divine. And, as in Genesis, the act unleashes chaos.

Frankenstein also indicates another reason for the continued marginalization of imagination even within the modern paradigm. The rise of modern science and subsequent rapid industrialization in the nineteenth and early twentieth centuries privileged technology and the objective science that was considered its basis. Imagination, championed by Romantic poets and artists, became associated solely with the aesthetic sphere. At the popular level, the imaginative came to be associated with "that which is not actually true," as in the word imaginary, and the use of imagination was relegated to the notion of daydreaming and other forms of fantasy.

In the twentieth century, the rehabilitation of imagination began with phenomenology and its assertion that the deepest level of meaning is how something is perceived in one's consciousness. As the notion of purely objective science has waned in the second half of the twentieth century, imagination has been restored to its rightful partnership with reason as an important way of knowing. This new attitude toward imagination is reflected in *The Structure of Scientific Resolutions*, as Kuhn points out that in paradigm shift, the new paradigm is identified not through the faculty of reason but through the power of human imagination.[29]

However, so deeply entrenched is the connotation of imagination as something trivial that in his seminal work *Stages of Faith*, James Fowler spends six pages preparing his readers for a definition of faith that identifies it with the use of imagination. Ironically, he is impelled to clarify the nature of imagination—despite the fact that the classic definition of faith in the Epistle to the Hebrews identifies it with the human capacity for imaging: "Faith is the revelation of what is hoped for and evidence of things not seen" (11:1).

During the past twenty years, theologians and religious writers have balanced our understanding of faith by returning imagination to its rightful position as a central aspect of the human faith experience, but before we turn to that phenomenon, it is important to note the effects of that marginalization of imagination on the way in which Catholicism entered the modern world.

CRISIS IN CATHOLICISM

While the Second Vatican Council was still in progress, Flannery O'Connor, with the acumen possible to the creative artist who did not abandon the imaginative, pointed out that "in the last four or five centuries we in the Church have over-emphasized the abstract and consequently impoverished our imagination and our capacity for prophetic insight."[30] This impoverishment left Catholic theologians unaware of the sociological and psychological impact of the changes in worship decreed by the Council. For it is the American Catholic response to liturgical change that most fully illustrates the nature of the crisis precipitated by the Council.

In measuring the impact of Vatican II on American Catholicism, it is important to keep in mind that when John XXIII summoned the Council that would meet from 1960 to 1965, Americans were not clamoring for change in their Church.[31] At the time the Council began, Catholics in the United States were enjoying the fruits of their efforts to join the American mainstream. During the previous half century they had developed an impressive physical Church that had succeeded in becoming an important part of American culture, and their cohesive and coherent philosophic system made them a beacon of hope in that culture. They were now at the pinnacle of success in America, success symbolized by the election of the first Catholic President of the United States in 1960.

The Second Vatican Council radically disrupted that security. As the Council which espoused collegiality mandated change autocratically, and the various practices that had been so cherished in their culture disappeared, American Catholics experienced the disintegration of an entire mode of expressing their faith. Ironically, because there were no major changes at the intellectual level of reformulation of doctrine or official teaching, the revisions of Vatican II, viewed from the limited perspective of reason alone, seemed innocuous. But the Catholic parish does not function solely at the intellectual level (indeed hardly at all) but in the pious experience of liturgical practices, the level at which there were the most radical disruptions. Liturgy is primarily a work of imagination. As Joseph Campbell explained in an interview with Eugene Kennedy,

It [liturgical renewal] was an effort to make ancient symbols and rituals more rational. And they threw out the Gregorian chant and other great symbolic achievements in the process; they disowned religious symbols that spoke directly to people without need of mediation. The old ritual of the mass spoke powerfully to people. Now the celebrant carries out a Julia Child sort of function at the altar.[32]

The widespread dissatisfaction with liturgical renewal in America among the laity was not caused by any rational preference for the Latin liturgy, but by a preference for a way of worship that had become meaningful to generations. Liturgy was:

the framework in which they [the laity] were accustomed to think of all things supernatural, the link in memory with exposure to spiritual things, with earlier aspirations; the holiday rite contained in every Holy Day and Sabbath, burial and marriage, Christmas and Easter.[33]

Logically, one would naturally assume that liturgy in the vernacular would be more understandable. But language functions differently in liturgy than in rational discourse:

> Even the Catholic who did not understand Latin was reading here a "language" both personal and shared—each rite or phrase meant what it suggested from repeated hearings in different places, different times, even different *selves* (drawing them back together into one self).[34]

Moreover, the renewal of liturgical life had profound sociological implications. Mass is the center of Catholic worship and was a focal point for dissatisfaction, but the renewal of Vatican II, limited by a reliance on reason that had marginalized the cultural expression of religion, eliminated a variety of activities that were part of American Catholics' self-expression in their pluralistic society, practices that had become an integral part of their religious identity. It is true that no doctrines were changed, but, as the sociologist Andrew Greeley has pointed out, the various practices of Catholicism, its "religious style," as it were, were products of the religious imagination that produced meaning for people in the irrational, inchoate ways by which religion is experienced.[35]

So although "fish on Friday" was a practice that was compulsively observed, for most Catholics in the United States it was also a way of reinforcing their identity in a land where they were the minority. The fact that Catholics had "made it" in the United States could be seen from the newspaper supermarket ads that proclaimed specials on fish for Fridays and during Lent. Thus, on first Sunday in Advent, 1966, when Catholics were told they could now choose whether or not to abstain from meat on Fridays, American Catholics did not wholeheartedly welcome this un-sought permission. It was just one of a host of changes that were taking their culture from them. Purging the calendar of saints of its legendary accretions was an eminently reasonable decision, but in the United States where St. Christopher graced every Catholic's dashboard, the saint's equivocal status was extremely disconcerting.

Change inaugurated crisis and, unfortunately, American Catholics, raised in an era of authoritarian apologetics, were ill-prepared for this crisis.[36] The lack of intellectual life that John Tracy Ellis had pointed out in 1955 also contributed to the confusion, There was no effective leadership at a moment in time when leadership was so badly needed. The pastors, formed in a Church that defined their role in terms of administration of the physical plant and the maintenance of orthodoxy among their flocks, could not hope to either understand or effectively deal with the myriad unconscious forces that were at work among the people—or within themselves.

The change in ritual, totally appropriate to a unified worldview that sees the supernatural participating in the natural world, was absolutely mind-boggling to people who were raised and educated with supernaturalistic frame of reference that neatly separated the two realms. In addition, at a time when religious affiliation was a central factor in self-identification, the Church inadvertently caused a crisis among its members—principally because of its failure to appreciate the significance of its rational decisions. The lack of "prophetic insight" that O'Connor spoke of was a direct consequence of the marginalization of the imagination.

Fowler's *Stages of Faith*, grounded in an appreciation of the importance of imagination in faith life, offers insight into the reason why American Catholics continue to obsess about the disruptions of Vatican II. The key is in what Fowler identifies as Stage 3 and Stage 4 in faith development. In Stage 3, which Fowler identifies as conventional faith, an individual's faith can synthesize values and information and provide a basis for identity. However, it is a conformist stage in which the individual is attuned to the expectations and judgments of significant others and does not have the confidence to rely on autonomous judgment to construct and maintain an independent perspective.[37] Obviously, this stage of faith development would be fostered by a hierarchical, authoritarian Church, and those with a Stage 3 faith life would be comfortable in the preconciliar Catholic Church.

The development of a Stage 4 faith, however, shifts the locus of ultimate authority from others to the self. For Fowler, Stage 4 represents a person-ally appropriated faith in which the individual has reflected on and chosen the values and responsibilities inherent in the explicit system to which he or she may give credence.[38] Interestingly, Fowler, in describing the factors that would contribute to a breakdown of Stage 3 and a readiness for the transition to Stage 4, mentions the significance of "marked changes, by officially sanctioned leaders, or policies or practices previously deemed sacred and unbreachable," and he uses as an illustration "the Catholic church changing the mass from Latin to the vernacular, or no longer requiring abstinence from meat on Friday."[39]

However, Fowler warns that if the individual in Stage 3 has become dependent on strong authority, that person's ability to develop autonomy may be impaired, especially in areas the person considers sacred. Thus, the post-Vatican II Church, lacking its formerly monolithic structure and authority, may no longer provide a sufficient locus of meaning for the

Stage 3 person who is unprepared or otherwise unable to negotiate the process to Stage 4 faith. This results in disorientation or even despair.[40] While people may accept the fact that "you can't go home again," it is easier to process that loss of security when the decision to leave has been one's own. Many Catholics, raised in a Church that fostered conventional faith, suddenly found themselves abandoned by that nurturing "mother." It is, thus, not surprising to discover the dominance of images of the death of a parent in postconciliar fiction of Catholic experience.

THE REHABILITATION OF IMAGINATION

Ironically, having delayed change for "four or five centuries," Catholicism embarked upon renewal at a most inauspicious moment. Even secular American society was overwhelmed by the revolution in consciousness now known as The Sixties. The Catholic Church, which had finally decided to open its windows for the fresh air of modernity, was in danger of being engulfed by the hurricane of relativism. However, it was also a time for renewed interest in the imaginative in secular life, an interest that has helped balance Catholicism's excessive reliance on reason. The right side of the brain became the hemisphere of choice, and Catholic education, which had focused almost exclusively on reason as a means of knowing, could only benefit from this epistemological emphasis.

Imaginative knowing is perhaps especially relevant to faith because the central metaphor for imagination is "vision"; the person experiences knowledge through imagination as a "new way of seeing." Paul makes the connection between seeing and knowing explicit in 1 Corinthians 13:12:

At present we see indistinctly,
as in a mirror, but then face to face.
At present I know partially; then I shall
know fully as I am fully known.

Following Vatican II, as Roman Catholic theologians sought an alternative to traditional theological education with its heavy emphasis on axiom and principle, they turned to imaginative knowing, increasingly important in contemporary culture, to create meaning for human experience. So recent American Catholic theology has included important studies that focus on the imaginative perspective by theologians like John S. Dunne, David Tracy, and Philip Keane.[41] A related development has been the use of narrative in theology in the work of theologians like John Shea and Rosemary Haughton.[42] Contemporary historians stress the fallacy of dichotomizing the work of the writer of fiction and that of the historian. *Both* fictionalize in imposing meaning on events and situations through the organization of narrative. For narrative in itself is one of our fundamental ways of establishing truth, as is evident from the development of gospel as a literary form witnessing to the truth of Jesus Christ. However, although narrative may be the ground of the gospels, the Church has never been happily wedded to the most modern form of narrative, the novel.

THE CHURCH AND THE NOVEL

The pre–Vatican II so-called "Catholic novel" was a contradiction in terms from a literary standpoint. The novel is a post-Renaissance literary genre, a reflection of the modern paradigm, the aesthetic expression of pluralistic culture. And Catholicism, retaining thirteenth-century categories, expected the novel to behave exactly like its predecessor in the classical paradigm.

The ancient storyteller, working within an oral culture, related the *mythos*, the traditional story accepted by that culture as true. The allegiance of the storyteller was not to fact or entertainment, but to the *mythos*, the story itself as preserved by the tradition and regarded as its truth.[43] In every story there were two important elements: the empirical, which connected the story to its hearers, and the fictional, which was designed to convey the message or purpose of the story.[44] The gospels provide an illustration of this pattern. Jesus' life is conveyed in events and details that convey a realistic picture of first century Palestine to readers. Simultaneously, Jesus' life is presented in a manner that transcends that particular culture and asks every reader ultimate questions, regardless of his or her particular culture.

If the gospels are the paradigmatic story of Christianity, subsequent stories should reflect allegiance to that *mythos*, reinforcing that primary narrative. And Western literature developed in precisely that manner. From the miracle and morality plays of the Middle Ages through Bunyan's *Pilgrim's Progress*, the gospel message was reinterpreted through fiction that employed the empirical reality of the contemporary culture. Literature was principally didactic and served to preserve the central *mythos*, connecting it to the historical moment. As the locus of interest in Western culture shifted to the potentiality of the human agent, narrative substituted allegiance to the *mythos* with an empirical allegiance to reality, combined with a fictional allegiance to the ideal—an ideal which from the Renaissance onward was dependent on authorial perspective rather than any central *mythos*. The novel is a product of that change. It has substantially the same elements as before, but meaning is not constrained by any central *mythos* or agreed upon larger story.[45]

As human potential became increasingly valued in the culture, literature began to challenge forces that were perceived as oppressive, among them religious institutions. The Church, now alienated from all literature that was no longer the servant of the *mythos*, responded by refusing to accept modern literary categories. Orthodox adherence to dogma by both author and text was the central critical criterion. A classic example of this mindset is a scene in James Joyce's *A Portrait of the Artist as a Young Man*, when some schoolboys ask their Jesuit teacher if Victor Hugo were not the greatest French writer:

> The priest had answered that Victor Hugo had never written half so well when he had turned against the church as he had written when he was a catholic.
> —But there are many eminent French critics, said the priest, who consider that even Victor Hugo, great as he certainly was, had not so pure a French style as Louis Veuillot.[46]

The Church's insistence on literature as a proof test of faith was a confusion of categories that resulted in an inability to appreciate the spiritual value of any literature that seemed contrary to Church teaching. Moreover, Catholicism continued to be informed by the classical paradigm that limits art to didacticism. So it is scarcely surprising that when the Catholic novel developed in the United States following the Civil War, it was "fiction with a parochial purpose," narratives produced "to give metaphoric reinforcement to ideology."[47] It is significant that scholars interested in the American Catholic novel have principally been cultural historians, for these parochial productions have proved interesting as cultural artifacts but generally have little literary merit. As Flannery O'Connor tartly observed,

> When the Catholic novelist closes his own eyes and tries to see with the eyes of the Church, the result is another addition to that large body of pious trash for which we have so long been famous.[48]

Locked into a perspective that judged all narrative in terms of its fidelity to the overriding *mythos*, American Catholic literary criticism, like its theology, was using thirteenth-century categories in a twentieth-century world. The so-called Catholic novel it promoted was a contradiction in terms because the novel form is, by literary definition, a product of the modern worldview. As the Russian critic Bakhtin explains, "A sealed-off interest group, caste or class, existing within an internally unitary and unchanging core of its own, cannot serve as socially productive soil for the development of the novel."[49] Bakhtin completes the sentence with the qualifier that the novel can develop if such a group is "shifted somehow from its state of internal balance and self-sufficiency."[50] In the culture of Catholicism in the United States, the Second Vatican Council initiated such a shifting and has produced a new Catholic novel, fiction derived from the emphasis on personal experience and knowledge rather than acceptance of the authoritative and absolute. However, a Church so steeped in preconciliar thinking is in danger of failing to appreciate this fiction.

THE CHURCH AND THE NOVELIST

I dwell on this problem of the Catholic novel because that wrongheaded perspective persists and limits appreciation of fiction of Catholic experience. Ironically, in a comment made well before he began his own lucrative career in fiction, Andrew Greeley forcefully argued against "the fashion of attacking American Catholicism or of ridiculing it," specifically naming Tom McHale's *Principato* and *Farragan's Retreat* as examples.[51] At the heart of this not untypical Catholic reaction to any writer of fiction who portrays the Church negatively is a remnant of triumphalism, an overidentification of the Church with the Kingdom to which American Catholicism is particularly prone.[52]

Another remnant of triumphalism is the need to identify "Catholic" writers, either by developing anthologies limited to fiction by Catholics or, worse, analyzing a writer's fiction on the basis of his or her standing in the Church. In a 1988 book about contemporary Catholicism, Bishop Norbert Gaughan rejects any value in John Gregory Dunne's *True Confessions* because Dunne left the Church and "fouled the Catholic nest" with his novel. Dunne is specifically criticized because the novel's prelate, Cardinal Hugh Danaher, must be, according to Bishop Gaughan, "a takeoff on the leadership" of Cardinal McIntyre of Los Angeles, speculation based solely on the fact that Dunne's novel is set in Los Angeles.[53] Almost unbelievably, the good Bishop mentions Greeley's *The Cardinal Sins* elsewhere in his book with nary a complaint about that obvious and abhorrent representation of Cardinal Cody of Chicago.[54]

Later in his book, Bishop Gaughan discusses Walker Percy, concluding that his novel *Lancelot* "expresses violently the resentment . . . of laymen" who feel the Church has "let the faith go to pot." This is a sentiment similar to that expressed in Dunne's novel, yet Percy is praised as an "outstanding

Catholic novelist," apparently because he "continues to remain within the Church."[55] It would seem that the ability to write an acceptable novel of Catholic experience is reserved to those who fulfill their Sunday obligation, according to Bishop Gaughan. The persistence of this type of intellectual provincialism among Catholics limits the appreciation of the important contribution of contemporary novelists who explore Catholic experience.

The situation of the writer who has been nurtured in the Roman Catholic tradition in the United States is particularly acute. Changes that affected the Catholic culture in the 1960's were felt in American culture as a whole with the loss of innocence much earlier in the century. Studies of that period show that when a coherent and transcendent structure of meaning loses significance, a feeling of dislocation occurs among people allied to that structure. As supernatural frameworks of meaning are eroded, individuals often feel rootless; they suffer from a sense of dispossession.[56] And these feelings of anomie are manifested in contemporary Catholic fiction.

Martin Wolfe, lapsed Catholic and central character in Philip F. Deaver's "Silent Retreats," is suffering from a spiritual and emotional malaise and impulsively phones a local rectory on his way to work. When he addresses the priest, he immediately thinks,

> Call a person "Father," it made you seem like the child, it made you seem innocent and the father all-knowing, like in the old days. It made life seem solid instead of liquid and gas. Intervention was possible, solutions existed and were only as far away as a rosary, a confessional, holy water.[57]

In the 1978 novel *Final Payments*, Catholics are described as feeling "like someone's broken into their home and stolen all the furniture."[58] Writing fiction as a way to cope with the loss of certitude and security, some writers only comment on the emptiness; others concentrate on getting the old furniture back, and still others are attempting to refurnish in various ways. The choice of subject, the decision to explicitly write about the Catholic experience, usually reflects an urge to acknowledge the value of some aspects of the tradition, even if only through mourning their passing. The need to refurnish rarely involves burning the house down. As one novelist mentioned in an interview,

> At its best, the Church is also a source of tremendous idealism and charity. It's a combination of the esthetic ideal and the ethical ideal,

both of which, to me, have a kind of purity that you don't find elsewhere.[59]

At a time when Catholicism is in need of a new paradigm, the patterns of vision provided by contemporary writers are especially significant. For new paradigms are not rationally deduced; they are imaginatively envisioned. The ability to see the lineaments of a new paradigm is an act of imagination, and novels that explore the Catholic experience should be central to envisioning a new paradigm for Catholicism.

THE CURRENT CATHOLIC MOMENT

Sometime during the 1960's a yet unknown American writer named John Kennedy Toole composed a wonderfully comic novel that is illustrative of the Church's situation in the modern world. In *A Confederacy of Dunces* the central protagonist is Ignatius J. Reilly, an unemployed (and unemployable) medievalist who has been aptly described by Walker Percy as "a mad Oliver Hardy, a fat Don Quixote, a perverse Thomas Aquinas rolled into one."[60]

Ignatius is convinced that "with the breakdown of the Medieval system, the gods of Chaos, Lunacy, and Bad Taste gained ascendancy" (p. 25). He is a personification of the premodern at odds with modernism. By analogy, Toole's narrative reflects the situation of the Church in the modern world, and Ignatius Reilly's remark in the final chapter could serve as a motto for the past twenty-five years in American Catholicism: "Once a person was asked to step into this brutal century, anything could happen" (p. 325).

A Confederacy of Dunces offers a challenge to both liberals and conservatives in Catholicism. The medieval Ignatius is fundamentally dysfunctional in contemporary society in spite of his impressive erudition. Yet the characters more in touch with the modern world are equally unable to cope with life. In fact, the apparently ineffectual Ignatius becomes the narrative focus for the redemption of other characters and represents the presence of grace, as it were.

Toole's ability to fashion a novel that reflects the conflicting modes of being that are at the heart of Catholicism's efforts at renewal shows the power of the imagination as a source of knowledge about reality. Fortunately, there has been a resurgence of the imaginative in Roman Catholic intellectual life, and that new awareness may yet lead the Church to prophetic insight. It is instructive to note that if Catholicism is in the process of a paradigm shift, the appearance of crisis is simply a symptom of the fact that the time for seeking the new paradigm has arrived. As Langdon Gilkey has commented:

> If the possibility of creativity arises *because* the old is being shaken and not despite that fact, then it is clear that the present confusion of authority, doctrines, law, customs, and usages of Catholic life must be accepted, faced, and understood in all its radical depth, and then interpreted positively to make that creativity possible.[61]

The Chinese character for the word crisis contains the characters for two other words that effectively gloss the meaning of crisis—danger and opportunity. It is often the danger that exists in crisis that is invoked by both liberals and conservatives alike. But crisis also involves opportunity, the opportunity to discover the new paradigm. However, as Gilkey points out, the chaos must be worked through and not simply negated. A scene from *A Confederacy of Dunces* is instructive here.

In the novel, Ignatius' principal intellectual activity is recording his perceptions and observations on Big Chief writing tablets, most of which eventually adorn his bedroom floor. At one point his mother enters the room and asks,

> "Ignatius, what's all this trash on the floor?"

To which her son replies,

> "That is my worldview that you see. It still must be incorporated into a whole, so be careful where you step." (p. 41)

The present task of Catholicism is similar to that faced by Toole's fictional medievalist. In order to function in the twentieth century, Ignatius Reilly must formulate a viable worldview. But he merely fulminates. There is no self-reflection, and he never attempts to integrate the texts he has produced. The chaos within Catholicism has similarly produced a lot of texts that may be helpful in the present crisis, but unless some effort is made to synthesize those texts, they may simply remain strewn about like Ignatius' Big Chief tablets.

NOTES

1. Jeanne Schinto, *Shadow Bands* (Princeton: Ontario Review Press, 1988), p. 45.

2. William Halsey, *The Survival of American Innocence: Catholicism in an Era of Disillusionment, 1920–1940* (Notre Dame: University of Notre Dame Press, 1980), p. 3.

3. Ibid., p. 2.

4. Ibid., p. 3.

5. David Lodge, *How Far Can You Go?* (Middlesex, England: Penguin Books, 1981), p. 6. The historian James Hennesey, in his *American Catholics: A History of the Roman Catholic Community in the United States* (New York and Oxford: Oxford University Press, 1981), confirms the novelist's vivid image of pre-Vatican II Catholicism with this more academic description:

> Salvation was conceived as an individual effort. The church, a juridical institution, supported the individual's union in grace with God by its sacraments and sacramentals and by making crystal clear what "you had to do" to avoid hell or an uncomfortable term in purgatory. (p. 266)

6. Halsey, p. 167.

7. Ibid., p. 168.

8. I used the image of Father O'Malley in a paper I presented on American Catholic fiction in 1985 ("The Demise of Father O'Malley: Reflections on Recent American Catholic Fiction"), a paper that was subsequently published in *U.S. Catholic Historian* 6 (Spring/Summer 1987), pp. 231–40. Only much later when reading Garry Wills' *Bare Ruined Choirs* (New York: Doubleday, 1972) did I discover that he alludes to Father O'Malley in a similar way. I offer the coincidence as evidence of the impact of American Catholic culture on two people who share a common history and tradition in the pre-Vatican II Church.

9. J. F. Powers, *The Presence of Grace* (New York: Doubleday and Company, Inc., 1956), p. 174.

10. Wills, p. 1.

11. Thomas Kuhn, *The Structure of Scientific Revolutions* (Chicago: University of Chicago Press, 1970), p. 175.

12. Ibid., p. 76.

13. Arnold J. Sparr, "From Self-Congratulation to Self-Criticism: Main Currents in American Catholic Fiction, 1900–1960," *U.S. Catholic Historian* 6 (Spring/Summer 1987), 213.

14. Wilfred Sheed, *Frank and Maisie: A Memoir With Parents* (New York: Simon and Schuster, 1985), p. 212.

15. Jay Dolan, *The American Catholic Experience* (New York: Doubleday and Company, Inc., 1985), p. 412. All information in this paragraph comes from Dolan, pp. 412–16.

16. Sheed, pp. 94–95.

17. Ibid., p. 92.

18. Hennesey, pp. 300–01.

19. Ibid., p. 288.

20. Max Weber, *The Sociology of Religion*, trans. Ephraim Fischoff. (Boston, Beacon Press, 1963), p. 152. Originally published in 1922, Weber's important work was revised by Johannes Winckelmann in 1956 in a fourth edition, and this English version is a translation of that fourth edition.

21. Dolan, p. 231.

22. Will Herberg, *Protestant-Catholic-Jew: An Essay in American Religious Sociology* (New York: Anchor Books, 1960), p. 31.

23. Dick Ryan, " 'Wonder Years' as Metaphor of Lost Innocence," *National Catholic Reporter* (December 30, 1988), p. 15.

24. Mary Gordon, "Getting Here from There: A Writer's Reflections on a Religious Past," *Spiritual Quests: The Art and Craft of Religious Writing*, ed. William Zinsser (Boston: Houghton Mifflin Company, 1988), p. 28.

25. James Fowler, *Stages of Faith: The Psychology of Human Development and the Quest for Meaning* (San Francisco: Harper and Row, 1981), p. 30.

26. This summary is loosely based on the more detailed account of the history of the concept of imagination in Western thought in Richard Kearney's *The Wake of Imagination: Toward a Postmodern Culture* (Minneapolis: University of Minnesota Press, 1988).

27. Ibid., p. 39.

28. Mary Shelley, *Frankenstein: Or the Modern Prometheus* (1818; reprint, New York: Bantam Books, 1967), p. 38. Throughout this study, fiction will be documented when first mentioned; thereafter citations will be indicated by page numbers within parentheses in the text.

29. Kuhn, p. 198.

30. Flannery O'Connor, *Mystery and Manners*, ed. Sally and Robert Fitzgerald (New York: Farrar, Straus, and Giroux, 1969), p. 203. This comment is from a talk presented at Georgetown University in 1963.

31. There seems to be much agreement on this crucial point. See, for example, Halsey, p. 176; Dolan, p. 390; Eugene Kennedy, *The Now and Future Church* (New York: Doubleday and Company, Inc., 1984), p. 46; and Richard John Neuhaus, *The Catholic Moment: The Paradox of the Church in the Modern World* (San Francisco: Harper and Row, 1987), p. 39. Indeed, in *Bare Ruined Choirs* (p. 71), Wills makes the unsupported but interesting claim that Vatican II was a theologians' rebellion, and the campaign for the vernacular in liturgy was inspired by resentment of the use of Latin in theology class more than in the Mass.

32. Joseph Campbell, quoted by Kennedy, p. 83.

33. Wills, p. 64.

34. Ibid.

35. Andrew Greeley and Mary Greeley Durkin, *How To Save the Catholic Church* (New York: Viking, 1984), p. xix.

36. Halsey, p. 6; and Dolan, p. 390.

37. Fowler, pp. 172–73.

38. Ibid., p. 182.

39. Ibid., p. 173.

40. Ibid.

41. John S. Dunne is noteworthy for his use of both the principle of the imaginative and primacy of personal story in theological reflection in his many books. David Tracy's *The Analogical Imagination* (New York: Crossroad Publishing Company, 1981) shows the affiliation between contemporary theological study and literary criticism, particularly in the work of Paul Ricoeur, while Philip Keane's application of the imaginative perspective to moral theology in his *Christian Ethics and Imagination* (New York and Ramsey: Paulist Press, 1984) contains preliminary chapters that provide an excellent overview of the importance of imagination in theological study. But there are many publications that stress the imaginative perspective in theology: For example John Coulson, *Religion and Imagination: In Aid of a Grammar of Assent* (Oxford: Oxford University Press, 1981); John W. Dixon, *Art and the Theological Imagination* (New York: The Seabury Press, 1977); Kathleen R. Fischer, *The Inner Rainbow: The Imagination in Christian Life* (New York: Paulist Press, 1983); Stanley Hauerwas, *Vision and Virtue: Essays in Christian Ethical Reflection* (Notre Dame, Ind.: Fides Press, 1974).

Greeley also emphasizes the imaginative in the sociology of religion in many of his books, especially *Religion: A Secular Theory* (New York: The Free Press, 1982) and *The Religious Imagination* (New York: Sadlier, 1981). These citations are meant to be representative rather than inclusive, illustrative of the interest in the imaginative among those whose concern is religious experience.

42. A readable and extremely thorough introduction to the theology of story is provided by William J. Bausch, *Storytelling: Imagination and Faith* (Mystic, Connecticut: Twenty-Third Publications, 1984).

43. Robert Scholes and Robert Kellogg, *The Nature of Narrative* (New York: Oxford University Press, 1966), p. 12.

44. Ibid., p. 13.

45. Ibid., p. 15. A more detailed discussion of this development of narrative in the Western literary tradition is provided by Giles Gunn, *The Culture of Criticism and the Criticism of Culture* (New York and Oxford: Oxford University Press, 1987), pp. 182–83.

46. James Joyce, *A Portrait of the Artist As a Young Man*, ed. Chester G. Anderson (1916; reprint, New York: The Viking Press, 1968), p. 156. The latter writer, perhaps not so familiar to us as Hugo, was a minor nineteenth-century French journalist and leader of the French Ultramontanes, a group that supported the Pope's claims to be spiritual head of the Church everywhere.

47. Paul R. Messbarger, *Fiction with a Parochial Purpose: Social Uses of American Catholic Literature, 1884–1900* (Boston: Boston University Press, 1971), p. 20.

48. O'Connor, p. 180.

49. M. M. Bakhtin, *The Dialogic Imagination*, trans. Caryl Emerson, ed. and trans. Michael Holquist (1934; reprint, Austin: University of Texas Press, 1981), p. 368.

50. Ibid.

51. Andrew Greeley, *The Communal Catholic* (New York: The Seabury Press, 1976), p. 145.

52. Tracy, 1981. Tracy points out that

there now exists among ecclesiologists a broad consensus that the church is not identical with the "kingdom of God." The importance of this theological consensus is crucial for undercutting any residual ecclesial triumphalism. (p. 23)

53. Norbert F. Gaughan, *Troubled Catholics: The Lessons of Discontent* (Chicago: The Thomas More Press, 1988), p. 138.

54. Ibid., p. 129.

55. Ibid., pp. 149–54.

56. Jackson Lears, *No Place For Grace: Antimodernism and the Transformation of American Culture, 1880–1920* (New York: Pantheon, 1981), p. 43.

57. Philip F. Deaver, *Silent Retreats* (Athens, Georgia and London: University of Georgia Press, 1988), p. 4.

58. Mary Gordon, *Final Payments* (New York: Random House, 1978), p. 101.

59. Mary Gordon in *Once a Catholic*, ed. Peter Occhiogrosso (Boston: Houghton Mifflin, 1987), p. 74.

60. Walker Percy, "Foreword," *A Confederacy of Dunces*, John Kennedy Toole (Baton Rouge and London: Louisiana State University Press, 1980), p. vi. Percy facilitated the posthumous publication of this novel; Toole committed suicide in 1969.

61. Langdon Gilkey, *Catholicism Confronts Modernity* (New York: The Seabury Press, 1975), p. 2.

2

Visions of Experience

And I saw it was filled with graves,
And tomb-stones where flowers should be:
And Priests in black gowns were walking their rounds,
And binding with briars my joys & desires.

William Blake

In 1789 the poet William Blake published his *Songs of Innocence*, poems reflecting the state of mind of the naive child who sees all of life as entirely beautiful and good. Five years later Blake combined his *Songs of Innocence* with *Songs of Experience* and included poems that reflect the contrary state, the ironic perception of the sordid reality behind the appearance of innocence—poverty, disease, oppression, and war. For Blake, the transition from innocence to experience is a natural process, and both states need to be comprehended, and ultimately transcended, for a balanced view of reality that prioritizes neither state. An exclusive focus on experience, on the horror in human life, is as misguided as the insistence of preserving innocence by failing to look at the negative. The negativism of the vision of experience, as exemplified in the lines from Blake's "The Garden of Love," cited above, is best understood as part of the process of development to a more complete vision of life.

The Blakean states of innocence and experience correlate well with the changing perceptions of American Catholics in the twentieth century, and Blake's contraries provide a useful context for fiction that is characteristically negative about the Church. As William Halsey and others have documented, twentieth-century American Catholicism provided a veneer of innocence for its adherents, a denial of experience in their culture. When that veneer cracked in the early 1960's, many American Catholics not only looked at their culture with the eyes of experience but at their Church as well. These visions of Catholic experience in contemporary fiction form a pattern that is best understood as a natural reaction to prolonged innocence and symptomatic of the discomfort engendered by the sudden loss of innocence.

In the Blakean cosmology only by integrating visions of innocence and experience can full vision be attained, and only by exploring the totality of the fictional presentation of American Catholicism will a true *sensus fidelium* be possible. The negative should not be an occasion for defensiveness but an opportunity for reflection.

SCHOOL DAYS

The vision of Catholic experience that has received the most public attention is not a novel but a play.[1] Performances of Christopher Durang's *Sister Mary Ignatius Explains It All For You* were picketed, and protests were vehement, yet the central revelation of disillusionment in the play is a classic expression of grief for lost innocence. Diane, one of Sister Mary Ignatius' former students, has come with three companions to visit their former teacher and, ostensibly, to embarrass the nun. Asked about the source of her anger, Diane begins:

> Because I believed you. I believed how you said the world worked, and that God loved us, and the story of the Good Shepherd and the lost sheep; and I don't think you should lie to people.[2]

In these lines Durang expresses the not uncommon experience of discovering that the formulaic responses of conventional Catholic religious training are insufficient to meet the conflicts of adult life. Diane's initial statement is followed by a long speech in which she explains her mother's extended agony while dying of cancer and her own seemingly futile prayers that the woman be delivered from her pain. In a hideous denouement to this recital of woes, Diane states that she was raped on the day of her mother's death. Faced with this overwhelming anguish, she can find no solace in the simplistic religious training of her childhood. The other three former students echo Diane's frustration and explain how the rigid dogmatism of their Catholic training provides little support for the complex and ambiguous life situations they have encountered as adults.

Despite protests against the play, Christopher Durang's four characters in search of religion are not anomalous in contemporary Catholicism. A 1976 study of Catholics in New York City revealed that these adults did not complain about liturgy or sexual prohibitions specifically, but about the fact that the Church teaching was unclear to them.[3] These cosmopolitan Catholics wanted leadership in living as committed Christians in the modern world, something their experience of church had not provided for them. This sentiment is echoed in many of the conversations with adult Catholics in Peter Occhiogrosso's *Once A Catholic*.[4] Notable among them is the film director Martin Scorsese who specifically identifies the difficulty of living a religious life in a secular society as the primary motivating force in much of his work.[5]

> The first, most important film to me was *Mean Streets*, which had the
> . . . theme: How do you lead a good life, a good, moral, ethical life,
> when everything around you works the absolutely opposite way?[6]

The opening line of that film, "You don't make up for your sins in church. You do it in the streets," reflects a perception of the failure of institutional religion to provide spiritual support. It is a vision of church similar to that of Christopher Durang.

Unfortunately for Durang, his artistic decision to symbolize the frustration of adult Catholics in a play with a classroom setting and a nun as its central character ignited the ire of those for whom the traditional Catholic school and the Baltimore Catechism are focal points in their preservation of innocence. The forceful opposition to *Sister Mary Ignatius Explains It All For You* is evidence not only of the persistence of Catholic aesthetic fundamentalism but also of an insistence on preserving icons of innocence. The preference for the creation of folklore to perpetuate an illusion of innocence is indicated by the popularity of such cartoons of pre-Vatican II life as *Growing Up Catholic* and the sitcom novels of John R. Powers.[7] In the Catholic adult there is a latent desire for the time when "Sister says" was the solution to problems, and this masked dependency was surely part of the overreaction to Durang's characterization of Sister Mary Ignatius, for those protests are at odds with the drama itself.

In *Sister Mary Ignatius Explains It All For You* there are no villains, only victims. Durang's Sister Mary Ignatius is revealed to be as much a victim of the system she so faithfully served as the former students who confront her. As an adult speaking to other adults, she can only repeat formulaic responses or pious platitudes. If there is any evil, it is in her absolute certitude that her repetitions are the sole deposit of truth and in her complete disdain for the very real suffering evidenced by the other adult characters in this drama. Dogmatism is clearly Durang's complaint rather than dogma, a dogmatism that leads to denial and repression of human feeling.[8]

This is clear from his companion one-act play, *The Actor's Nightmare*, published in book form with *Sister Mary Ignatius* and often performed with it. That *The Actor's Nightmare* does not elicit equal complaint from Catholics is evidence of the aesthetic fundamentalism at the heart of protests about *Sister Mary Ignatius*. Relying on more complex dramatic effects for its point, *The Actor's Nightmare* is little noticed by disgruntled Catholics, yet this play complements the vision of Catholic experience in *Sister Mary Ignatius*.

The Actor's Nightmare is a black comedy about an accountant named George who wanders backstage and is mistakenly identified as the leading man's understudy. Thrust into performances of Noel Coward's *Private Lives*, *Hamlet*, and Beckett's *Endgame*, the reluctant George fumbles through, reciting whatever is in his memory when he cannot get lines from the prompter. Significantly, the Act of Contrition is the only complete text he recalls, showing not only the power of rote memorization but the way guilt surfaces in the lives of adult Catholics.

That guilt is emphasized when the final scene that is announced is the execution of Sir Thomas More from *A Man for All Seasons* with George cast in the title role. The cryptic comment that "the executioner will play himself" is unsettling. George tries to halt the execution, changing the final speech to declare that Henry VIII can have all the wives he wants, but the executioner protests this departure from the script:

> I'm going to ignore what you've said and cut your head off anyway, and then we'll all pretend you went to your death nobly. The Church needs its saints, and school children have got to have heroes to look up to, don't you all agree? (p. 61)

As George imagines he is facing death, he tries to bargain with his malevolent God, declaring repentance for not having entered a monastery as he had promised in the third grade. Durang uses the play's death scene to unearth the burden of guilt George has internalized from his youthful experience of religion, an inheritance acquired from a training in which martyrdom was the ideal and any concession to self a failure. The playwright's concern is less with the sixteenth century than with a Catholicism that idealized violence in a variety of forms, not always with a clear principle at stake. The idealization of martyrdom is one aspect of excessive supernaturalism, and its embodiment in the classic Catholic injunction to "offer it up," regardless of the human suffering involved, led to a denial of the value of human feelings with a resultant violence to the person.

In the finale of *The Actor's Nightmare* George, with his head on the executioner's block, doggedly refuses to say the line that will cue the fall of the ax, but he is also unable to end the scene. Finally, deciding that the convention of such a staged nightmare always results in the actor's awakening as the ax falls, George cooperates to resolve the stalemate and says his line. The scene darkens, and, when the lights come up, all the other actors take a curtain call except for George, who lies on the stage, apparently slain. Things are not always as harmless as they seem to be, Durang indicates, either on the stage or in life.

The playwright's choice of specifically Catholic elements in these plays evidences a concern for faith experience. Both plays make it clear that simply abandoning religion will not conciliate its claims on an individual. Sister Mary Ignatius' former students return and engage her in dialogue, implicitly hoping for some support for their lives, and George's Catholic past surfaces in his moment of crisis. Durang's insistence on death scenes in both of these comedies indicates a serious purpose in dramatizing his vision of the effects of a Catholic past. His may be a bleak vision, but consigning one's religious heritage to the realm of pious idolatry or comic folklore is not a viable alternative. Not denial but the sincere effort to understand experience and transcend it contributes most to the perception of a new paradigm.

OUT OF THE CRADLE

Durang's concern with the tensions felt by adults formed in the pre-conciliar Church has affinities with the fiction of Tom McHale, whose fiction depicts the absurd world of "cradle Catholics" who are unable to reconcile belief and behavior. In two of his best-known novels, *Principato* (1969) and *Farragan's Retreat* (1971), McHale presents the dilemma of urban, ethnic Catholics, Italian and Irish respectively, who discover their alienation from the Church in the course of the narrative.

For both Angelo Principato and Arthur Farragan the essence of Catholicism is in the observance of its rules and obligations, and morality is measured solely in terms of such observance. Asked if his wife is a good woman, Principato muses,

Of course she was a good woman . . . one of the best. She followed
the Catholic format for living to the letter. Even had a Jesuit uncle
and deceased bishop uncle for extra credits.[9]

Ignored is the fact that despite their careful observance of the religious
obligations to fast, pray, and reproduce, husband and wife are locked in a
destructive, adversarial relationship that eventually ends the marriage in
law as well as reality.

Socrates' famous advice that the unexamined life is not worth living
would be paraphrased by McHale as "the unexamined Catholic life is the
only one possible." Both Principato and Farragan admit to functioning as
Catholics by exempting their religion from scrutiny. At one point in
Principato when Angelo is on retreat, the director engages him in a private
conversation, inquiring,

"Do you believe in the immortality of the soul, Principato?"

To which Principato can only respond:

"I'm a Catholic, Father. I've accepted the Church. I accept the dogma
she teaches."

Asked if he ever doubts, Principato can only admit,

"No, I don't think about it." (p. 124)

The central protagonist in *Farragan's Retreat* considers his religion as a
type of genetic inheritance, imagining that the strong Catholicism of his
parents "coursed through the blood, for his purposes, much like the
integralness of the Rh factor he had also inherited from them."[10]

The plot of *Principato* reflects conventions of religious practice separated from any vital faith experience. The principal event is the death of
the family patriarch, Joseph Principato, who is determined to preserve "the
Defiance," his long-held vow never to enter a Catholic Church or to be
reconciled to it. He writes three separate and contradictory letters to be
opened after his death to assure ambiguity about his final wishes, and he
complicates the situation by leaving all of his wealth to the Church while
simultaneously insisting on cremation rather than interment in what he
perceives as a final defiance. Son Angelo attempts to be faithful to the
demands of his defiant father, his outraged Irish in-laws, and the faith he
tries not to think too seriously about. He is not very successful in recon-

ciling these divergent forces, and, ultimately, he is alienated from family, home, and Church.

Like Durang, McHale's focus is excessive supernaturalism, which is reflected in his fiction as a habit of religious observance unconnected to life experience. For his characters, Catholicism is an isolated region of certitude and stability in a world of ambiguity and change. The resulting dichotomy between the strong emphasis on religious observance among ethnic Catholics and their disregard of their religion in actual life is the moral focus of McHale's fiction. In *Farragan's Retreat*, for example, the two most fervent Catholics in the Farragan family insist that their younger brother murder his only son because the son has fled the country to avoid military service. No one in this aggressively Catholic family questions the morality of this murder; in fact, the third Farragan brother, a priest, agrees to provide the alibi for his sibling in the murder plan.

McHale has an acute eye for the behavior of conventional cultural Catholics who neatly bifurcate their existence, often using Catholicism to support political or social ideology with little regard for philosophic consistency, as is reflected in Arthur Farragan's assessment of his recently deceased sister:

> Anna hated more than she could possibly love: Negroes and the Viet Cong, the unions and the Democrats; everything except her church, the Republican far Right, and Malcolm, her son, beside whom she had minutes before been laid to rest. (p. 206)

The creation of obviously stylized characters lessens the mimetic quality of McHale's prose and creates a surreal comedic tone that highlights his satire. In McHale's novels, as in Durang's plays, the distance between the absurd and the real is often difficult to discern, and authorial comment is made in that lack of distance.

Structurally, *Principato* and *Farragan's Retreat* use the deterioration of strong ethnic families to gloss the decline of the Church in its ability to influence the moral lives of its members. In both novels the central protagonist has an exceptionally strong parent but is unable to be similarly influential in his own children's lives. When Arthur Farragan thinks about his religion coursing through his bloodstream, he decides that the Church should eschew all proselytizing because the faith "was better extended through the blood." But then he thinks of his alienated only son who, in "receiving the gift of faith from his father, . . . had not even bothered to open the package before Farragan got it back in his face" (p. 132).

Angelo Principato and Arthur Farragan are both upright, well-intentioned

men, and their allegiance to the practice of their religion in the beginning
of these novels would gladden the heart of Sister Mary Ignatius. But, as
McHale reveals, theirs is an unexamined ritualism that they fail to integrate
with life experience. By the end of *Farragan's Retreat*, the formerly
staunch Farragan identifies his Church as

> that manure pile of platitudes that . . . [he] saw on the instant he had
> never in his lifetime considered leaving, since he had never in his
> lifetime dared to put it to the same test of honesty that Simon, his son,
> had already done and ended with. (p. 282)

Both Principato and Farragan embody the spiritual anomie that results
from the collapse of the classical paradigm with no intellectual preparation
for the modern world. The resulting chaos is even more apparent in *School
Spirit* (1976), in which the surreal comedy of McHale's earlier novels is
replaced by a sense of authorial despair.

In *School Spirit*, "Coach" Egil Magruder is seeking satisfaction for the
death of a student that occurred twenty-three years earlier in a Catholic
boarding school. It is difficult to understand McHale's perspective in this
strange book, for his central character, Coach Magruder, although seemingly motivated by a sense of justice, conveys a self-righteousness that is
unsettling. Everyone wants to forget the entire incident, including the dead
boy's mother, the current priest–headmaster, the school personnel, and the
former students. Indeed, as the novel progresses, it becomes clear that the
death was less the result of intentional malice than a schoolboy prank gone
awry. Magruder's mission begins to take on an aura of revenge rather than
justice as the narrative progresses.

To complicate matters, the three boys responsible for the incident have
grown into adults without strong moral values, so although Magruder's
presence ultimately results in their deaths, he is more catalyst than instrument of justice. Yet there is so little admirable in the depiction of the central
character that at the end of the novel it is difficult to know whether this
narrative has chronicled the ultimate triumph of justice or the chaos
perpetrated by an individual who masks his self-righteousness in the guise
of a seeker of justice.

Much less cohesive than either *Principato* or *Farragan's Retreat*,
School Spirit is a moral tale without a clear moral center. Its lack of form
is, in itself, its central comment. Magruder's demand for retributive justice
without regard for extenuating circumstances is as anarchic in this fiction
as the earlier decision to ignore the death of the unpopular student.

McHale's fiction becomes increasingly concerned with the question of maintaining a sense of absolute values in a world of increasing relativism. It is an issue that is never resolved for him and one that is certainly at the heart of the current dilemma in American Catholicism. However, McHale's fiction provides dramatic testimony to the fact that the attempt to insist on the preservation of innocence once experience has intruded is not only futile, it is often destructive. The old paradigm of "Catholicism past" cannot simply be stretched to include new awareness. For new wine, we need new wineskins.

FATHERS AND SONS

A collection of short stories by Philip F. Deaver provides a remarkable analogue to McHale's vision of Catholic experience but one that is less despairing. Although Deaver's fictional world is geographically distant from McHale's and concerns individuals of a later generation, he shares the former's depiction of a religious tradition that has lost currency in the modern world, a faith expression that fathers are unable to pass on to their sons.

In Deaver's *Silent Retreats* (1988), Catholicism exists in a wasteland of memory and desire for the Midwest males who confront their aging selves in the collected stories. The world that fathers bequeath to their sons, a concern with "the circularity of life," is a recurrent theme in Deaver's tales and most specifically delineated in the title story in this collection. For Martin Wolfe, principal character in "Silent Retreats," Catholicism exists in memory, memory of a time when: "intervention was possible, solutions existed and were only as far away as a rosary, a confessional, holy water."[11] But Wolfe's efforts to recapture that time in this story reflect the fact that there is no viable substitute for the loss of innocence.

A vague malaise, which often erupts into tears, directs Martin Wolfe to phone a local rectory, and he asks where he can make a "silent retreat." This tips the priest off to the fact that Martin is not *au courant*: he is not aware of the latest trends in Catholicism. Martin is informed that silence is now considered self-indulgent, and he is wasting his time if he is not currently practicing his religion. The conversation ends with no resolution for Martin, as the priest insists:

"You ought to start coming to mass. Do you have children?"
"What's this, the pitch? Right here on the telephone?"
"It's all we've got, you and me. Sorry." (p.8)

The suggestion that only the observance of rituals connects the priest and the individual Catholic indicates that the renewal of hearts and minds has not proceeded as expeditiously as the redesign of church buildings. In a 1968 study of the priesthood, Eugene Kennedy indicated that the spirit of Vatican II placed "strongly personalistic" demands on the priest, a challenge to avoid relating solely through ecclesiastical function or a tradition that made the priest authority on everything.[12] The character of the priest in "Silent Retreats" reflects an attempt at personalism gone awry. In spite of his agreeableness, Deaver's priest holds to the traditional authority role of "Father says." The accidents have changed, but the substance remains the same.

However, as Deaver's story indicates, the institutional Church remains a locus of meaning for Catholics, and the priest retains significance as its representative. After his abortive phone call, Martin's efforts to resolve his crisis—by going to see his young son at school and calling a childhood friend—end unsatisfactorily. He winds up drinking alone in a Chicago hotel. Finally, he is drawn back to the rectory he had called earlier, and the door is answered by the same priest he had spoken with in the morning. The priest is carrying a gun because, he explains to Martin, he was robbed of a collection the previous month. Martin responds, "You know, you might consider a dog. Experience tells me you can keep the poor from crowding in on you if you simply buy a large, well-trained killer dog" (p. 22).

There will always be points of tension between religious commitment and secular reality, but Martin's disillusionment when he notices the gun indicates an implicit expectation that those who publicly profess Christianity will reflect an uncompromising commitment to its ideals. With his sarcastic suggestion that the priest might consider a killer dog, Martin faces the sobering truth that there will be no help for him here. His expectations of the priest are a product of memory and desire. The rectory is still and dark as the story ends, reflecting Martin's increasing despair.

Earlier in the story, in his conversation with his young son, Martin had talked about baseball, about the fact that his own father had played baseball with him, as now he plays ball with his son, and he is the link between that man and his grandson: "And you and him, you never met. You're flesh and blood, but you never met. I'm the bridge between you" (p. 14). The sentiment is given fuller expression in a later story, "Infield," in which another father reflects on his youth and the fact that so often he and his friends played the same positions as their fathers in their Pony League days, "So there you are. The infield has continuity through the ages"

(p. 103). Unlike memories of baseball that are now revived in the lives of their sons, no comparable contemporary experiences of Church life exist in *Silent Retreats*. Martin Wolfe's visit to the rectory reinforces the point that Catholics today mourn the fact that they can't go home again.

The difference in tone between the fiction of Deaver and McHale reflects the difference in experience as well. McHale's biting irony is expressive of Catholics whose fundamental life choices were made in the pre-Vatican II era of innocence and for whom Catholicism was part of the structure of life itself. When the Church itself did the breaking off, when the anchor became a sail, Catholicism could no longer provide fixity and stability in a changing world. This experience is reflected in Deaver's autumnal prose with its elegiac tone. Now only "the infield has continuity through the ages."

Deaver's protagonists, a generation older than McHale's, reflect the effect of the breakdown of innocence in the lives of American Catholics. No longer envisioning Catholicism as some monolithic immutable structure of truth, they nevertheless turn to the Church in times of crisis. This fiction reflects no self-complacent autonomy, but a continued need for some official representation of the Divine in human life. A novel that serves as a classic document of this need is Wilfred Sheed's *Transatlantic Blues* (1978). The protagonist of this novel, fictional television personality Monty Chatsworth, is flying between New York and London. During the flight, he reflects on his disordered life and, in a spirit of reformation, yearns for a confessor. He finally settles for the tape recorder:

Perhaps now that we have arrogantly dismissed our other gods and sent them packing, our troubled hearts can still find something to say to the only two gods that remain: ourselves and our technology.[13]

At the end of the novel, Monty finds that technology is no solace, "You can't give me absolution, you blasphemous bastard. Somebody else has to. Somebody who doesn't exist anymore" (p. 304).

Sheed highlights the fact that the need for repentance is not absent in the modern world, but the Church no longer has a credible presence in meeting that need. A more educated Catholic who lives daily amid competing ideologies expects to encounter comparable strength in religion. Yet although the Church must define itself in the context of competing ideologies, the fiction of Catholic experience indicates that the Church does not image spiritual leadership effectively in contemporary society. This failure is the basis of two novels by John Gregory Dunne.

PRIESTS AND BROTHERS

In *True Confessions* and *Red White and Blue*, Dunne employs similar structural patterns. Both novels center on the relationship between two pairs of Irish Catholic brothers, one of whom is a priest, to express a vision of Catholic experience. In each novel, the story is narrated by the nonclerical brother who serves as a dramatic foil to his sibling, and the relationship provides Dunne with the structure for a commentary on both the ecclesial and cultural dimensions of Catholicism.

The 1977 *True Confessions* is in the tradition of detective fiction, and its narrator, Tom Spellacy, is a retired detective lieutenant reminiscing about a case he solved twenty-five years earlier. At the time of the crime, ca. 1950, the other Spellacy brother, Desmond, was Chancellor of the Archdiocese, a cleric on the fast track, whose career is undone in the course of the murder investigation. Tangentially involved in the murder is a gangster who is, coincidentally, a major contractor for the Archdiocese. Throughout the investigation, Dunne parallels the corruption within the police department with the corruption in the clerical culture. Using the detached tone of detective fiction, Dunne suggests that the incidents are venal—compromises made with a weak conscience, products of the breakdown of the ideal that the respective institutions represent.

The novel makes its most significant comment by indirection. Neither brother is purposefully evil but both accommodate evil in their lives. Dunne suggests that because evil is a fact of life for Tom Spellacy and he makes no claim to be immune from it, he is more aware of the choices and compromises he makes; whereas Des, whose vocation would seem to dictate a choice of good, rationalizes his self-deceptions and indulges in greater evil because he cannot consider his choices as openly—even to himself. For Dunne, the difficulty with preserving the state of innocence is that it is a deception; it simply masks the reality of experience. A Church that has trained itself in such self-deception would not be adept at dealing honestly with the world of experience, as Dunne's novel of the post-Vatican II Church indicates.

Red White and Blue (1987) is Dunne's vision of the Church of the 60's and 70's, and it is again the story of two brothers, the Brodericks, sons of a powerful and rich father. This time the secular brother, Jack, is a columnist turned screenwriter and the priest, nicknamed "Bro," has a similarly romantic lifestyle. Bro is the consummate priest-as-public-figure whose exploits are recounted on the evening news and in weekly news magazines. He is frequently referred to but rarely present in the narrative, which is principally the story of Jack and his relationship to a radical lawyer, Leah Kaye, whom he eventually marries and then divorces. The novel's plot culminates in the assassination of Bro and Leah together, and Jack hints that his brother had made plans to leave the priesthood.

As in *True Confessions*, Dunne makes his point in the contrast between the lives of the two brothers, Bro, an ordained Benedictine monk, has a more secular lifestyle than his screenwriter brother. His globe-trotting exploits are vaguely described but are clearly less pastoral than political. He is no Dan Berrigan, however, but the darling of the establishment, America's "public clergyman," the person sent on a mission whenever a collar is convenient.

Interestingly, in *True Confessions* Des Spellacy reforms through asceticism, leaving the chancery for a curate's life under a pastor known for his spiritual rigor, but Bro's end is an early and violent death. From the evidence of these novels, both written well after Vatican II, Dunne found more hope in the preconciliar Church. There his priest rediscovered his integrity; the life of the superficial priest of the "new" Church has no such positive conclusion.

In his fictional priests, Dunne images the institutional Church as a whole. Des Spellacy is a young priest on the fast track in *True Confessions*, and the portrait of Bro as the trendy priest in *Red White and Blue* is simply later manifestation of the same reality, clerical culture that has adapted itself to the values prevalent in society. In a culture with values that were consonant with the Christian tradition, the Church in the United States flourished. Now that American society is increasingly secularized, Dunne images a Church that is indistinguishable from the culture at large. In 1976, the sociologist Andrew Greeley commented,

> In the next ten years Catholicism, *as an ecclesiastical institution* in the United States, will continue in the course of its precipitous decline. At the same time, however, American Catholics, *as a community* in our society of pluralistic integration, will experience a dramatic increase in healthy self-consciousness and self-awareness.[14]

Fiction of American Catholic experience not only affirms the decline of the institutional Church that Greeley predicted, but the impulse to use the Catholic experience as a subject for fiction reflects the self-awareness he pointed to as well. Nowhere is the cultural tension generated by the decline of the institutional Church more apparent than in the fiction of Walker Percy.

RELIGION AND THE SOCIAL ORDER

Although the convert Percy had none of the concern for cultural Catholicism that comprises the vision of experience for Durang, McHale, and Dunne, his fiction is structured with the same concern for the role of Catholicism in contemporary society. All of Percy's central protagonists evidence a similar disorientation by the lack of stability in their world. Percy's fiction, dominated by images of insanity in the individual and apocalypse in the society, is marked by a concern for "shoring up the fragments" against the ruins of contemporary culture. And although Percy personally made a choice for Catholicism as a way to meaning in 1946, his fictional heroes have difficulty replicating that choice in the contemporary world.

In Percy's fiction, Catholicism is as disordered as the culture it inhabits. The most direct indictment of the Church occurs in two novels, narrated by the physician Tom More, that depict the collapse of the social order: The futuristic and apocalyptic *Love in the Ruins*, subtitled *The Adventures of a Bad Catholic at a Time near the End of the World*, published in 1971 and the more mimetic *The Thanatos Syndrome*, published in 1987.

The earlier novel fictionalizes the confusion of the 60's—in the Church and in America. In More's description, Catholicism, like Gaul, is divided into three parts:

(1) the American Catholic Church whose new Rome is Cicero, Illinois; (2) the Dutch schismatics who believe in relevance but not God; (3) the Roman Catholic remnant, a tiny scattered flock with no place to go.[15]

And the alliance of Church and culture is evident in More's fuller description of the American Catholic Church "which emphasizes property rights and the integrity of neighborhoods, retained the Latin mass and plays *The Star-Spangled Banner* at the elevation" (p. 6). Clearly this is the Church of Arthur Farragan's sister Anna.

The vision of society in *The Thanatos Syndrome* is less apocalyptic, and Percy's choice of a medical mystery thriller to structure his narrative signifies his theme—the tension between the powers of modern science and the mystery that is at the heart of the human condition. Percy's comments on Catholicism in this novel are indirect but insightful. Minor characters reflect the confusion of Catholics in conflict over pious practices, and they contrast with the central character, Dr. Tom More, a lapsed

Catholic faced with a personal ethical dilemma comparable to that of his famous martyred namesake.

Noticing some bizarre symptoms in his patients, More unearths a surreptitious plan to eliminate social problems through the chemical control of human subjects. Percy clearly links this project to the already legal "pedeuthanasia and gereuthanasia," which are widely practiced by the architect of the new plan. More's friend, the aged Father Smith, provides an indirect commentary on the situation with his apparently unrelated reminiscences of his experiences in Germany in the 1930's, a narrative that helps Percy make his point about the evil that can be done by people who misguidedly think they are doing good.

In spite of ethical decisions clearly influenced by his Catholic heritage, Dr. Tom More protests to the priest that he does not think much about religion and cannot return to the practice of his Catholicism. Father Smith reassures him. "Don't worry . . . It is to be expected. It is only necessary to wait and to be of good heart. It is not your fault."[16] Puzzled by this, More inquires further and is told, "You have been deprived of the faith. All of us have. It is part of the times" (p. 364). In Percy's vision, the institutional Church lacks a viable spiritual presence in the modern world, and its traditional values are preserved by the saving remnant, individuals like Tom More who have internalized their religious heritage and can represent the Catholic view, even when personally dissociated from the institution. It is now a faith of hearts and minds alone.

The Thanatos Syndrome is Percy's fullest explication of his vision of the contemporary Catholic diaspora, but his disdain for the institutional Church's inability to transcend the secular is evident in all of his fiction. Perhaps the most direct statement is in *Lancelot* (1977), when the title character speaks of his search for meaning to his priest–auditor:

> I cannot tolerate this age. And I will not. I might have tolerated you and your Catholic Church, and even joined it, if you had remained true to yourself. Now you're part of the age. You've the same fleas as the dogs you've lain down with.[17]

In his fiction, Percy is never more precise about his vision of Church, but his novels consistently image Catholicism as an institution that shares the ills of modern secularism and fails to provide viable spiritual leadership for contemporary Catholics. The pattern of Percy's novels shows the old paradigm in disarray and no new paradigm yet available. His vision of experience is one of alienation, insanity, and destruction.

His character Will Barrett's search for meaning, begun in *The Last Gentleman* (1966) and continued in *The Second Coming* (1980), is paradigmatic of Percy's fiction. As those two titles suggest, the preservation of a cultural inheritance is intimately related for Percy to its religious significance. In the contemporary world, Percy sees both culture and religion at risk. Lines from Yeats' poem "The Second Coming" effectively gloss the world depicted in all of Percy's fiction:

> Things fall apart, the center cannot hold;
> Mere anarchy is loosed upon the world,
> The blood-dimmed tide is loosed, and everywhere
> The ceremony of innocence is drowned.

In Percy's novel *The Second Coming*, cultural confusion is reflected in Will's inability to maintain mental alertness; in his only child, his daughter Leslie, with her androgynous name and born-again, Episcopalian fervor; and in the innocent Allison, recently escaped from a mental hospital, who seems to be the sanest individual in the narrative. In Will's escalating confusion and disorientation, he attempts to discern some sign from God and, in the process, comes upon Allison, who has begun life anew rebuilding a greenhouse. Will and Allison thrive in this symbolic Eden, and, in the final scene in the novel, Will (who has no religious affiliation) asks Father Weatherbee, an ancient Catholic priest, to perform a marriage ceremony between him and Allison. The elderly priest hesitates, and in his musing reiterates the Percy vision of experience in Catholicism:

> The trouble was catching on to the madness, the madness of the new church, the madness of America, and telling one from the other.[18]

Dismayed by Will's apparent lunacy, the priest recommends the enthusiastic Father Curl, the Episcopalian pastor of Will's daughter Leslie, but Will insists, "I perceive that you seem to know something—and by the same token Jack Curl does not" (p. 357). And in the final lines of the novel Will conflates Allison, the priest, and the God he serves, as he asks,

> What is it I want from her and him . . . not only want but must have? Is she a gift and therefore a sign of a giver? Could it be that the Lord is here, masquerading behind this simple silly holy face? Am I crazy to want both, her and Him? No, not want, must have. And will have. (p. 360)

For Percy the fact that "the center cannot hold" is a reason for concern, but his fiction charts the human impulse to find meaning that will renew the strength of that center. Percy's commitment to Catholicism's philosophic principles is evident in his fiction, and it is clear from *The Thanatos Syndrome* that he believes Catholic teaching can provide a locus of meaning for modern ethical decisions. But it is also evident that Percy does not see that happening in the contemporary world.

In Percy's fiction, the institutional Church is as uncentered as the rest of society. The old Church is no more; Fathers Weatherbee and Smith are dysfunctional; and Percy invests no wisdom in their clerical successors. In fact, at the end of *The Thanatos Syndrome*, Dr. More has been offered the directorship of St. Margaret's Hospice in place of the failing Father Smith. The novel ends with More undecided about taking either the position at St. Margaret's or a more lucrative association with a fellow psychiatrist. Percy indicates that no one is immune from having to define the self in relation to the culture, and only the remnant who can make the appropriate choices will preserve the spirit of Catholicism.

Thus, the visions of experience in postconciliar fiction of the Catholic experience evidence a longing for meaningful spiritual leadership. It is encouraging that this vision has already gone beyond the self-absorption characteristic of the initial awareness of the state of experience in which authority is often imaged as oppressive, with priests "binding with briars my joys & desires." There is no exaltation of autonomy in this fiction which mourns the loss of innocence. But neither is there any suggestion of a new paradigm for Catholicism. Beneath this fiction of a deteriorating institutional Catholicism, there is a persistence of the human need for relation to the Divine, as in the yearning for a stable order expressed by Deaver's Martin Wolfe and Percy's Will Barrett.

While Bishop Gaughan disparages Dunne, and Greeley criticizes McHale's negativism, the visions of experience in their fiction are, in fact, consonant with the documents of the Second Vatican Council. In *Gaudiam et Spes*, we are reminded, for example, that "It does not escape the Church how great a distance lies between the message she offers and the human weakness of those to whom the gospel is entrusted."[19] And, as Avery Dulles points out, principles of ecclesiology are normative, not descriptive, expressing "not what exists but what is intended to be."[20] Fiction that expresses a vision of experience is characteristically negative but simultaneously expresses hope that the Church might ultimately lead the way to the more balanced Blakean vision that blends innocence and experience.

NOTES

1. Fiction is a term commonly associated with the novel and short story, but in including drama as well I am following the lead of Northrop Frye who includes in the designation fiction all works that have internal characters and tell a story; see *Fables of Identity: Studies in Poetic Mythology* (New York: Harcourt, Brace and World, 1963), p. 21.

2. Christopher Durang, *Sister Mary Ignatius Explains It All For You/The Actor's Nightmare* (New York: Nelson Doubleday, Inc., 1981), p. 27.

3. James Hennesey, S.J., *American Catholics: A History of the Roman Catholic Community in the United States* (New York and Oxford: Oxford University Press, 1981), p. 331.

4. Peter Occhiogrosso, *Once A Catholic* (Boston: Houghton Mifflin Company, 1987). What is truly amazing about these interviews is the degree to which educated adult Catholics, many of whom have parochial school experience, have no knowledge of Catholicism commensurate with their secular learning. A case in point is Wilfred Sheed who, despite his apologist parents and the benefits of a Catholic education, reveals extensive confusion about the theology of the Sacrament of Reconciliation (pp. 56–57).

5. Ibid., p. 96.

6. Martin Scorsese as quoted by Occhiogrosso, p. 92. This interview preceded the making of *The Last Temptation of Christ* and the furor that film elicited. But in this interview Scorsese's explanation of his purpose in planning that film is instructive, revealing the personal religious dimension to the director's art:

> *The Last Temptation of Christ* . . . represents my attempt to use the screen as a pulpit in a way, to get the message out about practicing the basic concepts of Christianity: to love God and to love your neighbor as yourself . . . Maybe *The Last Temptation of Christ* could show that Jesus fought with the human side of His nature and let people say, "Hey, I identify with that" . . . That would've given some hope to people in the audience who had lost hope and had lost faith.

Film critics can determine whether or not Scorsese's execution of this intention reasonably reflected his purpose.

7. The novel is the most "elastic" of literary genres, usually defined as an extended work in prose fiction. There was a time when novels were considered either "popular" or "literary," but some contemporary works so strain the established conventions of the novel that they almost defy classification—and consideration as literature. John R. Powers, with his *Last Catholic In America* (New York: The Saturday Review Press, 1973), and his other extended monologues of Catholic folklore, is a case in point. Sadly, these subliterary Catholic comic books seem to sell well, reflecting the pervasive nostalgia for the residual culture of Catholicism in the United States.

8. While I made this observation on the basis of Durang's plays, he confirmed it in his interview with Occhiogrosso in *Once A Catholic*, p. 292.

9. Tom McHale, *Principato* (New York: The Viking Press, 1969), p. 113.

10. Tom McHale, *Farragan's Retreat* (New York: The Viking Press, 1971), p. 132.

11. Philip F. Deaver, *Silent Retreats* (Athens and London: University of Georgia Press, 1988), p. 4.

12. Eugene C. Kennedy, *Comfort My People: The Pastoral Presence of the Church* (New York: Sheed and Ward, 1968), p. 10.

13. Wilfred Sheed, *Transatlantic Blues* (New York: E. P. Dutton, 1978), p. 18.

14. Andrew Greeley, *The Communal Catholic* (New York: The Seabury Press, 1976), p. 2.

15. Walker Percy, *Love in the Ruins* (New York: Farrar, Straus and Giroux, 1971), pp. 5–6.

16. Walker Percy, *The Thanatos Syndrome* (New York: Farrar, Straus and Giroux, 1987), p. 363.

17. Walker Percy, *Lancelot* (New York: Farrar, Straus and Giroux, 1977), p. 157.

18. Walker Percy, *The Second Coming* (New York: Farrar, Straus and Giroux, 1980), p. 357.

19. Cited by Avery Dulles, *The Reshaping of Catholicism: Current Challenges in the Theory of Church* (San Francisco: Harper & Row, 1988), p. 152.

20. Ibid.

3

Visions of Passionate Intensity

The best lack all conviction, while the worst
Are full of passionate intensity

W. B. Yeats

The world of Blakean experience provides the background for another distinctive vision in fiction of the Catholic experience. The heightened awareness of oppressive structures in society, often an initial response to the loss of innocence in Blake's vision, is characteristic of the contemporary priest novel, a form that differs radically from its antecedents in the tradition of American Catholic fiction. Ironically, the fictional bulwark of orthodoxy now serves to subvert the institution.

Given the privileged status of the ordained person, it is not surprising that the character of the priest has been a significant protagonist in the traditional Catholic novel in the United States. However, in the parochial Catholic fiction of the past, the priest–protagonist functioned principally to promulgate the clerical stereotype, fostering the culturally approved norms for the Catholic priest. As Catholics moved into the mainstream of American life following World War II, so did their fictional priests.

The popular success of Henry Morton Robinson's novel *The Cardinal* (1950) reflects America's infatuation with things Catholic during the 1950's, a romance that persists, as is evidenced by the contemporary popularity of Andrew Greeley's fiction. Although the image of the priest presented by Robinson's *The Cardinal* differs greatly from the one offered in Greeley's *The Cardinal Sins* published thirty years later, both writers share the preference for literary romance within the context of the ostensibly realistic novel.

The novel is a fluid form with mixed antecedents, so the romance tradition can be combined with the novel's requirement for realism in a mode of fiction that is the nearest literary form to the wish-fulfillment dream.[1] Such dreams are best projected in the form of romance where the virtuous heroes and the beautiful heroines reflect ideals, while villains represent the threats to their ascendancy. In romance, good is always rewarded, evil is always punished, and it is always clear who wears the white hat. In the contemporary priest novel, however, it is often the wearer of the red hat who is the villain. Like all traditional romances, the priest novel concerns the structure of society, in this case ecclesiastical society, and the subtext is always the struggle for power.

During the first half of the twentieth century, the priest novel, principally formulated in this romantic mode, served to perpetuate the ghetto stereotype of the priest and the values of institutional Catholicism.[2] The idealized world of the Church was pitted against the evils of secular society in a determined effort to preserve innocence. Robinson's *The Cardinal* was both a culmination of that type of fiction and its quintessential expression. Its hero, Stephen Fermoyle, reflected the qualities American Catholics prized in their spiritual leaders—a combination of executive/administrator, spiritual leader (shepherd and counselor), gregarious friend, athlete, and heroic celibate.[3] As with all popular Catholic fiction of the period, the image of the priest in this novel served to preserve the values inherent in U.S. Catholic culture. It was a fiction in the best tradition of romance. Armed only with his shield of righteousness (i.e., adherence to official Catholic teaching), Stephen Fermoyle embodies the immigrant ideal of success with his ascendence to the College of Cardinals.

But the decade that began with the publication of *The Cardinal* also ushered in a trend toward a more realistic portrayal of the priest in fiction. The brief period of self-criticism in Catholic fiction prior to the Second Vatican Council marked the emergence of fiction that imaged the Catholic priest with more realism. Two of those novels won major literary awards; Edwin O'Connor's *The Edge of Sadness* received the Pulitzer Prize in 1962, and J. F. Powers' *Morte D'Urban* was the 1963 recipient of the National Book Award. This led one student of the priest novel genre to speculate in 1969 that fiction of clerical experience, freed from the constraints of the ghetto stereotype, would enjoy a literary renaissance.[4]

Alas, that has not proved to be the case. As history shows, periods of excessive control are often marked by periods of excessive reaction to that control, and this trend in American Catholicism is best illustrated in the contemporary priest novel, a form dominated by a "sacerdotal school" of priests and former priests. Polemical preconciliar fiction designed to bolster traditional values is countered with similarly polemical postconciliar fiction that speaks with equal authority and absoluteness— but against the institution rather than as its bulwark. The concentration on maintaining the institutional stereotype has been replaced by a more subtle and individualistic stereotype that presents the priest as romantic hero challenging the hierarchy.

This trend precedes the Second Vatican Council. Indeed, a novel published in 1960 provides an example of the cultural climate in which the Church would enter the modern world in the United States. William Michelfelder's *Be Not Angry*, a story of a priest's marriage—with his pastor's blessing—presents the disparity between law and love in the best tradition of literary romance. Love is a good, and law, represented here by Church law, is the evil to be overcome. In *Be Not Angry*, Father Bowles' decision to leave the priesthood for the love of a woman is less startling than the approval of his pastor, Monsignor Murchie. Murchie, on his deathbed, responds to Father Rosenbrock, a character who represents the legalistic mentality:

> You are a good priest. You would not do what Bowles has done. Nor would you condone, in your private heart, what I have done in sending him away to the woman. All this you think, and rightly believe. It is doctrine; it is precept . . . yes, even creed. But creed, Father, is not compassion. Nor is canon the same thing as charity.[5]

Murchie's speech is emblematic of the "Sentimental Love Ethic," a romanticized, anti-intellectualism that sees life in terms of absolutes. It is the response to life most closely associated with the period known as The Sixties.

Periods of excessive control inevitably lead to expressions of liberation. In the decline of Puritanism, eighteenth-century American fiction canonized the Sentimental Love Ethic: an anti-intellectual belief that simple feeling is closer to God's truth than educated intelligence.[6] That belief, a symptom of the decline of the authority of Puritanism, is repeated in the contemporary American fiction of Catholic experience during a time of similar decline in the authority of the Church.

The critical response to *Be Not Angry* is indicative of the cultural climate in which the Church in the United States would attempt to enter the modern world within the decade. *Time*'s reviewer praised *Be Not Angry* because it "earnestly pleads that human love is a work of God as surely as is the priestly vocation," and the *Saturday Review* noted that the novel was "passionately committed to belief in a power greater than the disciplines of a church or the practices of a faith."[7] Both comments could readily apply to any one of Greeley's novels. For the fiction that derives from this substitution of the Love Ethic for positive law continues to reflect, not a desire to come to terms with the forces of modernity, but a romantic, anti-intellectual stance that seduces readers through sentimentality. As the *sociologist* Greeley commented in 1976,

> The fideistic anti-intellectualism of the monsignor, the novice master, the seminary rector, and the renaissance monarch archbishop has been replaced by the new anti-intellectualism of the romantic.[8]

Ironically, within four years, Greeley the *novelist* began his career with romantic fiction, which was as popular as Robinson's *The Cardinal* but derived its underlying ethos from the same source as Michelfelder's *Be Not Angry*—the facile Love Ethic that sentimentalizes the moral world.

The sentimental romance, masquerading as a realistic novel, tends to convince the passive reader because of its undialogized voice of authority.[9] But meaning in the novel form is achieved heuristically rather than apodictically. The text that seeks to manipulate the reader does so at the expense of its competence. As Wayne Booth has noted, although there is some degree of rhetoric in fiction, a controlled effort to produce significance, "signs of the real author's untransformed loves and hates are almost always fatal."[10] Booth's phrase "untransformed loves and hates" is an apt description of the fiction I refer to as informed by "passionate intensity," the thesis novel in which plot and character are subordinated to the service of an authorial thesis that has persuasive power. Unfortunately, such a thesis-ridden fiction tends to appeal to readers with a desire for passive consumption, those who would be most likely to unwittingly digest the underlying authorial thesis along with plot developments.[11] A classic illustration of the novel of passionate intensity is James Kavanaugh's *The Celibates*.

THE SEXUAL CELIBATE

Kavanaugh's 1985 novel *The Celibates* depicts the same reductive dualism that Michelfelder had promoted twenty-five years earlier, law versus love. Kavanaugh, the impassioned author of the nonfiction *A Modern Priest Looks At His Outdated Church* (1967), has scarcely modulated the strident tone of that earlier work, and the title of Kavanaugh's 1967 book clearly indicates the lines of his romantic novel published eighteen years later. In *The Celibates*, the institution is all wrong (out-dated) and only the author (a modern priest) understands the situation. The subtext of this story of two Michigan priests is that the requirement for celibacy is an abomination, and, in maintaining this discipline, the insti-tutional Church destroys people.

The difficulty is not the subtext per se, but Kavanaugh's inability to frame a believable fiction. Plot and character development are subordi-nated to the author's untransformed loves and hates. Thesis is all. To promote his belief that no one can live a celibate life, Kavanaugh depicts two priests, one highly sexed, the other rather asexual. Ultimately, of course, he will show that both men are forced from their ministry by the authoritarian hierarchy. But along the way, he asks readers to admire some rather questionable behavior.

Father Ted Santek's sexual needs are so strong that he seduces teenage girls in his parish and, in one scene, makes sexual advances to an emotionally disturbed nun who has come to him for counseling. When parish life becomes too restrictive for his sexual exploits, he becomes an Air Force chaplain and enters into a secret liaison with a woman he has rescued from the destructiveness of the convent. When she pressures him to leave the priesthood, so they can marry and have children, he makes a brief attempt at secular life (during an Air Force leave) but cannot adjust to the demotion in status he experiences in trying for entry-level jobs, explaining, "I miss the priesthood already. It's like I'm nothing without it."[12] Kavanaugh reveals more than he intends. It is obvious that he sees Ted Santek as a modern priest whose sexual needs are repressed by the archaic attitudes of the outdated Church toward human sexuality. But what he presents is a man who embodies patriarchy as much as the institution he disdains. Deriving power and self-esteem from his privileged role, Santek simply desires to legitimize his exploitation of women.

Kavanaugh's other plot line reinforces this reading. Santek's seminary classmate Father Gerry Beauvais, an aesthetically oriented musician, seems to have little need for sex. However, he is victimized by clerical jealousy when a new Bishop comes to power and, posted to an isolated rural parish, suffers an emotional breakdown. Kavanaugh seems to be relying on the stereotype of the high-strung aesthete, for nothing in the fiction prepares the reader for Beauvais' sudden instability. Of course, that instability is a plot device designed to provide Beauvais with a need for a nurturing woman. Enter the woman.

Kavanaugh expects the reader to believe that the retiring, experienced, and wise pastor would provide a beautiful divorced woman in her early thirties as the new pastor's housekeeper. Beauvais, desolate because of his exile, is strengthened by this woman's supportive presence, but when the Bishop comes for Confirmation and orders him to dismiss his attractive housekeeper, Beauvais' ego strength is exhausted, and he winds up in a catatonic despair. The reader must also believe that this woman, Peggy, manages to get Beauvais hospitalized and reactivate the former pastor to manage the parish without anyone from the Chancery ever finding out about Beauvais' illness.

In an increasingly sentimentalized plot, Peggy fights the inadequacy of the state mental hospital and its psychiatrists, finally caring for Beauvais entirely by herself in the rectory while the elderly pastor carries out the sacramental duties. Gerry Beauvais and Peggy are thus bonded emotionally, and when he reassumes his pastoral responsibilities, they function as a couple—except for the fact that they are not physically intimate because Gerry intends to remain a celibate priest. Peggy is the idealized woman of patriarchy, supportive yet subordinate. Ironically, Kavanaugh, in his passionate intensity for an end to the requirement for clerical celibacy does not seem able to depict healthy male–female relationships in his fiction.

The Celibates, like *Be Not Angry*, presents only victims and their allies. Thus, the undramatized villain seems even more nefarious. Michelfelder has Father Bowles' pastor support the priest's decision to marry, and Kavanaugh extends the pattern even further with his portrait of the sympathetic Bishop. When Santek visits the Bishop to argue for Beauvais' innocent relationship with Peggy, he also reveals his own sexual liaison and defends it. Kavanaugh would have his readers believe that the Bishop allows both men to continue their lifestyles, so impressed is he by Santek's candor. Only several years later, under pressure from the villainous Vatican, are both priests forced to resign.

In spite of the narrative energy with which Kavanaugh tells his tale, the problem with this novel lies in the implausible situations the author concocts and his manipulation of characters in the promotion of the Sentimental Love Ethic. But both the genre's inherent realism as well as Kavanaugh's credibility as a former priest serve to mask the contradictions in this simplistic tale. In the guise of a passionate plea for a married priesthood, the actual subtext in this fiction is a demand for autonomy. The United States prizes individualism, and fiction of passionate intensity that focuses on Catholic experience castigates the Church for any restriction of personal autonomy. It is not surprising that this fiction is principally authored by the ordained, for this is inherently a clerical class struggle— cassock against crozier.

THE CHURCH AGAINST ITSELF

The fiction of passionate intensity does not simply seek to disestablish the authority of the Church; it appropriates that authority for its own purposes. In the present cultural climate, the Catholic Church is one of the last vestiges of traditional authority, and fiction of passionate intensity is not authored only by the sacerdotal school. Novels of Catholic experience can create a fiction that appropriates authority to sacralize special concerns, as can be seen in Patricia Nell Warren's *The Fancy Dancer* (1977). This novel predates *The Celibates* but employs similar conventions in support of a different authorial thesis.

Warren's novel tells the story of a young Montana priest, Tom Meeker, who discovers his homosexual orientation in a dramatic encounter during his first parish assignment. The requirement for clerical celibacy is irrelevant, according to this fiction, as are distinctions between heterosexual and homosexual love. "All that matters is whether love is real," Father Meeker explains in a sentiment one could readily expect to find in *The Celibates*—the Sentimental Love Ethic writ large.[13]

Like Kavanaugh, Warren sees the institution as oppressive, so her revisionist theology is promoted by young attractive priests. Father Meeker is the modern priest, as is his gay classmate and Dignity chaplain Doric Wilson, and they must deal with an outdated Church, the stodgy older clergy represented by Meeker's irascible but dim pastor and his conservative and cranky spiritual director. Like Kavanaugh, Warren provides official approval for her perspective by creating an enlightened Bishop who demonstrates his tacit approval by offering Meeker a non-parochial assignment that will eliminate the parish nosey parkers and enable him to enjoy the sexual lifestyle of his choice.

By creating a protagonist who is a priest and by having his Bishop implicitly approve of his sexual activity, Warren, like Kavanaugh, appropriates the status and authority of the Church against itself and in support of her perspective. Despite what you may read in the newspapers, this fiction proclaims, important people in the Church are not opposed to homosexual love relationships.

The popularity of this fiction of passionate intensity with its prominent Love Ethic reflects the shift in the American cultural climate during the past generation. And it is in the atmosphere of moral relativism in which the Sentimental Love Ethic inevitably dwells that the Church must maintain its presence. Simply reasserting authority will not suffice. American culture's espousal of the Love Ethic, apparent in the reviews of *Be Not Angry* in 1960, has increased in the past thirty years. The romance tradition that once helped perpetuate the ghetto stereotype of the priest and promote the values of the institutional Church is now used to subvert the institution. The imaging of the Church in this popular fiction of passionate intensity provides authority for the elimination of moral norms. This is readily apparent in the work of James Carroll.

WAR AND PEACE

The title of J. F. Powers' short story collection *Prince of Darkness* contrasts interestingly with that of James Carroll's mammoth novel *Prince of Peace* (1984). For Powers' concern with the insidious compromises individuals often make that undermine their idealism is conspicuously absent from Carroll's fiction. *Prince of Peace* is an encomium to romantic self-expression, a character study that somehow excludes the necessity for character in its hero—or character development by the author.

The exuberance of romanticism is apparent in the ambition of the novelist, who attempts a cultural history of the United States in the sixth and seventh decades of the twentieth century. This is combined with a look at Catholicism during that same period and a biography of a fictional antiwar priest, Michael Maguire, who is intended as an embodiment of the age. Unfortunately, Carroll's focus on the individual as a symbol is undercut by his inability to create a viable character. His passionate intensity for the new age of secular sanctity is reflected in his florid prose and his inadequate character development. In the story of Michael Maguire, Carroll attempts to reveal an individualistic Christianity superior to any of its orthodox manifestations, but Carroll's reach has clearly exceeded his grasp.

There is little in the novel to affirm the narrative assertion of Michael Maguire's moral superiority. The Maguire who enters the seminary is a Korean War veteran, a hero who has spent twenty-two months as a prisoner of war. Yet during his diaconate assignment in a New York City parish he becomes involved in a political contretemps that antagonizes the Cardinal, and he lets one of the parish nuns take all the blame rather than risk being denied ordination to the priesthood. The nun eventually leaves her order and marries Frank Durkin, Maguire's childhood friend and the novel's narrator. It is possible that Carroll intended this episode to indicate that the war hero Maguire had been emasculated by his seminary education. Yet Maguire's moral behavior as the supposedly noble antiwar priest is even less admirable. As in Kavanaugh's fiction, the Love Ethic is not too loving when looked at closely.

It is not clear what makes Maguire heroic, except for Carroll's florid praise. Even his public antiwar stance is precipitated by an adolescent conflict with the Cardinal rather than any moral conviction about war. Although Maguire, as a representative of Catholic Relief Services, has been in Vietnam and has seen the situation first hand, he is content in his subsequent assignment as a curate in a quiet, suburban New York parish, until he winds up in a power struggle with the Cardinal.

One day a young man named Nicholas Wiley reappears in his life. Maguire had originally met Wiley when the latter was a reporter for the *Catholic Worker*, and the priest had realized that in spite of the young man's obviously sincere idealism, he had severe psychological problems. These problems had led to his expulsion from the Catholic Worker house, and his attempts to join other pacifist groups were similarly unsuccessful. Maguire provides a refuge for Wiley in the parish until the day when Wiley immolates himself in front of the United Nations as an act of sympathy with the Vietnamese Buddhists.

Maguire is interviewed by the press and foolishly allows himself to be drawn into a public conflict with the Cardinal in a dispute about whether or not a funeral Mass can be offered for Wiley. Carroll's romantic impulses make his supposedly realistic scenes ludicrous. Maguire retains an unbelievable naïveté about the political realm that indicates idiocy more than innocence. His immediate commitment to antiwar activity seems less a memorial to Nicholas Wiley than an adolescent rebellion against the Cardinal. In Carroll's obvious desire to depict the institutional Church as corrupt and repressive, he relies on the undialogized voice of authority rather than development of plot and character, but the novel form establishes its meaning from the latter rather than the former.

Once Maguire challenges the Cardinal, Carroll seems to expect the reader to accept all subsequent behavior as heroic. Not only does the priest refuse to accept the consequence of his actions, but in resisting incarceration he causes his best friends, Durkin and Carolyn, to lose the $20,000 they had pledged for bail, their life savings. He has betrayed Durkin, who learns from the FBI that Maguire and Carolyn have been lovers for three years. Yet when the pain of that knowledge impels Durkin to reveal Maguire's whereabouts, Durkin sees himself as a type of Judas to Maguire's Christ figure. The more competent reader might assume Carroll intends Durkin as a classic unreliable narrator, with meaning expressed in the reader's identification of the narrator's fallible perspective. But Durkin's perspective is consistent with a similar ethic in Carroll's earlier novel *Madonna Red* (1976).

In this earlier novel, Carroll attempts to write both a political thriller (IRA assassin against British ambassador in Washington, D.C.) and a commentary on Catholicism (assassin is the cousin of a Catholic priest who foils the assassination attempt). The subplot of *Madonna Red* involves a radical nun who has lied to the Cardinal about reports of her openly presiding at Mass. At the end of the novel, the priest–hero, who has been assigned to investigate the nun's actions, defies the Cardinal and refuses the assignment, a mystifying action and completely unmotivated in the book.

The reason for the hero's transformation from establishment lackey to revolutionary is lost in Carroll's eclectic mix of literary modes. The linear codes of the thriller do not invite complex character development, so the reasons for the priest's dramatic change of heart remain unclear. In an interview, Carroll commented that *Madonna Red* was the precursor of *Prince of Peace*,[14] and both novels do share the implicit notion that once authority is seen as fallible, the individual is free to create his or her own moral world according to whim. In spite of Carroll's florid encomia to his hero Michael Maguire, the author cannot seem to manage a credible fusion of plot and character to provide meaning as is the convention in fictional representation.

Confusion about character development seems to be the result of authorial myopia rather than any attempt at narrative subtlety. Carroll's facile assignment of all evil to the institutional Church and all good to Michael Maguire betrays the anti-intellectual romanticism at the core of his narrative. In *Prince of Peace* intentionality is all; personal sincerity is the only measure of morality. Yet, if history (of which Mr. Carroll seems so fond) has any lesson for us in the twentieth century, it is about the evil done by misguided individuals who assumed they were blameless.

Unfortunately, visions of passionate intensity sell well. The mass market readily absorbs the fictional voice of authority that speaks in absolutes. Authorial conviction is persuasive. The image of the Church presented by Kavanaugh, Warren, and Carroll retains an aura of reality that, for many readers, authenticates that image. Hence, the *New York Times* reviewer of *Prince of Peace*, while critical of the literary lapses in Carroll's novel, nevertheless assumes that the novelist presents an accurate picture of the Church:

> I like "Prince of Peace" best as fictionalized social history because it connects recent events into a coherent and credible statement of what has divided American Catholicism.[15]

This reviewer does not hesitate to accept Carroll's presentation of the institutional Church as "a politically ambitious corporation run by autocratic and cynical executives," so taken is he by this insider's view of the Church.[16]

The mark of good literature is that it does not simply reflect reality, it illuminates that reality for the reader. In the fiction of passionate intensity the authors manipulate the form to present a thesis subliminally, without the need for logical proofs and coherent evidence in support of their position. Verisimilitude, the adherence to realism inherent in the novel form, is used to create an illusion of truth without having to support those assertions. And, unfortunately, the more authoritative the authorial voice, the more it appeals to the passive reader, and the more likely it is that its premises, however intellectually vacuous, will be accepted. This is perhaps most pronounced in the fiction of the prolific Andrew Greeley.

THE GREELEY MYTH

The presence of untransformed loves and hates is nowhere more evident than in the fiction of Andrew Greeley, the priest of the Chicago Archdiocese whose novels have been a sensation of the past decade. It is difficult to examine this fiction from any intellectually viable perspective because questions of its literary value have been obscured by both the author and some of his critics who indulge in *ad hominem* attacks, and by Greeley himself with his relentless defensiveness. Nowhere is this more apparent than in Father Greeley's autobiography, *Confessions of a Parish Priest* (1987), a text that not only details his life but is perhaps even more concerned with this dynamic writer's untransformed loves and hates. This self-portrait, when read in concert with the Greeley novels, provides insight into "the Greeley Myth," the actual foundational story that the author is continually retelling.

The Greeley Myth is the priest's own phrase for the pattern of false assertions he ascribes to his enemies, particularly fellow clergy. It is also an apt description of the underlying pattern of his fictional work, a pattern that reveals the passionate intensity at the heart of these novels. The claims made by the author about the significance of his fiction are contradicted by the dominant motifs in his novels.

According to Father Greeley's account of his career, in the late seventies he noted the important work in narrative theology being done by his fellow priests David Tracy and John Shea who, along with Greeley himself, were reminding the Church of the theological importance of story and its presentation of meaning through metaphor. Father Greeley then decided the time had come to produce some contemporary theological narratives and, after establishing a liaison with Bernard Geis and Warner Books, produced *The Cardinal Sins*.[17] The rest is history, as they say—sixteen novels followed in nine years.

Father Greeley's "comedies of grace," as he calls his novels, therefore, have, the author insists, theological significance, a fact that critics consistently ignore and misinterpret, much to his annoyance. Undeniably, Greeley intends to convey some religious message in his novels; this is indicated by the theological notes that often preface or follow the narratives. Greeley characteristically attributes the fact that reviewers and literary critics fail to appreciate the theological significance of his fiction to either obtuseness or ill will:

> If in fact I must say it repeatedly [i.e., that his are "theological novels"] the reason is that many people have personal hang-ups that prevent them from seeing the obvious, and some people are sufficiently malicious as deliberately to deceive others about the subject matter of my stories.[18]

However, one of the basic principles of literary criticism is that judgment is concerned with the finished work rather than claims of purpose. As D. H. Lawrence succinctly admonished, "Never trust the artist. Trust the tale." Without calling into question Father Greeley's intentions in writing these novels, the fact remains that the discipline of literature evaluates texts according to their competencies, not according to the author's descriptions of them.[19]

Looking more closely at the tale rather than the teller, as D. H. Lawrence advises, one discovers a fiction of passionate intensity that is far more insidious than could be apparent to reviewers of individual novels, especially the early ones when the foundational myth was still in its formative stages. The myth that informs Greeley's fiction can be easily summarized: Eroticism is the primary sacrament of the human encounter with God. There is a corollary of this in the motif of the suffering woman, depicted through a proliferation of sado-masochistic sexual scenes in which pain is inflicted on women, always for a salutary purpose. A secondary motif is the plight of the intelligent and gifted male, who is always persecuted and maligned by his mediocre associates. All three motifs—the erotic as primary sacrament of the encounter with God, sexual violation and physical pain as salvific for women, and male accomplishment as a target for the envious—pervade his fiction.

In Dickens' *David Copperfield* the title character introduces his narrative with the comment, "Whether I shall turn out to be the hero of my own life, or whether that situation will be held by anyone else, these pages will show." For Greeley, there is clearly no "or" involved; in his novels the maligned hero always suffers from slings and arrows modeled on those suffered by his author (in events endlessly recounted in his autobiography, *Confessions of a Parish Priest*). From Kevin Brennan in *The Cardinal Sins* (1981) through Seamus Desmond in *Angel Fire* (1988) and Neil Connor in *St. Valentine's Night* (1989), competent male characters (not coincidentally often priests and academics) are maligned by the envy of their less talented colleagues and associates.

In this fictional motif of misunderstood and reviled genius, the victims enjoy increased recognition and success in spite of the envy of their peers. Seamus Desmond, one of the most recent incarnations of this motif, not only wins the Nobel Prize but has his intellectual acumen acknowledged by the supernatural being who is the other central character in this tale, his guardian angel, Gabriella. She even tells Professor Desmond that he would "make a better pope than a lot of the people who've had the job."[20] As noted earlier, romance is the closest literary form to wish-fulfillment fantasy.

This authorial self-dramatization takes on a decidedly unpleasant cast when Greeley's antagonism toward the hierarchy colors his fictional depictions of its members. The author's disclaimer of such intentionality in *The Cardinal Sins* is paradigmatic of the glibness with which he attempts to extricate himself from criticism. In his autobiography, he comments:

> It was also asserted with serene confidence that the book was based on my conflict with Cardinal Cody. No one who knew anything about Chicago could possibly think that Pat Donahue, my cardinal, had anything in common with Cardinal Cody, besides the red hat.[21]

This remark is so blatantly disingenuous that it insults the intelligence of any competent reader. Comments about the character representing Cardinal Cody in that novel are clearly directed at the *other* Cardinal in that book, Daniel O'Neil. Reading Greeley's account of Cody's administration in *Confessions of a Parish Priest* confirms any suspicion that O'Neil is modeled on Cody. Greeley attributes to O'Neil every negative fact and rumor associated with Cardinal Cody. But, as Greeley's subsequent novels have shown, *The Cardinal Sins* is no *roman à clef*; Greeley's characters simply embody his personal undisguised loves and hates. His undialogized fiction substitutes the *mythos* of the self for the once universally accepted *mythos* of the culture.

Unfortunately, the more passive readers to whom these slick narratives appeal are internalizing not only Greeley's unvarnished hostile opinions of the Catholic hierarchy, liberation theologians, nuns, feminists, academic administrators, and other assorted villains of the Greeley mythic system, but they are also absorbing his theology of sex, a view Greeley propagates with the same glibness that characterizes his self-defense. While scarcely anyone would defend the Church's well-documented, poor record in dealing with human sexuality, elevating the erotic to the status of prime sacrament as Greeley does seems equally unhelpful. In fact, his glib allusions to *sex, human sexuality, passion, eroticism,* and *love* as though they are interchangeable terms helps obscure the very real problems in his fixation on the sexual. As David Tracy comments, *"eros* will be transformed but not negated by divine *agape.* That transformation is *caritas."*[22] But just as Greeley bombards the reader with his untransformed loves and hates in his characterizations, his sexual theme is equally untransformed. It is eros, not caritas that is the dominant expression of his fiction.

In fact, Greeley's sexual preoccupations owe less to the Christian tradition than to the Marquis de Sade. For, like de Sade, Greeley's theology of sex is simply a reversal of traditional proscriptions, a reaction to a repressive past through the creation of a world in which "whatever has been suspect, outcast, and denied is postulated as the source of good."[23] There are indeed theological ramifications to Greeley's fiction, but not the ones he blithely proposes. In his landmark study of *Love and Death in the American Novel,* Leslie Fiedler argues:

> The anti-intellectualism of the sentimental code, its theory that simple feeling is closer to God's truth than educated intelligence, could exist only in the decline of Puritanism and is, indeed, a symptom of that decline.[24]

The parallel with the present moment is inescapable. The prevalence of the Sentimental Love Ethic in this fiction of passionate intensity is a product of the decline of authority in American Catholicism. Unfortunately, Greeley's fiction, which appeals to a wide readership, allies religion with the baser human instincts. For in spite of the theological purposes that Greeley projects onto his fiction, the actual sexual images in these novels reflect a consistent objectification of the female, a practice characteristic of pornography.

The objectification of his female characters, all of whom are consistently described in terms of their sexual attractiveness, is the most obvious manifestation of this pornographic perspective in his novels. I am not the first to point this out, of course, and Greeley's defense is an appeal to verisimilitude; that is how men initially think of women.[25] However, in his fiction, the obsession with female physical desirability is not limited to the male characters. In *Lord of the Dance*, the adolescent heroine Noele Farrell is rebuked for coming into her parents' bedroom without knocking, and she protests:

> "Mo-*ther*, I know Daddy isn't home, and I know you don't have a lover, and"—she whistled appreciatively—"and you're totally beautiful in that pale gray teddy. Like, I wish I had the figure for things like that. Lucky Roger!"[26]

Note that for Noele the human need for personal privacy is limited to the demands of the erotic, and she admires her mother's body with a clear reference—"Lucky Roger"—to her father's sexual enjoyment.

A similar preoccupation with homoerotic thoughts colors the opening pages of *Happy Are Those Who Thirst for Justice* (1987) when another teenager, Fionna Downs, is thinking of her Mexican companion Luisa as "the immigrant girl, fifteen and totally gorgeous in her comic-opera naval uniform, like really voluptuous, you know."[27] And when her mother arrives on the next page of the novel wearing a strapless dress, Fionna's comment is, "Pretty shoulders and boobs" (p. 4). Because lesbians are featured as villains in the Greeley myth, these comments by his teen heroines are indicative of the author's limited ability in creating consistent characters.

This obsessive concern with women's erotic appearance is pervasive in Greeley's novels, and the so-called development of a woman character simply replaces one form of objectification with another. One of the most derogatory presentations of a major female character in Greeley's fiction is Suzie Quinlan in *Happy Are the Meek* (1985). She is initially introduced on the second page of the novel by the Greeley oracle Blackie Ryan:

> Suzie [never Susan or Suzanne, nor Sue for that matter] Wade Quinlan is one of the memorable fluffheads of our era. Not totally unattractive, mind you, until she opens her mouth. Pink cotton candy at a circus.[28]

After a conversation with Suzie's supposed lover, Blackie comments, "I concluded that he had yet to possess himself of poor addle-brained Suzie. Admirable if needless restraint. From the first day of her existence the woman had been trained for submission." (p. 7) It is important to note that these opinions are expressed by Greeley's idealized priest, his most reliable narrator. And when Blackie thinks about having a conversation with this woman three pages later in the novel, he expresses reluctance in an especially revealing comment:

> If you are a celibate and do not plan to go to bed with a woman, her conversation takes on a certain importance. If Suzie Wade could put together three consecutive sentences, it would surprise me. (pp. 10–11)

If a male is not celibate, Greeley has his alter ego assert, a woman's conversation is irrelevant. In this fiction, physical coupling is not expressive of a relationship; it *is* the relationship.

Equally interesting is Greeley's way of showing Suzie's transformation at the end of the novel. She has been redeemed and is now a sedate Sue, rather than Suzie. Visiting Blackie to consult with him about her selection of college courses as she prepares to further her education, the woman is now described by the priest in a different way:

> She clung to the catalog the way a little girl would cling to her dolly. Her tan suit and thin beige sweater, mannish in their style and cut as the fashion section of the *New York Times* had demanded a week ago, said "college professional." Labor Day sun and makeup obscured her pallor. (p. 243)

Sue's redemption does not preclude her continued objectification, although now the emphasis is on her clothing rather than her body. Blackie continues to perpetuate the myth of her mindlessness, attributing to her a slavish adherence to the dictates of fashion experts. She is compared to a little girl clinging to her dolly, but one who is wearing mannish fashions.

Women have no core personality that can develop, this fiction suggests. Their physical appearance is determined by the particular experts to which they give obeisance. This view of women is consistent with the abuse with which they are redeemed in the Greeley myth. In this novel Sue's transformation is effected through graphic scenes in which she and her daughter Laurel are tortured by a mad priest. Violence against women is one of the more compelling aspects of the Greeley sexual myth.

Scenes of sado-masochism proliferate in this fiction. This, for example, is a description of one of Maureen Cunningham's sexual encounters in *The Cardinal Sins*:

Fredo DeLucca was hurting her, deliberately, skillfully, precisely. She reveled in the experience of pain and pleasure, enjoying the sharp stab of agony that repeatedly leapt through her body.[29]

The scene continues in a similar vein, ending with the comment, "It was an experience she wanted again" (p. 232). In *Ascent Into Hell* (1983), the radical nun Liz seduces the priest Hugh Donlon, but theirs is an unhappy union, principally because of her feminist confusion (feminism is one of the consistent negatives in the Greeley mythic system). Near the end of the novel, Greeley inserts a totally gratuitous scene that becomes standard in his subsequent fiction. Hugh and Liz wind up in a Third World country, and coincidentally Laura Kincaid, the innocent daughter of their friends, is there working as a Peace Corps volunteer. The country's leader stages a mock capture of the American party, apparently for the sole fictional purpose of presenting this scene:

The men tore off Liz's and Laura's clothes. Fabric that would not tear was cut away with the bayonets. Naked and terrified, the two women were pushed from soldier to soldier, slapped, fondled, pinched, and squeezed. When they tried to resist, they were beaten, but just enough to intimidate them into passivity again. Dark fingers pawed at white flesh, amusing themselves, taking their time, stretching out their own pleasure and the women's pain and humiliation as long as they could. Torture as foreplay it seemed.[30]

Hugh's response to being forced to watch the abuse of both his wife and the innocent girl is to conclude, "So this was Liz's Third World. He hoped she was happy with it" (p. 301).

While this is only an isolated scene in *Ascent Into Hell*, abuse of women becomes increasingly prevalent in four subsequent novels and is the major motif in three of them. In *Lord of the Dance*, Greeley's sixteen-year-old heroine Noele Farrell is graphically and brutally beaten, raped, and sodomized. *Virgin and Martyr* (1985), the story of the nun-turned-radical Cathy Collins, eventually depicts her actual torture in the imaginary country of Costaguana, but because much of the novel is predicated on her having been martyred, Blackie Ryan's belief that her still living body had been torn apart by a chain saw in the courtyard of a South American military barracks is a recurrent image in the book. Two of the novels in the Beatitudes series also revolve around the abuse of women. In *Happy Are the Meek*, Suzie and Laurel Quinlan are stripped and tortured by a mad priest in a scene that extends over several chapters. And *Happy Are the*

Clean of Heart (1986) begins with the vivid scene of a drugged and helpless Lisa Malone being stripped and tortured by an anonymous assailant whose identity is the crux of the novel.

Lest one think that Father Greeley is simply having some innocent fun to help increase sales, he provides a rationale for this abuse. Physical abuse and sexual violation is the process by which his female heroines mature. After the attack on Noele, she is visited in her hospital room by Father "Ace" McNamara, a priest and psychologist, one of the "good" in the Greeley mythic system.[31] When the priest advises Noele that "there are going to be some tough times" ahead in her recovery, she responds, "That goes with being a woman. We have to learn to live with being raped and things like that" (p. 345). The priest sacralizes this sentiment with the remark, "This is Passion Sunday . . . suffering goes with being human" (p. 345).

Like Noele, Cathy Collins in *Virgin and Martyr* understands that abuse is part of being a woman. Following Cathy's escape from Costaguana, she and her future husband Nick Curran have intercourse for the first time since her horrifying experience of having been repeatedly raped and tortured for two months. At once point he unthinkingly slaps her playfully. Immediately realizing how inappropriate even the slightest connection of sex and violence is in light of Cathy's recent experience he apologizes, but Cathy replies,

> "A man should swat his woman's rear end occasionally. That's one of the things it's for. . . . Remember when you spanked me for pouring sand in your lemonade?"[32]

The still contrite Nick asks, "Did I hurt you then?" to which the "impish" Cathy replies, "I loved every second of it" (p. 521).

The reason women in the Greeley myth welcome physical abuse is because it is salutary. In *Lord of the Dance* Father Ace, counseling Noele after her horrifying experience, explains:

> Some people also have to learn that even though they are cute and smart and popular and maybe a little psychic, they please God the most by learning to live with suffering and tragedy. (p. 356)

This notion that violated women are purified is repeated in *Virgin and Martyr*. In this novel Blackie Ryan, Greeley's consummate priest, explains the value of Cathy Collins' traumatic experience to Nick: "It seems to have facilitated her maturation. . . . Maybe it was a *felix culpa*" (p. 526). When the shocked Nick responds, "That's cruel" (one of the few understatements in Greeley's fiction), the good priest advises, "A tortured and adult Cathy is better than an untortured and juvenile Cathy" (p. 526).

Greeley claims that Blackie represents the priesthood at its best, even repeating a comment that Blackie represents Greeley's own image of God. Thus, Blackie's comments seem to be a reliable expression of the authorial philosophy underlying the consistent images of violated women in Greeley's fiction.[33] In his notion of women's redemptive suffering Greeley is consistent. He has fashioned a seamless garment, but it is a garment that has not been in vogue since the time of the Third Reich.

As in his exaltation of the erotic, the "moments of grace" Greeley refers to in his novels are simply not achieved in the manner he asserts. In *The Cardinal Sins*, the moment Greeley points to as theologically significant occurs when Ellen comes to Kevin for sacramental confession after many years of anger at the Church. His response to her genuine contrition is the remark,

And the damn-fool Church says, "Ellen Foley Curran Strauss, we really didn't notice you were gone, because we never let you go." (p. 210)

The entire scene is highly charged with sentiment, and Kevin's remark indicates Greeley's alliance with Kavanaugh and Carroll, the romantic exaltation of the Sentimental Love Ethic.[34] The old Catholic dictum that "error has no rights" has been replaced by the new age belief that "law has no rights." Obviously Ellen's confession is not a situation for condemnation, but the scene trivializes her sincere contrition. Kevin's response makes her seem like a toddler who has had a tantrum rather than an adult admitting a mistake. With the patriarchal attitude that characterizes Greeley's fiction, Kevin deprives Ellen of her desire for reconciliation by telling her that it is not necessary.

Greeley's second novel provides a model of the manner in which theological significance is presented in his novels. The author asserts that *Thy Brother's Wife* (1982) reflects a Holy Thursday theme. It is about commitments, "perhaps wisely made, sometimes poorly kept but still kept nonetheless."[35] Yet the narrative offers a banal tale about people who sleep around, with the added dimension that one of them is a future Cardinal. It is about commitments, but one fails to see how the illicit sexual activities of various characters is spiritually edifying. However, the author who can claim that the cover art of this novel, a vivid photograph of a sensuous woman dangling a gold cross in her mouth "represents the oral incorporation of God in the Eucharist" and thus points to the secondary theme of Holy Thursday, is clearly capable of any rationalization.[36]

Undeniably, Greeley provides a good read, comparable to the very successful fiction of Sidney Shelton and Jackie Collins and with about as much theological significance. Yet the best-seller actually has a religious meaning but not in the sense Greeley asserts. As Fiedler points out,

> Best sellers are by and large holy books, and the age of the best seller is an age unable to confess its true religion except in terms of commodity fiction.[37]

Enormous sales are a symptom neither of having written an exceptionally fine novel nor an exceptionally bad one, but of having provided a readable text that is extraordinarily consonant with the spirit of the culture. The success of Robinson's *The Cardinal* in the early 1950's was due to its affirmation of the Catholic success story in American culture. This Horatio Alger tale of Stephen Fermoyle, who becomes prince of the Church, mirrored the realization of the American Dream for Catholics and the emergence of the Church from the ghetto. The disarray in the U.S. Catholic culture occasioned by the Second Vatican Council and its aftermath disturbed not only Catholics, but other Americans for whom the Church had represented the last outpost of certitude and innocence in a confusing and complex world. The success of Greeley's novels is a reflection of the widespread wish to be once more in touch with a stable and secure Catholic culture. And Greeley's development of the idealized Ryan clan responds to that desire and should insure him continued popular success.

Unfortunately, the appeal of a stable and secure Catholic culture in this fiction is deceptive. Although it is in the nature of romance to present idealized images, Greeley's undisguised loves are created through the diminishment of his hates, and the Church and most of its official representatives fall into the latter category. His sentimentally idealized clergymen, for example, are presented with a simultaneous disparagement of their real-life counterparts. Blackie Ryan is "far too wise and far too gentle to be like any existing rector of Holy Name Cathedral" and Sean Cronin, "too courageous, honest, and outspoken to be like any known archbishop of Chicago."[38]

In addition, his fiction panders to the darker side of American life. In a society where unrestrained and irresponsible sex is a social as well as moral problem, he sensationalizes the erotic. In a society where abuse of women is rampant and the legal system is only beginning to revise archaic codes that discriminate against abused women, he provides graphic scenes of abuse and has his priests rationalize the need for this brutality. In a society where Catholicism must envision a new paradigm for the third millennium consonant with the Good News, his fiction offers a sentimentalized family Church with an idealized clergy—the old paradigm romanticized.

The difficulty with the fiction discussed in this chapter is that issues that require nuance, dialogue, and reflection are presented to unsuspecting readers in an undialogized mode of fiction that speaks authoritatively. This reductive presentation of these authors' untransformed loves and hates also has a certain power. As Greeley the sociologist so forcefully stated in both *The Religious Imagination* and *Religion: A Secular Theory*, people act more in response to the unconscious images they develop than through rationally acquired principles of behavior. And fiction, which functions through the creation of images rather than through discursive argument, can be particularly effective in influencing its readers' beliefs and behavior.

NOTES

1. Northrop Frye, *Anatomy of Criticism* (Princeton, New Jersey: Princeton University Press, 1957), p. 186.

2. Hugh Rank, "The Image of the Priest in American Catholic Fiction, 1945–65" (Ph.D. diss., University of Notre Dame, 1969). This is the major thesis of Rank's dissertation. Stated explicitly in the preface, it is developed with minute attention to individual novels throughout his important study.

3. Ibid., p. 7.

4. Ibid., p. 408.

5. Quoted by Rank, p. 301.

6. Leslie Fiedler, *Love and Death in the American Novel* (New York: Stein and Day, 1966), p. 79.

7. *Time* 76 (August 29, 1960), 71; *Saturday Review* 43 (August 13, 1960), p. 37. Cited by Rank, p. 302.

8. Andrew Greeley, *The Communal Catholic*, p. 50. Romantic anti-intellectualism in the Church is also the principal theme in the title essay of Greeley's *Come Blow Your Mind With Me* (New York: Doubleday and Company, Inc., 1971), pp. 17–25.

9. The term "undialogized" is a favorite of the Russian critic M. M. Bakhtin. Referring to literary language that is authoritative or absolute, it reflects the same premodern epistemology as preconciliar Catholic thought and is, of course, inimical to the novel form, a product of modern epistemology.

10. Wayne Booth, *The Rhetoric of Fiction* (Chicago: University of Chicago Press, 1961), p. 86.

11. A similar point about the linear codes that restrict plurality and thereby appeal to more passive readers is developed by Frank Kermode, *The Art of Telling: Essays on Fiction* (Cambridge: Harvard University Press, 1983), pp. 72–74.

12. James Kavanaugh, *The Celibates* (New York: Harper and Row, 1985), p. 190.

13. Patricia Nell Warren, *The Fancy Dancer* (New York: Bantam Books, 1977), p. 182.

14. Michael J. Farrell, "James Carroll's Fiction's Priestly Pursuits," *National Catholic Reporter* (May 12, 1989), p. 30.

15. Webster Schott, "Maguire the Mettlesome Priest," *New York Times Book Review* (November 4, 1984), p. 44.

16. Ibid.

17. Andrew Greeley, *Confessions of a Parish Priest* (New York: Pocket Books, 1989), p. 478. Elsewhere in this book (p. 203), Greeley admits to turning to fiction in the hope of finding a wider audience than he had found for his nonfiction publications.

18. Ibid., p. 484.

19. In responding to his critics, Father Greeley often invokes the defense of the "scholarly" study of his work by Ingrid Shafer, principally *Eros and the Womanliness of God* (Chicago: Loyola University Press, 1976). However, this book is, by Professor Shafer's own admission, scarcely "scholarly." As she points out in her introduction, "I have no intention of limiting myself to analytical arguments." Thus, the text is riddled with methodological problems. For example, when it serves her purpose, Professor Shafer cites scholarship in support of the Greeley perspective. Accordingly, she notes that the eminent literary scholar Northrop Frye credits the unique Christian perspective with the importance of the female in romance (p. 124). But she faults Frye for insisting on keeping separate the Romance tradition and Christianity (p. 125). Shafer's argument is that Greeley, as a Catholic priest, has a better perspective on this issue than the acknowledged scholar whose work on the structure of romance is the standard in the field (Northrop Frye, *The Secular Scripture: A Study of the Structure of Romance* [Cambridge: Harvard University Press, 1976]). It is this blithe shift from scholarship to personal bias that mars this supposedly "scholarly" study.

In addition, although Greeley frequently cites Shafer's work to counter literary critics' negative assessments of his fiction, *Eros and the Womanliness of God* is not a literary study and answers none of the critics' objections to the Greeley novels. Although Shafer raises the question of literary merit in her prefatory attacks on the critics who have failed to understand the Greeley theological vision, she does not provide literary analysis but a detailed explication of Greeley's major theological themes and symbols, a type of "reader's guide to the fiction of Andrew Greeley." However, as is evident in her negation of Frye, this is a reading of the fiction that privileges authorial assertion.

20. Andrew Greeley, *Angel Fire* (New York: Warner Books, 1988), p. 230.

21. Greeley, *Confessions*, p. 500.

22. David Tracy, *The Analogical Imagination* (New York: Crossroad Publishing Company, 1981), p. 432.

23. Fiedler, *Love and Death*, p. 34.

24. Ibid., p. 79.

25. Greeley, *Confessions*, p. 122. A literary critic who presents a similar view of Greeley's treatment of women is Mary Zeiss Stange, "Little Shop of Horrors: Women in the Fiction of Andrew Greeley," *Commonweal* (July 17, 1987), 412–17.

26. Andrew Greeley, *Lord of the Dance* (New York: Warner Books, 1984), p. 28.

27. Andrew Greeley, *Happy Are Those Who Thirst for Justice* (New York: Warner Books, 1987). p. 3.

28. Andrew Greeley, *Happy Are The Meek* (New York: Warner Books, 1985), p. 2.

29. Andrew Greeley, *The Cardinal Sins* (New York: Warner Books, 1981), p. 232.

30. Andrew Greeley, *Ascent Into Hell* (New York: Warner Books, 1983), p. 300.

31. In his "Disclaimer" at the beginning of the novel *Lord of the Dance*, Greeley notes that none of the characters speaks with his voice "save occasionally Father Ace." Because these sentiments are among the fictional priest's few significant remarks and because they are in the same spirit as those of Greeley's other fictional alter ego, Blackie Ryan, it might be assumed that the lines cited are among the "occasions" when character speaks for author.

32. Andrew Greeley, *Virgin and Martyr* (New York: Warner Books, 1985), p. 521.

33. Greeley, *Confessions*, p. 498.

34. Interestingly, Greeley castigates both Kavanaugh and Carroll (*Confessions*, pp. 290–91) in an indictment of priests who leave the priesthood. His comments about *Prince of Peace* are revealing, because he clearly distorts the text to make an unfounded assertion about its author. This comment coming from a writer who relentlessly complains about critical responses to his own fiction reminds one of the beam and the mote.

35. Greeley, *Confessions*, p. 495.

36. Ibid., p. 491.

37. Fiedler, *Love and Death*, p. 46.

38. These are the standard descriptions of Monsignor Ryan and Cardinal Cronin that preface each of the novels in the "Beatitudes" series, the "Blackie Ryan books."

4

Visions of Innocence Restored?

Fair Quiet, have I found thee here,
And Innocence, thy sister dear?

Andrew Marvell

The character of the priest has emerged as an amateur sleuth in contemporary American detective fiction. Initially, the focus on the priest–detective appears to be a corrective to the prevalence of the Sentimental Love Ethic in the postconciliar priest novel. The detective novel, a literary form dependent on an externalized moral order, seems an ideal palliative. But in literature, as in life, appearances are often deceiving. The fictional American priest–detective is related less to his apparent ancestor in crime, Chesterton's Father Brown, than to the upheaval in contemporary Catholic culture.

In spite of the popularity of the British Father Brown, the American priest–detective's appearance in fiction was delayed until Father Roger Dowling began solving crimes in the 1977 novel *Her Death of Cold.*[1] The priest's emergence in American detective fiction is a product of literary, cultural, and religious change and provides important insights into the current moment in American Catholicism.

During the first half of this century, the American tradition in detective fiction was not conducive to the development of a priest–detective. It was a tradition grounded in the hard-boiled private investigators of Dashiell Hammett, Raymond Chandler, and Ross MacDonald.[2] The world of such novels combines harsh realism with sensational, often violent, events, and the detective–hero is physically, as well as intellectually, tough. This distinctively American mode of the detective novel reflects the culture's idealization of rugged individualism. The American private detective usually operates in an adversarial relationship to the police who disdain these amateurs in their world.

On the other hand, the British detective, a product of a traditional, structured society with an established Church, tends to be either an official representative of the police (Roderick Alleyn, Adam Dalgleish, Inspector Wexford, Henry Tibbett) or a brilliant eccentric (Sherlock Holmes, Hercule Poirot, Jane Marple, Peter Wimsey). So Chesterton's priest with his "face as round and dull as a Norfolk dumpling" is well suited to the British tradition of the eccentric amateur.[3] It is a tradition that prizes deduction rather than physical action and where class differences alleviate the tension between professional and amateur.

Conversely, the American detective's adversarial relationship with the law reflects the American fascination with rugged individualism. The detective-as-loner in American fiction affirms a view that justice depends on the individual outside the law by emphasizing the detective–hero's success and police inefficiency.[4] Although the brilliant eccentric is not unknown in American detective fiction (Nero Wolfe is perhaps the most vivid example), superiority to the police is always emphasized. During the first half of the twentieth century, the traditionally anti-establishment role of the American detective would exclude the Catholic priest, the representative of a Church that was engaged in the effort to enter the American social mainstream, a Church in which singularity was not a virtue. Both the violence and the frequent erotic encounters associated with the hard-boiled detective–hero would also mitigate against the creation of an American priest–sleuth.

Current American detective fiction features three prominent priest–detectives and two series featuring a nun–detective. Changes in the culture and in the Church account for this phenomenon. Detective fiction, like other popular art forms, reflects the society in which it is produced, and the vast cultural changes experienced in U.S. Catholicism in the 1960's and 1970's mirrored social and intellectual changes in the entire culture. The American detective story and its heroes changed radically during this time.

Perhaps as a reaction to the violence of a society torn by wars, two other strains in American crime fiction gained ascendancy in the years following World War II. The crime as puzzle to be solved, a predominant emphasis in the work of Ellery Queen, Rex Stout, and Earle Stanley Gardner, became more popular. In addition, the police procedural novel, epitomized in Ed McBain's 87th Precinct series, helped balance the continued presence of the hard-boiled private investigator. The increasing use of technology in solving the mystery emphasized teamwork, and a fiction of the cooperative group interested in securing justice developed along with the standard American image of the lone private investigator.

The concept of heroism is subject to cultural change, and this is reflected in fiction, especially formula fiction like the detective story. In the past twenty years women have been increasingly depicted as detective–heroes, and two of the current popular American private detectives are modeled on their hard-boiled male counterparts. Sue Grafton's Kinsey Milhone and Sara Paretsky's V. I. Warshawsky are independent operators of their own agencies, well able to handle both the violence and eroticism common to hard-boiled tradition. Both characters are clearly a product of the psychic shift in American understanding of gender resulting from the Women's Movement.

A similar cultural shift accounts for the new priest–detective. Despite its appearance of realism, the detective story belongs to the literary mode of fantasy. It is, as Jacques Barzun observed, "the romance of reason."[5] Like all romances, it appeals to the reader's need for wish fulfillment—but of a very specific type. The experience of the classic detective novel is primarily cathartic, symbolically granting the human wish for restoration and renewal. In mythic terms, the crime is the act of social disruption by which innocence is lost, and the job of the detective is to restore the state of innocence. From the cultural perspective, the U.S. Catholic culture lost its innocence in the aftermath of the Second Vatican Council, and, interestingly, since 1977 three priest–detectives have appeared on the American literary scene where formerly there were none. The need felt for a restoration of innocence is surely one factor in this fiction's popularity.

From the mythic perspective, the priest is an ideal detective, and the poet W. H. Auden describes the crime milieu in distinctly religious terms:

It must be an innocent society in a state of grace, i.e., a society where there is no need for the law, no contradiction between the aesthetic individual and the ethical universal, and where murder, therefore, is the unheard of act which precipitates a crisis (for it reveals that some member has fallen and is no longer in a state of grace). The law becomes a reality and for a time all must live in its shadow, till the fallen one is identified. With his arrest, innocence is restored, and the law retires forever.[6]

Prior to the 1960's, American Catholic culture preserved its state of innocence and had no need to admit the detective into its ranks. Today, however, not only is the detective a priest, but frequently it is the Church that is most responsible for the crime, the "member which has fallen and is no longer in a state of grace." Clearly innocence has been lost, and the apparent restoration of lost innocence through the ecclesial detective is illuminating. While the form would encourage an attachment to the residual ethos of innocence, the character of the priest–detective in contemporary American fiction clearly reflects an emergent ethos that casts institutional Catholicism in the role of villain.

From the literary perspective, one would expect the priest–detective novel to provide an alternative vision to the Love Ethic, which predominates in contemporary priest novels. The sentimental exaltation of love over law as though they are mutually exclusive concerns engenders a moral relativism that is inimical to the detective mode which necessarily emphasizes justice and operates with an externalized moral order. Because the detective is a heroic figure in this genre, the priest–detective should provide a needed prominence and definition to the role of the priest in society, a need indicated in the fiction of Walker Percy, John Gregory Dunne, and Wilfred Sheed (see Chapter 2). But this is not the case. Nowhere in contemporary literature is the current confusion in U.S. Catholicism more prominent than in this form of detective fiction.

The detective novel is formulaic fiction that involves the use of archetypal story patterns in terms of specific cultural materials.[7] The emphasis on Catholicism in the American detective story, a phenomenon of the past decade, is a prime example of specific cultural material being incorporated into the form of the detective story. In formulaic fiction, the archetypal story patterns (the conventions) and departures from those patterns, are extremely illuminating indicators of authorial vision.

Popular literature is especially responsive to cultural influences, and the formulaic pattern of the detective novel serves to highlight those influences. On the current scene there are three priest–detectives and two nun–detectives solving crimes, and a close look at the lineaments of this fiction informs the contemporary crisis within Catholic culture. To begin at the beginning is to look first at McInerny's Father Roger Dowling.

RETURN TO THE GOLDEN AGE

Roger Dowling, who made his debut in *Her Death of Cold* (1977), is the creation of Ralph McInerny, the author of numerous novels of Catholic experience in addition to his critically acclaimed Father Dowling books.

Roger Dowling appears in his first novel "impeccably dressed in clericals, his Roman collar seemingly a centimeter higher and a shade whiter than anyone else's."[8] And it is consistently clear throughout the Dowling series that orthodoxy is measured by the preservation of traditional externals of Catholic culture. Father Dowling not only regularly recites his Office, he uses a Latin breviary. He prays frequently, preferably in the presence of the Blessed Sacrament, and "a day without the recitation of the rosary would have been a dead day to him."[9] He provides one Latin Mass each week for his parishioners, using the new rite because it is "simply too much of a hassle to get permission to say the Tridentine Mass."[10] And, as his cohort police lieutenant Phil Keegan says of his daily Mass, "Dowling could be trusted not to stage any liturgical extravaganzas. A straight simple Mass, done at a brisk but reverent pace."[11]

But Dowling is idealized for more than liturgical purity. "A Dante scholar of sorts," Father Dowling embodies a medieval worldview with its unambiguous moral order and universally accepted recognition of the truth of that order.[12] In fact, Roger Dowling's present assignment as pastor of St. Hilary's Church is indirectly a result of the failure of society at large to retain a sense of the hierarchical order and the commitment to personal responsibility such a worldview entails. For Roger Dowling is a degreed canon lawyer who was a rising star in his diocese, an important member of the Marriage Tribunal for many years. Alcoholism led to his exile to the relatively obscure parish of St. Hilary in the small Illinois town of Fox River. And the cause of that alcoholism is related less to the rigid strictures of Church marriage law, which Dowling was obligated to apply to the cases that came before him, than to the prevalent failure of people to acknowledge their personal responsibility in relation to that law.

It is not the legal system, secular or ecclesiastical, that is the evil in this fiction; it is the human refusal to submit to law. For, as we learn in another novel, Dowling feels that "litigation is often a protest against personal responsibility, a refusal to accept the consequences of one's own free choices."[13] Caught between the Scylla of an unyielding canon law and the Charybdis of bewildered litigants who cannot fathom the worldview on which that law is based, much less accept it, Roger Dowling retreats to the comfort of alcohol: "It was when the marriage court no longer seemed to deal in anomaly but only with life very small that he began to drink."[14]

Alcoholism ruins his promising ecclesiastical career, but, once rehabilitated, Dowling is free to do "the work for which he had been ordained."[15] From the evidence of the text, it appears that the work for which Roger Dowling has been ordained is a preservation of the past. Aside from helping Keegan solve crimes, Dowling principally is occupied in maintaining the parish as primarily a clerical domain. In one novel, he is reported to be preparing young people for Confirmation, a fact that upsets one new parishioner who mentions that in her former parish the entire family was involved in this celebration where it included many activities beyond catechesis. Dowling ignores her plea for such "witless innovations," and sticks to his orthodox preparation of "soldiers of Christ." Of course, in the fiction this reluctant parishioner is won over, although McInerny gives no reason why she should be.[16] Apparently Catholics really do want to leave the parish entirely to their priests—at least that is the message these novels promote.

With a collar "a shade whiter than anyone else's," Roger Dowling represents the True Church in Exile. This is emphasized by Phil Keegan, an ex-seminarian equally committed to the preservation of the faith of his youth. In one novel, Dowling is away on retreat, and Keegan attends the noon Mass celebrated by his temporary replacement Father Bovril, a presider who attempts such radical innovations as having members of the laity serve as lectors. Keegan is displeased:

> It was always a safe haven when Dowling was the celebrant. Bovril was different in that Bovril was exactly what Keegan would have found in most of the parishes in town, in the state, in the country, and for all he knew, in the world.[17]

Interestingly, Keegan, from whom McInerny elicits most of his judgments about the state of the Church, is described much like Tom McHale's Angelo Principato: "Keegan's faith was blind. He accepted it all. But the truth was he preferred not to talk about it."[18] The attitude that McHale disparages, McInerny seems to celebrate. If the culture promotes a worldview at odds with the medievalism of neo-Scholasticism, then Catholics should simply obey the Church blindly. Clearly, McInerny's detective series reflects a longing for the restoration of innocence, the Golden Age of Catholicism Past.[19]

Dowling's adherence to customs and traditions of the past is part of the attempt to recapture an intellectual and social milieu that has disappeared. This is most apparent in the contrast between Father Dowling and Chesterton's Father Brown. Like his predecessor in detecting, Father Dowling's primary interest is in the soul of the criminal rather than the solution to the crime. However, whereas Chesterton's priest–detective converts even the infamous Flambeau, Dowling is as unsuccessful at getting murderers to accept responsibility for their behavior as he was with litigants before the marriage court. Despite this experience, Dowling assumes the existence of a universally accepted, objective moral order, a position at odds with the reality of contemporary pluralism.

Throughout the novels, the priest attempts to minister God's mercy to people who do not recognize their need for it. Unfortunately, in Dowling's attempts to right the wrongs of contemporary relativism, the novels seem more located in the political right than mere theological conservatism. Dowling often seems more anti-liberal than anti-evil, as in this comment:

> Above all, the doer must be protected from the suggestion that he could not have acted otherwise, that something in his psyche or surroundings or genes or upbringing explained the action. Better an unapprehended murderer who knew what he had done and was genuinely sorry before God, than a caught culprit condemned to years of thought control as he was programmed for re-entry into society by technicians who regarded him as a machine.[20]

Against the Sentimental Love Ethic that disparages law, McInerny insists on an inflexible recognition of the claims of law. For Roger Dowling the question of obedience to law is central to the character of the individual person. Faced with postconciliar abuses of canon law, "the product of cynicism parading as mercy," Dowling asks himself the rhetorical question:

> Is there a human self distinct from the history of its deeds, a self that can be freed from what it has done, from what it is, and still be, still exist?[21]

This central theme that pervades the Father Dowling series is an obvious reaction to the Sentimental Love Ethic that trivializes law and creates a distorted view of reality. Thinking about his experience on the Marriage Tribunal in *Second Vespers*, Father Dowling concludes:

> The guilty party is each of us. No man is without sin. No court, no code of law, can undo the past, make what we have done as if it had never been. We are what we have done. A new self can be created only by a prolonged sequence of deeds, not by a ruling, not by a judgment that events which occurred never really happened.[22]

By maintaining the True Faith in all its manifestations—clerical dress, liturgy, canon law—Roger Dowling is Church Past in Exile. Unfortunately, McInerny diminishes the moral power of his presentation by forcing the Fox River pastor to bear the burdens of all his author's complaints about contemporary society, especially its ecclesiastical dimension. This is clear in McInerny's most obvious departure from the conventions of the detective novel. Father Dowling himself represents the "innocent society in a state of grace" in this fiction, so there cannot be any restoration of innocence. Society at large refuses to accept the priest's priorities, and Church Past in Exile is limited to the rectory study where the pastor watches the Cubs in the company of Keegan. This vision of the saving remnant in isolation is McInerny's consistent emphasis, as can be seen in his subsequent development of a nun–detective.

Writing under the pseudonym Monica Quill, McInerny has produced several creditable mysteries featuring Sister Mary Teresa, a septuagenarian who is to religious life what Father Dowling is to the priesthood. She is one of only three remaining members of the fictional Order of Martha and Mary, a community that has been decimated by the decision to "engage in allegedly more meaningful work."[23] Sister Mary Teresa is the only one who has remained in the original habit, and is thus "a reassuring symbol in a world that seemed to change with such dizzying rapidity."[24] She is, appropriately, a medieval historian, and the superiority of Sister Mary Teresa as a symbol of Church Past is implicit in the pattern of the novels.

The two young nuns who complete the small community, Sisters Kim and Joyce, represent the modern religious world. They are well-meaning, pleasant women, but they are never able to solve the crimes. This is especially apparent in Sister Mary Teresa's principal assistant Sister Kim, a doctoral student in history whose relatively unstructured routine frees her to spend time checking on clues for the elderly sleuth. The senior nun and her junior assistant are very evocative of Nero Wolfe and Archie Goodwin, except that Kim is not allowed Goodwin's intelligence or competence. Only Sister Mary Teresa, the emblem of the Church's glorious past, is able to solve the crimes and restore innocence.

It is apparent in the fiction that in the character of Sister Mary Teresa, McInerny is attempting to restore the Golden Age of Catholicism. In one novel this is especially explicit. Sister Kim feels "drawn back into a better time" she can only know from the elderly nun's description:

> More than once Sister Mary Teresa had suggested that the Thirties, Forties, and Fifties would one day be recognized as a golden period in the history of the Catholic Church.[25]

Sister Mary Teresa's life shows "how brilliance can flourish even in the apparently restrictive corridors of the convent."[26]

Unfortunately, as in the Dowling series, McInerny's vision begins to appear less allied to traditional Catholicism than to the political conservatism of the radical right. Certainly Sister Mary Teresa's insistence on the need for capital punishment belongs to a more contemporary political agenda than to Thomism.

> Sister Mary Teresa took it as a religious obligation to hunger and thirst after justice and she had no patience with those who became sentimental on the subject of punishment. She had a little lecture on capital punishment to counter maudlin denials of the moral responsibility of the human agent.[27]

How the "religious obligation to hunger and thirst after justice" makes capital punishment a moral imperative is made clearer in the casuistry in another novel:

> You and I—society—do not have the power to forgive a murder. God does that. And the death penalty does not interfere with God's mercy. It may be an instrument of it.[28]

McInerny's efforts are so focused on the Church Past, the restoration of a culture, the lost Golden Age of American Catholicism, that he completely discounts contemporary society. If the residual ethos is to have meaning in the modern world, those values must find expression in a modern context. An example of an attempt to influence the dominant culture with residual values can be seen in the nun–detective series authored by Sister Carol Anne O'Marie.

SISTERS IN CRIME

While the nun–detective is not a new phenomenon, the debut of the fictional Sister Mary Helen in the 1984 *A Novena for Murder* marked the first nun–detective created by an actual religious sister, Sister Carol Anne O'Marie. While Sister Mary Helen wears a modern habit and is certainly less conservative than Father Dowling and Sister Mary Teresa, she embodies traditional Catholic values in the modern world more effectively than other ecclesial detectives. She restores innocence to a fallen world in both secular and Catholic terms.

Like Sister Mary Teresa, Sister Mary Helen is a septuagenarian, but unlike McInerny's nun, Mary Helen has made her peace with the modern world. She has chosen to abandon the traditional habit for modern dress, shocking her contemporaries in the community. Her explanation is typically pragmatic, "Well, I figured life would go on with or without me . . . so I might as well go with it."[29]

Yet she is discriminating about change, neither accepting blindly nor resisting obstinately. Forty years earlier along with the habit, Sally O'Connor had received the religious name Mary Helen, and, she explains, the latter name signifies her identity after all these years. Given the option to return to her baptismal name, Sister Mary Helen retained her name in religion. "Besides," she explains, "a seventy-five-year old Sister Sally sounds ridiculous."[30] Sister Mary Helen is, however, not simply Sister Mary Teresa in modern dress. The differences in the basic patterns in the two series reflect important differences in authorial perspective.

In McInerny's fiction, Sister Mary Teresa sits in splendid isolation. Like Nero Wolfe, she seldom leaves the house but sends Sister Kim on errands and has her bring suspects to the convent for questioning. Sister Mary Teresa's eminence and isolation are clearly intended to highlight the glory of the past when American Catholicism insulated itself from the world and preserved its medieval worldview. This self-cloistered and coifed nun can solve crimes that baffle the modern world, just as a return to the Golden Age will restore order to a confused society, according to the implicit message of this fiction.

On the other hand, Sister Mary Helen not only does her own leg work, she enlists others in her cause. One of the strengths of Sister Carol Anne's fiction is her depiction of the relationship among the three "sisters in crime" who cooperate in each mystery. Sister Anne comes close to being a stereotypical postconciliar young nun in her jeans and moccasins, but she is provided with intelligence and good sense and is an equal partner in the detecting triumvirate. The third regular ally is Sister Eileen, several years younger than Mary Helen and the realist of the group. Her cynical comments about Mary Helen's enthusiasm for detection rescue the fiction from taking itself too seriously, for the success of these novels is in maintaining a tone that invites the reader to become involved in a self-consciously fictional mode meant primarily for enjoyment.

The first two novels in this series, *A Novena for Murder* (1984) and *Advent of Dying* (1986), depict murders at the sisters' college, and in both novels the murderers are brought to justice in the classic simplicity of the detective genre. Like most amateur detectives, Sister Mary Helen associates with the police, and it is in this relationship that this fiction provides the most telling contrast to McInerny's detective fiction. For Sister Mary Helen does not merely identify murderers, her presence in the fiction promulgates traditional Catholic moral values through the subplots involving detective Inspector Kate Murphy.

The homicide team of Dennis Gallagher and Kate Murphy is involved in each of Sister Mary Helen's adventures, and in the first novel the paternal Gallagher is concerned about his partner, the daughter of a fellow policeman, now deceased. Kate is living with a fellow detective, Jack Bassetti, and everyone wants them to marry except Kate. When the team is called to investigate a murder at the sisters' college, Kate's alma mater, Gallagher's first thought is that perhaps getting back in contact with the nuns will "straighten her out" about her relationship with Jack. The Catholic perspective of the Kate Murphy story is unfailingly traditional. *A Novena for Murder* ends with the marriage of Kate and Jack, *Advent of Dying* ends with Kate's enthusiasm for motherhood, something she had resisted throughout the novel, and *The Missing Madonna* (1988) recounts Kate's attempts to conceive a child.

The Sister Mary Helen novels reflect the mythic pattern Auden identified. The sisters' college is an enclosed world of innocence into which evil intrudes. Law enters (Gallagher and Murphy aided by the detective–heroine, Sister Mary Helen), the evil is expelled, and innocence is restored. However, the specifically Catholic dimension extends the restoration of innocence beyond the campus to the alumna, who has become confused by the different values proposed by secular society. Kate Murphy, para-digmatic Catholic-in-the-world, is restored to innocence (returns to the faith community) through her association with Sister Mary Helen in solving crimes. One commentator complains that Sister Carol Anne "doesn't portray sin well," yet concludes that her novels "make innocence fashionable, attractive, alive."[31] In this regard, Sister Mary Helen, gender difference notwithstanding, is the most authentic contemporary incarna-tion of Chesterton's Father Brown.

Unfortunately, Sister Carol Anne's weakness is plotting, an element essential to detective fiction. This weakness destroys *The Missing Madonna*, as both competent police procedure and common sense are sacrificed to a flawed plot, seriously detracting from the credibility of the principal characters. In the novel, a woman is missing, and her friends suspect foul play. Yet the author expects readers to believe that experi-enced detectives, as well as the very pragmatic and intelligent Sister Mary Helen, would accept the unverified explanation of one individual, espe-cially when his story rings false in many particulars. It is interesting that this latest novel also has the weakest "Catholic" subplot involving Kate Murphy.

It might be hoped that Sister Carol Anne O'Marie can retain the form of her first two novels, for she creates a fictional world in which the residual Catholic ethos interacts positively with the dominant culture in

American society. And that is certainly the minority vision in the Catholic detective novel, as is evident from the work of the sacerdotal school of Kienzle and Greeley.

CASSOCK VERSUS CROZIER

Two years after Father Dowling began his career as a detective in fiction, William X. Kienzle's Father Robert Koesler helped the Detroit police solve *The Rosary Murders* (1979). Like Roger Dowling, Father Koesler prefers clerical dress in all but the most informal situations ("bed, bath, beach, and golf course"[32]) and he, too, recites his breviary in Latin. In *Kill and Tell* (1984), the fictional Father Koesler discovers the existence of his clerical counterpart, Father Dowling:

> Koesler was about the same age and disposition as the fictional Father Dowling. Both were in their mid-fifties; neither cared for canon law; both thought the good old days really were the good old days more than less, and neither understood the very young new Roman Catholic clergy.[33]

The contradiction between surface and substance here is indicative of a consistent pattern in the Koesler series. While Fathers Dowling and Koesler may share a preference for clerical attire, Roger Dowling's commitment to law, canon and secular, is explicit in McInerny's fiction. The association that author Kienzle suggests is either based on his own misreading of the Dowling fiction or is part of a conscious attempt to confuse surface and substance in his own novels.

Kienzle creates a deceptive fiction with a priest–detective who seems to embody a commitment to tradition, while the pattern of the fiction reveals a bias against the institutional Church, inevitably the true villain in most of the novels in his popular series. In *The Rosary Murders*, the psychopathic murderer of priests and nuns is less relevant to the narrative than his motivation for the crimes, the inability of a confessor and a nun to deal with the plea for help by the murderer and his daughter who were engaged in an incestuous relationship. When the daughter commits suicide, the father carefully plans an intricate series of murders of priests and nuns as revenge.

In a Father Dowling novel, the murderer's plan would reflect the typical modern inability to assume personal responsibility for evil, trying to alleviate his own sinfulness by projection. In the Father Koesler fiction, the plot emphasizes the abuse of authority in the Church, which is ultimately responsible for the crime. At the heart of Kienzle's fiction is a pervasive anger at the authoritarianism he apparently sees as the central problem in Catholicism.

In *The Rosary Murders*, Kienzle reinforces his obvious point about the abuse of power in the Church in his reversal of the detective story's formulaic ending. Rather than the traditional meeting of the principals to explain the details of the now-solved crime, Kienzle emphasizes the negative image of the abusive confessor by creating a final scene in which another man confesses incest and meets with a similarly outraged and implacable confessor, thereby suggesting that the motivating incident was not anomalous.[34]

Father Koesler's contribution to the solution of crimes is in his ability to provide the police with significant clues because of his arcane and esoteric knowledge of canon law and pastoral practice. This, combined with Koesler's tendency to daydream and reminiscence, results in an enormous amount of information about Catholic tradition and pious practices being given to the reader. All this information, and the priest–detective's centrality, creates an impression that this is a very Catholic detective series, committed to orthodoxy. However, the dialectic in Kienzle's detective novels between good and evil pits Koesler and other good members of society against the Church as the central evil. In addition to the initial *The Rosary Murders* in which callous confessors caused the crime, other novels in this series depict the rupture of the fabric of society being caused by the Church itself.

In *Mind Over Murder* (1981), the evil is in the stringent Catholic marriage laws, as well as in the abuse of authority. In *Deathbed* (1986), the Church's ethical standard demands the closing of a valuable inner-city hospital, thereby engendering a worse evil, and in *Marked for Murder* (1989), the killer is actually a priest, a man who has been victimized by archaic canon law. *Assault With Intent* (1982) is an uneven conflation of mystery and slapstick involving a group of former seminarians who attempt to harm the priests who dismissed them years earlier. What angers them now is that, with the current shortage of priests, the seminary is retaining equally inept men. In almost every novel, actions by the Church are the cause of violence, either directly or tangentially. Even in novels that have a more secular explanation for the crime, Kienzle never fails to offer a negative view of the Church. *Kill and Tell*, for example, portrays a vain and materialistic auxiliary Bishop whose disdain for the law provides the killer with the murder weapon.

Ostensibly, Father Koesler is satisfied with the Church. But the reader soon discovers that Koesler's satisfaction is in his enjoyment of priestly fellowship and clerical privilege. Preferring to be addressed by his title (but addressing the laity familiarly, of course), Father Koesler is most comfortable among his fellow clerics. The narrative frequently shows priests dining together, often in fine restaurants, especially after a day of golf, and Father Koesler's conversations and frequent daydreams are peppered with nostalgic tales about the experiences of priests. In *Eminence* (1989), the clerical mystique is elevated in significance as Koesler's inability to feel a priestly camaraderie with the villain, who is masquerading as a priest, is the only means of identifying the culprit. Kienzle prepares the reader for this "solution" with an encomium to priestly fellowship that crystallizes the implicit clericalism of the earlier novels. At the airport, when the police are attempting to apprehend the villain no one can clearly identify, Koesler casually notices another priest, and Kienzle reports:

> There was a priest who was approximately Koesler's age. They did not know each other, but they nodded and smiled at each other. Oh, the incomparable camaraderie of the priesthood! No one but a priest could fully appreciate it.[35]

This would be innocuous except for the fact that this "incomparable camaraderie" appears to dictate the priest–detective's moral perspective. The second and third novels in this series provide a case in point.

In *Death Wears A Red Hat* (1980) the victims are members of Detroit's underworld who exploit others—an organized crime leader, the head of an illegal drug empire in the city, a notorious pimp, the head of the numbers operation in Detroit, a sadistic abortionist, and a con man who preys on the elderly. Father Koesler discovers the identity of the murderer, an ordained permanent deacon, who admits to the killings. The deacon even brought suspicion on Koesler by leaving a clue that pointed to the priest as the killer and, finally, when Koesler is on the verge of identifying him, he assaults the priest. Koesler wrangles with his conscience over whether or not he is obliged to identify the murderer to the police (ironically, for someone who disdains canon law, he is always invoking it to resolve personal dilemmas), but in spite of six admittedly premeditated murders,

> It was impossible for Koesler to perceive his friend as a murderer. For the moment, Koesler preferred to look upon it as an as-yet undefined form of justifiable homicide.[36]

Even as a misapplied notion of the means justifying the end, it would be hard to credit this thinking because the underlying evil was not abolished—let alone seriously undermined—by the elimination of a few of its practitioners.

The fact that the deacon's ordination, his special status in Kienzle's clerical mind-set, might help explain this permissiveness is indicated by the very opposite reaction of Father Koesler in his next adventure, *Mind Over Murder*. This novel highlights the psychological sadism of Monsignor Thompson, the head of the diocesan Marriage Tribunal. In an interestingly contrived plot, the priest mysteriously disappears, and Kienzle leads the reader to believe that one of Thompson's many victims has finally murdered him. At the end it is discovered that the disappearance was part of an intricate plan to expose the cleric's sadistic behavior. Monsignor Thompson is not physically harmed but is disgraced when his diary is leaked to the press.

The author of this revenge, a powerful millionaire named Lee Brand, gathers Thompson's various other victims for a celebratory dinner and also invites Father Koesler who helped solve the mystery. However, Koesler is not as generous to this character assassin as he was to the multiple murderer in the previous novel. When the other guests have departed, the priest confronts his host:

> Mr. Brand, as a Catholic you must know that it is the teaching of our Church—*your* Church—that each person has a right to a good reputation whether such reputation is deserved or not, unless the person himself or herself publicly destroys that reputation. But you have taken it upon yourself to destroy a man's reputation by innuendo and the revelation of his most private thoughts.[37]

Brand's crime was stealing Monsignor Thompson's diary and making sure the press discovered it. Because Thompson had used the diary to gloat about the various ways he had destroyed the hopes of many of the people who had come before the Tribunal by failing to take action or otherwise humiliating them unnecessarily, the revelation of his own narrative of events was sufficient to destroy his career.

Koesler's cavalier attitude toward the multiple murders by the deacon and commitment to "what he considered his priestly obligation" to correct the character assassination of Monsignor Thompson betrays the clericalism that is at the heart of this fiction. The vacillation in moral perspective, a fatal flaw in detective fiction, is not readily apparent because the essential dialectic between Koesler (the good) and the magisterium (the bad) is consistent. The conventions of the detective mode reinforce the central dichotomy in this fiction.

While McInerny would restore the Golden Age of Catholicism with its medieval worldview, Kienzle seems to desire a liberal Church with a restored innocence of priestly fellowship, a special society of privilege and honor for the clergy. Or is Father Koesler such a traditional priest, stalwart representative of the True Faith, in order to enlist "the Church against itself" in another variation of the priest–novel that subverts the institution?[38]

Certainly the pattern of the novels is unmistakable. Author Kienzle manipulates the conventions of detective fiction to fashion an ongoing indictment of institutional Catholicism. In a fictional form that requires an externalized moral order, Father Koesler represents the "innocent society in a state of grace" while the institution and its law is the fallen member "no longer in a state of grace." So corrupt is this institution, according to the dynamics of the fiction, that the best Koesler can accomplish is to remove individuals from the influence of the "fallen member" of society. We read that "in practice, Koesler bent church law as far as he feasibly could *to serve the needs of individuals.*"[39] In each novel, then, Father Koesler redeems some unfortunate victim of the institution's villainy.

A recurring subplot in this series, the relationship between two investigative reporters, Joe Cox and Patricia Lennon, highlights the moral matrix of the Kienzle novels. Sister Carol Anne O'Marie's subplot involving Kate Murphy illustrates the traditionalism at the heart of her fiction. In Kienzle's subplot, he reveals the Sentimental Love Ethic at the center of his novels.

In *The Rosary Murders*, Lennon and Cox are introduced as having been together only two weeks. Both reporters have been previously married, and by the third novel *Mind Over Murder*, Pat Lennon, a lapsed Catholic, is inquiring about an annulment of her former marriage to marry Joe Cox in the Church.

In *Mind Over Murder*, Pat Lennon becomes one of the victims of the nasty Monsignor Thompson. After explaining her case to a priest at the Marriage Tribunal, Lennon is assured that she has significant grounds for annulment. At this point Thompson takes over the case because he has a preference for attractive women and takes some delight in apparently professional discussions that force them to describe intimate details of their sexual habits and practices. Predictably, the self-assured reporter refuses to submit to this treatment, and Thompson dismisses her, assuring her there will be no annulment without her cooperation. She consults Koesler who simply tells her that Thompson has full authority, and her fate is in his hands. A novelist who creates recurring characters needs to be faithful in their representation, and in this instance, Kienzle subverts both Lennon and Koesler to the demands of his plot.

Koesler has already demonstrated his disdain for canon law, and in this novel he is aware of Thompson's reputation for harassing litigants. He does not encourage Lennon, and, uncharacteristically, insists that she has no option if she does not cooperate with Thompson. On the other hand, Lennon is an intelligent and skilled investigative reporter and has balked because she knows that Thompson is clearly exceeding the requirements of the case in his questions. Is it Koesler's inherent clericalism that prevents him from encouraging Lennon to use her professional skills to develop a formal complaint against Thompson? What is more strange is that Koesler, who confronts Lee Brand because of "his priestly obligation," feels no priestly obligation to help Lennon resolve her marriage problem in spite of the fact that she has tried to initiate the process and has been treated unfairly by the venal Thompson.

Although Cox and Lennon appear in many of the eight subsequent novels, Father Koesler seems to have forgotten that Pat Lennon had expressed a desire to have her marriage regularized. Apparently law can only fail to serve the needs of individuals. It is not the simple fact of their remaining unmarried that is most disturbing in this fiction but the way Kienzle idealizes this relationship. Cox and Lennon live in a luxury apartment and share fascinating work that they discuss over leisurely Sunday brunches. One of the most revealing descriptions of their relationship is in *Deathbed*:

> Both felt they had chanced upon something rare and free: a relationship that found them loving each other and growing in that love. It was the epitome of what one might hope to find in an exemplary marriage. Neither wished to chance mucking up what they had by getting the certificate that society expected them to acquire stating they were married.
>
> In addition, their sex was great.[40]

If this passage sounds familiar, the reader is identifying yet another manifestation of the Sentimental Love Ethic. Kienzle's commitment to the Love Ethic is less apparent than that of Kavanaugh or Carroll because he is writing in the form of detective fiction. In a form which requires a concern for an externalized moral order, Kienzle creates a fiction of moral relativism.

Yet there *is* a submission to law in this fiction, and the very next paragraph of this text highlights the distinction Kienzle makes:

> The obvious pitfall, of course, was that their jobs frequently placed them in direct competition. By now, they had worked out some ground rules. Each recognized that if their self-made rules were not scrupulously observed, it could easily mean the end of their personal relationship. So the rules were scrupulously kept.[41]

One does not undercut established morality without providing an alternative, and Kienzle's choice seems to be situation ethics. It is no authorial lapse that Cox and Lennon live together "without benefit of clergy" but a part of the moral vision pervasive in the Father Koesler series—a version of the Sentimental Love Ethic that is promoted as modern Catholic morality because its principal proponent is cast in a traditional image of the conservative priest. The moral vision in Kienzle's novels is actually closer to that of a very different priest–detective, Greeley's Blackie Ryan. For, as in all Greeley's fiction, the novels that feature this amateur sleuth principally expound the author's radical commitment to his self-styled law of love.

THE RYAN FAMILY DETECTIVE

> Praise the Lord and pass the black leather garter belts. Andrew M. Greeley, the priest known for his novels about the carnal clergy and lascivious laity of Chicago, has adapted his racy style to the mystery genre.[42]

Thus the first "official" Blackie Ryan novel, *Happy Are the Meek* (1985), was greeted by the *New York Times*' critic Marilyn Stasio. Although each of subsequent mysteries in the Beatitudes series is billed as "a Father Blackie Ryan" novel, readers of the Greeley *oeuvre* know that Blackie actually began his career in fiction in *Virgin and Martyr* (1985) and is a character in other Greeley novels as well. For, as Stasio's comment indicates, the Beatitude novels are less a classic detective series than an application of the Greeley myth to the mystery genre. The priest–detective Blackie Ryan is best understood in the context of the Ryan family saga, which is continually evolving, according to Greeley himself.[43]

There is a literary cliché that only God loves his characters more than the author J. D. Salinger, but that saying should be amended. As much as Salinger idealizes his fictional Glass family, he cannot hold a vigil light to Greeley's adulation of the Ryans. They embody the American success story for Chicago's Irish Catholics, not simply preserving their ethnic and religious heritage as they enter the American mainstream but waving it like a banner proclaiming their distinctive identity. In his *Confessions of a Parish Priest* (1987), Greeley admits that the Ryan clan composes a matrix for his imagination (p. 496) and claims that they are a symbol for the Church, "loyal faithful, tender, zany, resolute" (p. 499). In fact, they seem to be more of an alternative to the Church. They constitute the Perfect Church, as opposed to the Fallible Church in Need of Reform, the target of much Greeley criticism. In the evolving Ryan family saga, the Ryans' perfection is always in counterpoint to the Church's villainy.

The first four installments of the Ryan *mythos* present the redemption of characters who have suffered abuse from the Church and its official representatives. Cathy Collins of *Virgin and Martyr* is brutalized not only by the South American terrorists, but, earlier in the novel, she is the victim of a repressive and sadistic religious formation. She is later victimized by both the former priest she marries and the charismatic priest who exploits her wealth. In Greeley's *Confessions*, he explains that Anne Reilly of *Angels of September* (1986) "has been savaged by the Church through much of her life," and the male protagonists in *Rite of Spring* (1987) and *Patience of A Saint* (1987) "have been pushed around by the Church for much of their lives" (pp. 497–98). All these people are ministered to by the beneficent Ryan clan "with affection, persistence, and ingenuity" (p. 499). Indeed, Greeley asserts, "The Church has a long way to go before it comes close to that model" (p. 499). Thus, the Ryan family, embodying virtues the Church has yet to attain, is Greeley's Perfect Church.

And, traditional Catholic that he is, Greeley needs a hierarchy for this idealized Church, so each of the three Beatitudes novels has the prefatory note:

Monsignor John Blackwood Ryan, PhD., is far too wise and far too gentle to be like any existing rector of Holy Name Cathedral.

Sean Cronin is too courageous, honest, and outspoken to be like any known archbishop of Chicago.

Thus, not only are the priests of the Perfect Church introduced, but their counterparts in the Fallible Church in Need of Reform are described by implication. For Greeley, Blackie Ryan represents "the priesthood at its best" (p. 498), and the novels are vehicles for displaying that wonderfulness.

It is an interesting comment on the image of the priest in contemporary American culture that Greeley makes him a detective in order to idealize him. As Dorothy Sayers pointed out long ago, in modern society "the detective steps into his right place as the protector of the weak—the latest of the popular heroes, the true successor of Roland and Lancelot."[44] Thus it is that in spite of the perfection of each of the Ryans, Greeley confidently says that "Blackie holds all the stories together" and is "the central figure in the saga" (p. 496). Blackie is a detective in order to fulfill his symbolic role as "protector of the weak," the Perfect Priest of the Perfect Church.

In Blackie's first appearance in fiction, Greeley allies him with Chesterton's famous priest–sleuth:

> Blackie looks like a modern Father Brown, short, pudgy, cherubic, with curly brown hair, apple cheeks and an expression of impenetrable composure. He is the kind of utterly unimportant-appearing person that you wouldn't even notice if he was on the elevator when the door opened and you walked it.[45]

But unlike Father Brown—or Father Dowling—Blackie Ryan has no need to minister to criminals because there are no secular criminals in Greeley's mythic system. In the Sentimental Love Ethic, law is the central evil, so in the Greeley detective fiction, innocence is restored without need of legal intervention. In *Happy Are The Meek* the murder is justifiable homicide, and the perpetrators of the crimes in *Happy Are the Clean of Heart* (1986) and *Happy Are Those Who Thirst For Justice* (1987) are presented as insane. As in the Kienzle mysteries, the central evil in all this fiction resides in the Fallible Church In Need of Reform.

For Greeley, as for Kienzle, detective fiction is less a means for asserting the presence of a moral order in the face of contemporary secularism than for presenting the villainy of the Church. The traditional work of the fictional detective is not only to identify the culprit but, in doing so, to expunge evil and restore innocence. In their fiction, Kienzle and Greeley present the institutional Church as the evil to be purged. Thus, detective fiction, which ideally would be a vehicle for asserting an accepted moral perspective to counter the relativism of the Sentimental Love Ethic in contemporary priest novels, is subverted by both writers. Because the conventions of detective fiction lead readers to expect a traditional moral order, this fiction is perhaps even more subversive than other priest novels that promote the Sentimental Love Ethic.

Thus, the popular form of detective fiction provides a microcosm of contemporary attitudes within Catholicism in the United States and offers insight into the cultural significance of these attitudes. Kienzle's and Greeley's attempts to establish the Sentimental Love Ethic as the dominant ethos are, of course, the ruling passion in the fiction of passionate intensity already discussed. But, although the form of the detective novel highlights the difference between Ralph McInerny's retreat to the residual ethos of preconciliar Catholicism and Sister Carol Anne O'Marie's attempt to articulate an emergent Catholic ethos, that difference is not always easily identified in less formulaic fiction.

NOTES

1. For an overview of the clerical crime novel see Catherine Aird's essay on clerical detective fiction in *Murder Ink*, ed. Dilys Winn (New York: Workman Publishing Company, 1977), pp. 467–69 as well as the systematic review of the genre, *Mysterium and Mystery: The Clerical Crime Novel* by William David Spencer (Ann Arbor and London: UMI Research Press, 1989), especially the "time line," pp. 320–21. Ralph McInerny, *Her Death of Cold* (New York: The Vanguard Press, 1977).

2. For a fuller discussion of this characteristic American detective fiction, see George Grella, "The Hard-Boiled Detective Novel," *Detective Fiction: A Collection of Critical Essays*, ed. Robin W. Winks (Englewood Cliffs, NJ: Prentice-Hall, Inc., 1980), pp. 103–20.

3. G. K. Chesterton, *The Father Brown Omnibus* (New York: Dodd Mead and Company, 1961), p. 5. This famous description of Father Brown appears in the first story, "The Blue Cross," of the initial 1911 collection, *The Innocence of Father Brown*.

4. John G. Cawelti, "The Study of Literary Formulas," Winks, p. 142.

5. Jacques Barzun, "Detection and the Literary Art," Winks, p. 145.

6. W. H. Auden, "The Guilty Vicarage," *The Dyer's Hand and Other Essays* (1948; reprint, New York: Random House, 1968), p. 150.

7. Cawelti, p. 124 ff.

8. McInerny, *Her Death of Gold*, p. 27.

9. Ralph McInerny, *The Seventh Station* (New York: Vanguard Press, 1977).

10. Ralph McInerny, *The Basket Case* (New York: St. Martin's Press, 1987), p. 25.

11. McInerny, *Her Death of Cold*, p. 42.

12. Ibid., p. 26.

13. Ralph McInerny, *Bishop As Pawn* (New York: The Vanguard Press, 1978), p. 17.

14. McInerny, *Her Death of Cold*, p. 28.

15. McInerny, *The Basket Case*, p. 101.

16. McInerny, *Bishop As Pawn*, pp. 49–50, 65–66, 111, 183.

17. McInerny, *The Seventh Station*, p. 57.

18. Ibid., p. 61.

19. The "Father Dowling" who appears on television, however, belongs to another genre—and another culture. McInerny has no connection with the television version of his priest–detective (as he informed me in a personal conversation), so the video Dowling is apparently designed to appeal to the popular cultural image of Catholicism. In the interest of Catholic verisimilitude the priest's first name has been changed from "Roger" to "Frank," and his suburban parish of St. Hilary is now the inner-city St. Michael. Dowling has been allowed to keep his cantankerous housekeeper (perhaps because she is already a true Catholic stereotype), but in the interest of the television detective genre, Phil Keegan is gone and the police are extraneous, for television has added a young nun

sidekick who accompanies "Frank" Dowling everywhere in his sleuthing because, we are asked to believe, the priest cannot drive! The daring duo of "Father Frank" and "Sister Steve" are a bumbling Batman and hip Robin, as television perpetuates cartoon Catholicism. While McInerny's Dowling books may not appeal to the popular imagination (they have, interestingly, not appeared in paperback), the television Dowling is an absurdity with dramatic car chase scenes and implausible plots. It almost makes McInerny's Golden Age appealing.

20. McInerny, *Her Death of Cold*, p. 81.

21. Ibid., pp. 27–28.

22. Ralph McInerny, *Second Vespers* (New York: The Vanguard Press, 1980), p. 39.

23. Monica Quill, *And Then There Was Nun* (New York: The Vanguard Press, 1984), pp. 73–74.

24. Ibid., p. 13.

25. Monica Quill, *Sine Qua Nun* (New York: The Vanguard Press, 1986), p. 153.

26. Ibid.

27. Monica Quill, *Let Us Prey* (New York: The Vanguard Press, 1982), p. 197.

28. Monica Quill, *Nun of the Above* (New York: The Vanguard Press, 1985), p. 127.

29. Sister Carol Anne O'Marie, *A Novena for Murder* (New York: Charles Scribner's Sons, 1984), p. 110.

30. Ibid.

31. Spencer, *Mysterium*, p. 163.

32. William X. Kienzle, *Shadow of Death* (New York: Ballantine Books, 1983), p. 106.

33. William X. Kienzle, *Kill and Tell* (Kansas City and New York: Andrews, McMeel and Parker, 1984), p. 141.

34. William X. Kienzle, *The Rosary Murders* (New York: Bantam Books, 1979), pp. 291–93.

35. William X. Kienzle, *Eminence* (Kansas City and New York: Andrews, McMeel and Parker, 1989), p. 282.

36. William X. Kienzle, *Death Wears a Red Hat* (New York: Bantam Books, 1980), p. 267.

37. William X. Kienzle, *Mind Over Murder* (New York: Bantam Books, 1981), p. 295.

38. I make this suggestion not solely on the basis of the contradiction between this apparently conservative priest who is meticulous about proper clerical attire and etiquette but who evidences such obvious hostility toward the institutional Church, but because of the authorial design suggested by that contradiction. Koesler's "conservatism" is limited to personal habits rather than patterns of thought, so his character is either poorly drawn or is purposefully dichotomized. The latter is suggested by a minor but interesting detail. When Koesler "discovers" Father Dowling's novels in *Kill and Tell*, the sixth novel in this series, Koesler is suddenly depicted reading his breviary four pages later—in Latin. Because this is new information about Koesler, never mentioned in the previous novels, it appears that the reference to Dowling and the adoption of his manner of reading the Office is a conscious attempt to make Koesler appear more similar to Dowling than he is in fact.

39. Kienzle, *Death Wears a Red Hat*, p. 123; italics are mine.

40. William X. Kienzle, *Deathbed* (Kansas City and New York: Andrews, McMeel and Parker, 1986), p. 93.

41. Ibid.

42. Marilyn Stasio, review of *Happy Are the Meek*, by Andrew Greeley, *New York Times Book Review* (September 29, 1985), p. 46.

43. Andrew M. Greeley, *Confessions of a Parish Priest*, p. 496. Subsequent citations from this autobiography will be indicated by page numbers in parentheses within the text.

44. Dorothy L. Sayers, "The Omnibus of Crime," Winks, p. 56.

45. Andrew M. Greeley, *Virgin and Martyr* (New York: Warner Books, 1985), p. 75.

5

Visions of Reconciliation

The Gods are hard to reconcile;
'Tis hard to settle order once again.

Tennyson

As might be expected, the disruptions in Catholic culture begun in the 1960's spawned various attempts in literature to provide meaning for this experience. For some writers, witnessing what they saw as a dissolution of their religion, there was an attempt to fictionalize a solution. Liberal or conservative, these authors share a "vision of reconciliation," an attempt to merge the Catholic past and present and provide a context in which claims of the past are allied to present concerns. Their work, however, illustrates the aptness of Tennyson's line from "The Lotus-Eaters"—"'Tis hard to settle order once again."

THE GOLDEN AGE IN MODERN DRESS

While Ralph McInerny's priest–detective, Father Dowling, represents an impulse to retreat to the Golden Age, his nondetective fiction attempts to apply traditional Catholic approaches to life to contemporary situations. In two novels written before he began his detective fiction and two written since that time, McInerny has shown that his vision of the way the past and present are to be reconciled is unwavering. The 1973 novel *The Priest* provides an important foundation for this vision.

The Priest is McInerny's longest, and perhaps most successful, novel. Although it covers a comparatively brief time span (one summer), it provides a panoramic view of Catholicism in transition. McInerny has an acute perception of the weaknesses in the various groups that clamor to be recognized as representing the True Faith, and he presents a series of memorable portraits in this novel. The focal character is Father Frank Ascue, who returns from doctoral study in Rome to the fictional Midwest diocese of Fort Elbow expecting to be the new moral theologian at the diocesan seminary. Instead, his Bishop, known for capricious assignments, inexplicably sends him to a local parish as second assistant.

As Ascue becomes acquainted with his new parish, the reader meets the assorted members of the postconciliar Church. These include Ascue's classmates—one a dissident priest destined to marry before the end of the novel, the other a pompous and complacent cleric anxious to reap the privileges of his priestly vocation while sowing as little as possible; an energetic but dissatisfied young nun who will become the bride of the dissident priest; an ambitious auxiliary Bishop, angling for his own diocese; a liberal pastor on the fast track; the organized Catholic right (a group called "Te Deum" that is, predictably, misheard as "tedium"); a married couple of liberal bent with intellectual pretensions; and Ascue's own family—his sister and brother-in-law, a liberal Catholic feminist and a confused (and adulterous) husband, and their college-age daughter, who is impregnated by a seminarian "testing his vocation."

To his credit, McInerny portrays all of these types vividly and without obvious bias in favor of either the conservatives or the liberals, and he provides an excellent sample of the wide diversity of people and opinions huddled under the Catholic banner. Unfortunately, among all these vivid cameos, Frank Ascue becomes obscured. Caricature rather than characterization seems to be McInerny's strength, so Ascue remains as one-dimensional as all the characters around him. He drifts through associations with all the people in the novel, and those associations only bewilder him. By the end of the book, he is questioning his vocation. With little self-reflection by Ascue in the narrative, there is no preparation for this crisis. McInerny resolves the dilemma abruptly in a brief but telling incident.

In the final pages of the novel, Ascue makes a retreat and encounters an enigmatic elderly priest, Father Leo, who pronounces sentence on the contemporary situation in the Church. "We are being punished," Leo tells Ascue, explaining, "You and I. Priests, the laity. God is punishing us, Father. We have much to answer for."[1] In Leo's cryptic words, Frank Ascue reads an indictment of his current confusion. He had been concerned with others' actions, he reasons, and now he must be penitent and resolve not to judge. In this spirit of self-abnegation, Ascue decides to continue in the priesthood.

Frank Ascue seems to have refocused his life as the novel closes, but there is no indication how this renewed cleric will function in the contemporary Church. McInerny seems better able to depict aberration than balance, and the final scene of personal resolution seems incomplete. *The Priest* highlights postconciliary confusion but achieves resolution solely in terms of the personal interiority of the central character.

In a subsequent novel, McInerny identifies the ills for which punishment is being meted out according to Father Leo in *The Priest*. For McInerny, authority must be responsibly enforced as well as obeyed, and deviations from this hierarchical orderliness are at the heart of the Church's problems. His 1975 novel, *Gate of Heaven*, focuses on a group of priests who are members of the fictional Order of St. Brendan. The novel's title refers to the Order's retirement home, Porta Coeli, and the action centers on the residents of that home, a group of retired priests who gain an unexpected voice in the development of the community's nearby college.

The college is headed by one of the Order's most ambitious younger members, Father Hoyt, who runs not only the college but the community as well through his manipulation of the weak and ineffectual provincial Father Faiblesse. However, Hoyt's decision to demolish the original campus building (known as Little Sem) to make room for a new dormitory runs into unexpected opposition.

Because of a condition in the long-forgotten bequest, the fate of the building requires the unanimous agreement of all living founding members of the community. For some of these elderly men, Little Sem, the building in which they spent the first years of their religious life, takes on a metaphoric significance. They feel as discarded by the community as the building that faces demolition, and they resist the change with their only remaining power—a veto. Ultimately, Little Sem is demolished, but the elderly priests indirectly cause the downfall of the ambitious Father Hoyt as well. The conflict galvanizes the passive provincial who finally begins to assert his lawful authority, and a proper hierarchical order is thereby restored to the Order of St. Brendan.

This novel makes more explicit the perspective of *The Priest*, which is that obstinate resistance to change is as destructive as mindless change. The Founder's deathbed admonition had been, "Let go," advice that applies to the urge to wield power as much as to blind loyalty to the past. Yet, in spite of the apparent balance in the central message of this novel, the older priests are all portrayed with greater depth and compassion than the younger members of the community, betraying an authorial bias toward the past that will become pronounced in McInerny's subsequent novels. This bias is not simply a sentimental nostalgia. The moral matrix of McInerny's vision is the importance of responsible use of lawful authority and obedience to that authority. It is at the center of the Father Dowling novels and illuminates the essentially reactionary vision at the heart of McInerny's apparent attempts at reconciling Church past and present in *Connolly's Life* and *Leave of Absence*.

Connolly's Life (1983) is McInerny's story of conversion among the intellectual left. The character of Michael Connolly, dissident theologian and philandering priest, is reminiscent of the postconciliary stereotypes in *The Priest*. Connolly's character is clearly designed to embody McInerny's vision of the clerical ills in postconciliar Catholicism, and the crux of the novel is in the enactment of Father Leo's warning at the end of *The Priest*, "We have much to answer for." Repentance is the central theme of *Connolly's Life*.

The major event in the novel occurs one day at O'Hare Airport when Connolly misses his plane. He had already checked in and received his boarding pass, so when the plane crashes, the priest is presumed dead. By the time he learns of his reported death, Connolly is already in the midst of a personal crisis of sorts because the reason he missed his plane is that a woman had collapsed in the airport bar where he had gone for a preflight drink. When he noticed the rosary that had slipped from the woman's handbag, the tell-tale sign of a Catholic, Connolly identified himself as a priest. But neither victim nor onlookers would credit the claim of the casually dressed Connolly, and he compounds the problem by his inability to remember the words of absolution.

So shocked is he by this failure that rather than try to board the next flight, he retreats to the airport hotel where he eventually learns of the plane crash and his presumed death. He thinks about notifying the press that he has survived, but, instead, still troubled by the incident in the airport and now further disturbed by the thought of his near brush with death, he begins a private retreat at the O'Hare Hilton. The "death" of Michael Connolly results in his rebirth as a priest through a renunciation of his postconciliar activity:

> What have we all been up to since 1965? I suppose 1968 was the crucial year. I've been accused of trying to make Catholicism easy, and empty. My accusers are right.[2]

He eventually travels to Italy to see his old friend Jim Clark, a professional writer and the novel's narrator, and there, while he is trying to decide how best to live the rest of his life in piety, Connolly is murdered in a bizarre case of mistaken identity.

This somewhat improbable plot succeeds largely because of McInerny's choice of point of view. The story is told by Connolly's friend Clark, a complex and intriguing character. A self-proclaimed agnostic, Clark has been Connolly's friend since they were in the minor seminary together. Clark's subsequent loss of faith, attributed to Connolly's dalliance with Clark's wife, further compounds the priest's depravity. Clark's faith has been undermined by the liberal left, embodied in Connolly, who also becomes, by indirection, a symbol of all that ails contemporary Catholicism.

Thus, in spite of his secular lifestyle, Clark becomes the oracle for orthodoxy, the individual Catholic disenfranchised by liberal Catholicism. For example, when Clark and Connolly lunch with Notre Dame University's then-president, Father Hesburgh, Clark's evaluation of the two priests reflects the fiction's subtext:

> Sympathetic as the two priests were, there was something in Hesburgh that Connolly lacked, and that was unquestioning loyalty to the Church. I have never met a man with such confidence that everything is going to turn out all right. Perhaps that came from the never-missed daily Mass. . . . Hesburgh remained a champion of clerical celibacy, and I for one never saw him in anything but clerical clothing. (p. 146)

Except for the name and the reference to "his university," Father Dowling, rather than Father Hesburgh, could be the subject of these words. Note, however, that Connolly is not directly compared to Hesburgh, simply diminished by the comparison. McInerny's strategy in having the theological left undercut either by indirection, as in this passage, or directly by its representative, the converted Michael Connolly, successfully promotes the conservative cause without any apparent authorial intrusion. But the cause of the traditional past is undeniably the motivating factor in this fiction.

The major moral point McInerny makes in this novel is that actions have consequences, consequences for which the individual must bear responsibility. Father Dowling had once rhetorically asked himself, "Is there a human self distinct from the history of its own deeds, a self that can be freed from what it has done?"[3] This novel is, at one level, a dramatic response to that question. Apparently freed by a plane crash from the person he had become, Connolly later dies as an indirect result of having long ago betrayed his friend Clark. Residual punishment for sin is very real in this book.

The novel functions best as a satire of the Catholic left, especially dissident theologians. But the plot indicates McInerny's scope was wider, and in the development of this narrative the author betrays the classical vision that is actually at the heart of this supposedly modern tale. From the literary perspective, the two major characters are sacrificed to the underlying theological imperatives. The major development of the novel is the conversion experience of Michael Connolly, and it is especially well presented in the text through Clark's reading of Connolly's journal, a device for authenticating the essentially interior experience yet bringing it into the public forum. By the final pages of the novel, Connolly is a sympathetic character for the reader, a character who is then suddenly and violently murdered. It is an especially ironic murder, because Clark was the intended victim.

Connolly's death is a plot device designed to reinforce the religious message. Unfortunately, the theological imperative conflicts with the demands of fiction. The priest was saved from the airplane crash in order to save himself. Because the novel records that he has made a general confession, and his only plans for the future are for a pious life in pursuit of sanctity, his death is not tragic from the theological perspective. In the novel, however, this ending is as reassuring as the standard parochial school exemplum about the young child who is hit by a car and killed on the way home from his or her First Confession (or First Communion). It has a similar theological basis and about as much literary merit. The random murder of a character the reader has come to like, a character who is in the process of renewing and changing his life, is as unsettling in literature as it is in life.

The other character who is subverted by McInerny's theological preoccupation is the narrator, Jim Clark. As a professed agnostic who expresses a residual commitment to traditional Catholic ideals, he seems to be a character in search of a conversion experience. Clark's complaints are less about the nature of God or traditional Catholic teaching than the liberal theology Connolly represents. Yet when the converted Connolly enters the novel, the development of Clark's character seems to end. During the final third of the novel, his principal purpose appears to be to read Connolly's journal and thus inform the reader of the priest's thoughts and feelings.

The first-person narrator of a novel can be either dramatized or undramatized in fiction, but once that "I" appears, he or she becomes a presence to whom the author must be faithful. When that narrator is as central to the plot as Clark (betrayed husband and friend) is and exhibits such an intriguing attitude (professed agnostic committed to traditional Catholicism), he obviously is a dramatized narrator. Then it becomes inexplicable why McInerny treats him as a stock figure for the final third of the book, using Clark principally to report action and move the plot forward, finally ending in two ambiguous scenes with his former wife. The interesting persona of the earlier part of the novel deteriorates. Clark, like Ascue in *The Priest,* dominates the narrative by his presence, yet his story, too, is unsatisfying.

In McInerny's emphasis on theological meaning, he often fails to sufficiently dramatize his characters. He creates types rather than people. But in the realistic novel, where the emphasis is on an individual, as in *The Priest* and *Connolly's Life,* the diminishment of character detracts from the fiction. This is also the central problem in *Leave of Absence.*

The McInerny emphasis on the importance of commitment is the moral center of *Leave of Absence* (1986). It is the story of two Catholic women, Andrea and Vera, friends from childhood, and their experience of the Church. Andrea becomes a nun and, like Michael Connolly, loses her way in the postconciliar Church. There is some question about whether she leaves her community or her community abandons her, but the result is that she has an affair with Vera's husband Edward, and the latter's marriage disintegrates.

The novel begins *in medius res* with Vera off to Europe on a leave of absence from her law firm to come to terms with the betrayal of both her friend and her husband. In Europe she returns to the practice of Catholicism and comes home to America intrigued with the idea of becoming a nun. She actually visits the local Carmelites but is advised that her canonical marriage would impede any plans for religious life.

The clue to McInerny's intentions in depicting these two women is in their names. We are told in the novel that Andrea means "manly," but the character Andrea as described is anything but manly in physical appearance. The designation refers to her feminist ideology. Like Greeley, McInerny sees feminism as a perversion of the feminine. And, of course, to disturb one link in the great chain of hierarchical structure that supports McInerny's world is to inaugurate chaos. "The politicization of religion, that was what Andrea's feminism had meant."[4] A redefinition of women's role in society is necessarily negative in his fiction. "Religion as resentment. Nuns had been repressed by priests, women by men" (p. 205). Vera means "faith," and the name is also evocative of the Latin *veritas,* "truth." The third-person narrative is related through Vera's perceptions, and she is clearly the theological and moral center of the book, as she returns to the True Faith and her true husband. But in idealizing Vera, McInerny betrays both female characters by his obvious manipulation for theological purposes.

McInerny's depiction of Vera is informed by an allegiance to the Golden Age that is no longer tenable in either the Church or the secular world. Vera, returned from Europe, is drawn to religious life and has no desire to return to her husband. "Whether or not the Carmelites would have her, she knew how she wanted to live her life. Edward now seemed a threat" (p. 205). Amazingly, in the next scene Vera and Edward are reunited as husband and wife, with no apparent motivation in the plot except Vera's Catholic belief that their union is permanent.

As in *Connolly's Life*, characterization is principally directed by theological motives. At the end of the novel, Andrea is abandoned to her feminism, living with another former nun whose marriage to a priest ended in ruin. Her transition from nun to feminist seems to encompass Andrea's purpose in the novel. Adopting an ideology that challenges traditional norms places her beyond McInerny's pale. But Vera, McInerny's ostensible heroine, suffers more from the novelist's theologizing. The tone of her reunion with Edward suggests a mutual entrapment rather than the renewal of romance:

> Poor Edward. They had linked their lives once and for all, for better or worse, and it did no good to kick against the goad. He had tried to escape and failed. (p. 208)

The novel ends with Vera visiting a downtown Chicago church, mourning her lost vocation and imaging her husband as the millstone of her spiritual longing:

> She wanted to be a saint, a heroine, someone like Edith Stein. But she had Edward and vice versa. She sat in a pew and closed her eyes, holding back the tears. (p. 210)

Vera is not only depicted as returning to her marriage out of a sense of obligation rather than any relationship with Edward, but this ending suggests that a life of prayer is denied to her because of her prior commitment to marriage. This is the Golden Age writ large; supernaturalism in modern dress. Vera's relationship with God will be enacted, apparently, solely in fidelity to her marriage vows, the sacrament of her state in life. The life-denying aspect of this legalism is mind-boggling. McInerny does better satirizing the foibles of Catholics than he does attempting to project Golden Age theology onto the modern world.

This is not to say that the past has no claims on the present, but McInerny's essentially satiric vision masks an uncompromisingly reactionary view that would simply impose the past on the present, a practice that would be as destructive in life as it is in fiction. While McInerny's conservatism is well documented in fiction, Eugene Kennedy is principally known as a liberal voice in American Catholicism. Yet his first novel, *Father's Day* (1978), clearly an attempt at a vision of reconciliation, betrays a residual clericalism that is disconcerting. The fiction reflects an implicit commitment to the preservation of the clerical past.

THE GOLDEN BOY AT THE GOLDEN DOME

In the scene in *Connolly's Life* when Jim Clark and Michael Connolly lunch with Father Hesburgh, the narrator comments, "It was difficult, talking with the president of Notre Dame, not to share his serene conviction that his university was emblematic of the Church in America." (p. 145) Kennedy obviously shares this conviction, for *Father's Day*, set at Notre Dame, is an obvious effort to chronicle the story of the Catholic Church in America in microcosm. Unfortunately, Kennedy, an able commentator on the American Church in his nonfiction, is largely unsuccessful in this ambitious task.

As a writer of fiction, Kennedy's initial faux pas in this novel was to attempt to tell the tale through a first-person narrator, a retired Notre Dame professor named Austin Kenna. Perhaps Kennedy was aiming for the kind of authenticity that personal commentary conveys, but the span of this novel, both in time and space, is too broad, and the awkwardness of the narrative stance calls attention to the contrived nature of the story itself. The symbols are just too obvious, from the setting at Notre Dame, "altar of religious devotion and symbol of Catholic determination and achievement in American society" to Father Thomas Kinsella, the fictional President of Notre Dame in 1983, a contemporary version of the ghetto stereotype of the Catholic priest, "the classic golden boy of the clerical world."[5]

On the literal level, *Father's Day* is the intergenerational saga of the Kinsella family, Chicago Irish Catholics, stalwart representatives of the Immigrant Church in America. The narrative traces the rise of Thomas Kinsella's father, P.B., from his undergraduate years at Notre Dame beginning in 1929, through his emergence as a leader of men and a corporate magnate. All of this is told in flashback, as the narrative begins with P.B.'s son Tom, President of Notre Dame, who on a football weekend in 1983 is dealing with a campus disorder, his father's difficulties with the

U.S. Attorney, and the Vatican's offer to make him the next Archbishop of Chicago.

In this story of P.B. and Tom, his priest–son, it is also apparent that Kennedy is trying to tell the larger story of the American Church, attempting to reconcile Church Past—"the good old days when the Church was a great disciplined presence and there was no faltering, there were no conflicts in the young about doing their own thing, or finding their true selves" (p. 13)—and Church Present, as represented in this novel by Father Thomas Kinsella.

Kennedy, a trained psychologist, seems oriented less to problems with Church law than to the conflict of the human person attempting to reconcile faith experience with life situations. However, in fictionalizing the issues of power and love with which Thomas Kinsella is concerned in this novel, Kennedy is disconcertingly inconsistent.

As P.B.'s heir, Thomas Kinsella is attracted to power, and it is clear that the latter's success in the Church is attributable to the same talents that made his father a success in the secular world:

> Becoming Archbishop of Chicago was a family affair, after all. How like a medieval family filled with kings and popes, dreaming every night of power—and this, what a finesse of power! The kind of move his father loved, the way Patton loved battle, and, if the truth were told, Thomas was good at such moves himself, although he did not let himself think about it much; power came naturally out of the fingertips of those who had a feel for it. (p. 158)

But Thomas does not become Archbishop of Chicago. In spite of family pressure to accept the appointment, the Notre Dame President decides that he is content in his present position and refuses the Vatican's offer.

This independent decision seems to be Kennedy's attempt to depict Thomas Kinsella as having transcended the obsessive grip of the Immigrant Church, but it is difficult to understand the meaning of Kinsella's decision to remain as President of Notre Dame as any reconciliation with his own urge to power. Granted, he does not automatically grasp for greater power by accepting the post offered, but the Notre Dame presidency is scarcely a powerless position, as he himself observes when reflecting on the charge that he is obsessed with power:

> He loved the power the presidency gave him, not only at Notre Dame but also because of the doors it opened—at the White House, the foundations, everywhere. (p. 474)

If Kennedy intends Kinsella's refusal of the Chicago see as a moment of reconciliation for the priest in terms of his urge to power, he has not successfully dramatized such a resolution. This is especially apparent in terms of the other conflict the priest is supposedly resolving, his attitude toward love.

According to the novel, Tom and a famous actress, Maria Moore, have loved one another for fourteen years, becoming physically intimate seven years after their first meeting. At one point in the novel, a wise confessor tells Tom, "Maybe you discovered your humanness. That is what love lays bare in us" (p. 297), and it is possible that the relationship with a woman is Kennedy's attempt to indicate the importance of the feminine for psychological wholeness in the male celibate. But there are divergent views of this relationship presented in the novel, and they are never reconciled. Kennedy has another priest confront Kinsella with the self-serving nature of his relationship with Maria Moore: "Come on, Tom, the woman makes most of the sacrifices in these relationships. Do you ever admit that to yourself?" (p. 255). Although Father Thomas Kinsella seems to recognize the truth of this assertion in the lines that follow in the novel, he proceeds to reform by insisting that he and Maria attempt to maintain an intimate but platonic relationship. Father Thomas Kinsella is the heroic celibate, a classic depiction of the stereotypical priest–hero, and the issues raised about Kinsella's clerical self-absorption are ignored in favor of an unrealistically romantic ending that glorifies the preconciliar clerical stereotype.

If Kennedy intends this saga of the Kinsellas to illuminate the Irish Catholic experience in the United States, the conclusion must be "like father, like son." The commitment to patriarchy will continue.[6] In Father Thomas Kinsella he has embodied most of the traditional ghetto stereotypes of the priest, especially the able administrator and the heroic celibate. He has adorned his novel with various aspects of contemporary culture— the homosexual priest in search of identity, the pervasiveness of the drug culture, religious enthusiasm among Catholics—but ultimately he has provided, in his hero, an image of the Immigrant Church in modern dress. Ironically, in his 1984 study of American Catholicism, *The Now and Future Church*, Eugene Kennedy insists that "Redecorating the old institution simply will not do," but this is all that is accomplished in *Father's Day*.[7] It is more a nostalgic encomium to the past than any insight into the "now and future."

This inconsistency is no anomaly, however. In *The Now and Future Church*, Kennedy wrote of the end of the Immigrant Church in the United States and its culture of clerical authoritarianism. Yet in his 1989 novel

Fixes, when the central character, Father Michael Tracy, defies an unresponsive hierarchy that has ignored his petition for laicization and marries, he and his bride are almost immediately destroyed by a terrorist bomb. Literary convention mitigates against the arbitrary destruction of the hero, so Kennedy's authorial decision to annihilate the couple is, from the literary perspective, an alliance with the authority that would deny Michael Tracy the right to marry. While Kennedy the commentator on contemporary Catholicism consistently critiques the institutional Church, Kennedy the novelist betrays a disconcerting allegiance to its patriarchal model. Although Kennedy's authorial bias toward the past may be the failure of technique in an inexperienced novelist, it is a disconcertingly salient feature of the fiction of the more accomplished novelist Jon Hassler.

THE MYSTERIOUS DIMENSION

Hassler's *North of Hope* (1990) is ostensibly the story of a middle-aged priest with a vocational crisis who resolves his dilemma. Hassler's hero, Father Frank Healy, bears a strong resemblance to Kennedy's stereotypical heroic celibate Thomas Kinsella. While Kinsella's crisis is whether or not to become Archbishop of Chicago, Healy is perplexed about his vocation to the priesthood. He has been an educator for twenty years, but with the closing of the boarding school that he administered, he is suddenly thrust into the challenges of pastoral life and experiences a mysterious psychological crisis. Precisely why an excellent teacher and able administrator should find pastoral life such a problem, especially since he has been assigned to the elite Cathedral parish, is unexplained in the text. The implication is that this is Healy's first exposure to the postconciliar Church, having been insulated by the cloistered academic environment during Catholicism's crisis. In the parish of the very liberal Bishop Baker ("call me Dick"), Healy experiences a vague anomie and, rejecting the help of a female therapist the Bishop suggests, trusts his own instincts and asks for a return to his "roots," his home parish in the remote north.

In his new assignment, Healy encounters his childhood sweetheart, Libby Girard, a woman enmeshed in destructive relationships, and the narrative focus shifts to concentrate on Healy and Libby. The priest eventually saves Libby and affirms his vocation, but, like Thomas Kinsella, he is the heroic celibate, affirming a deep love for the woman but insisting on a platonic relationship. In Frank Healy, Hassler has invested all the qualities of the preconciliar clerical stereotype, and in true Chuck O'Malley fashion Healy solves all problems, and indeed exceeds his own expectations:

More and more of his people were receiving the Sacraments; he sensed a heightened regard for the Eucharist and he might be the only priest in the diocese—indeed in America—to report an upswing in the number of confessions.[8]

While Hassler tries to present a more modern pastoral person—"He was not so much their leader as their center. They were not his followers; they were his family" (p. 442)—nevertheless, his fiction suffers from the underlying bias for the stereotypical heroic celibate, product of a supernaturalistic understanding of the priesthood.

The solution of his relationship with Libby Girard is similar to that of Thomas Kinsella with Maria Moore. Healy assures the confused Libby, "don't forget, my feeling for you never changes. Since 1949 you've been the woman in my life" (p. 513). But, like Kinsella, he defines their relationship as "love on a higher plane" (p. 512), and the unfulfilled Libby is left to her fantasies of intimacy. Lunching with Healy and her daughter, Libby keeps the conversation going "far into the afternoon, pretending all the while that they were a family of three" (p. 514). The novel ends with Healy's continued midnight phone calls to assuage his need for psychological intimacy, while refusing Libby her desire for physical intimacy.

Although Hassler clearly intends to depict Healy as the model postconciliar pastor, his fiction is informed by the supernaturalistic model in which the priest is a divine mediator. This is clear in the awe of the rejected Libby who concludes:

He [Healy] had a dimension she lacked, a mysterious dimension from which he drew strength, a spiritual dimension she'd never believed existed until she saw it in him. And because she lacked that dimension but needed it nearby, she couldn't imagine being out of touch with him. (p. 513)

Thus, Healy's midnight phone calls can be regarded as pastoral work, enabling the spiritually deficient Libby to remain in touch with the mysterious dimension she lacks. Like McInerny's Vera who reluctantly returns to her husband, Libby's relationship to Healy is ruled by the imperative of Church discipline. Despite the modern trappings with which Hassler invests his plot, *North of Hope* is an encomium to the supernaturalism of the classical paradigm of Catholicism.

Andrew Greeley's enthusiasm for *North of Hope* as "a hymn of praise to the Catholic priesthood, neither traditional nor modern, but perennial" is scarcely surprising in light of Greeley's penchant for exploiting female characters in his own fiction and his persistent defense of clerical celibacy in his nonfiction.[9] The perennial aspect of priesthood that Greeley exalts in *North of Hope* is, unfortunately, the vision he shares with other members of the sacerdotal school, a vision that locates the essence of Catholicism in the activities of its priests, affirming the patriarchal structure with its privileged cast of men who have access to the "mysterious dimension" denied to others. This may explain why Hassler's earlier effort to present a Catholic heroine resulted in a conspicuously less successful novel.

CATHOLICS ON THE ROAD

Hassler's *A Green Journey* (1985) recounts the visit to Ireland by the recently retired parochial school teacher, the indomitably conservative Agatha McGee, on a packaged tour sponsored by the liberal Bishop Baker (who asks Agatha to call him Dick, as he later makes the same request of Frank Healy). While Agatha's central purpose is meeting her Irish pen pal, James O'Hannon, the Bishop hopes to use the time together to enlist the former teacher in his efforts to close parochial schools in his diocese. The plot provides Hassler with an opportunity to portray two intelligent and articulate Catholics discussing change in the Church. But having created the situation, the author fails to supply the dialogue his plot promises. Instead, Hassler subverts the novel with a reliance on gender-role stereotyping, sentimentality, and slapstick.

The first problem with this novel is in the stereotyping of Agatha McGee, ostensibly the central character. The seemingly well-adjusted educator who can handle conflict with the Bishop with aplomb and who is depicted as a generous, socially conscious Christian, is also prey to adolescent romantic illusions about her Irish correspondent. Originally writing to James O'Hannon in response to his complaint about modern liturgy in a conservative Catholic newspaper, Agatha soon begins to dream of a romantic liaison with the Irishman. When offered the opportunity of a trip to Ireland, she accepts, secretly hoping to enact her dream of romance. The character of Agatha McGee is distorted by the male author's fantasy of the unfulfilled female. This is made increasingly obvious when Agatha discovers that O'Hannon is a priest. So extreme is her disappointment that she must be rescued from despondency by the good Bishop who effects a reluctant truce between Agatha and O'Hannon.

Along the way, Hassler provides several occasions for a discussion of contemporary issues in the Church but strangely shies away from all of them. For example, when Bishop Baker seeks out O'Hannon to confront him about his deception, the Irish priest reminds the Bishop of the

loneliness and isolation of the clergy. O'Hannon explains that the corre-
spondence with Agatha was an attempt to meet his strong need for
psychological intimacy with a woman. Just when the reader assumes that
Hassler will allow his sensitive Bishop to engage in a serious conversation
with the unhappy priest, the author announces that Bishop Baker is a
notorious hypochondriac, and a silly sequence follows in which Baker
assumes that he and O'Hannon have eaten poisoned mushrooms. What
begins as a possibly intelligent discussion of the problems of personal
development exacerbated by enforced celibacy degenerates into a rush to
the hospital and an evening of stomach-pumping. The poisoned mushroom
escapade is unrelated to any plot development and seems to be Hassler's
authorial technique for subverting his own plot and characters.

Similarly, although there is ample opportunity for significant exchanges
between Agatha and Bishop Baker, they engage in only a few remarkably
obscure conversations about the Church. Yet as they return to the United
States at the end of the novel, Agatha has agreed to the Bishop's request
that she return to her school to help effect its peaceful closing. However,
the reader discovers that the wily teacher is confident she can subvert the
Bishop's plans and keep the school from closing.

The "green journey" symbol is one of hope through passage, but if
Hassler intended to suggest that Catholicism is going through a time of
transition during which new structures and relationships will naturally
evolve, he does not successfully dramatize that process in his fiction.
Ultimately, this is a superficial book recounting the deed of caricatured
Catholics unable to do more than reflect stereotypes. It is disappointing
because Hassler's initial characterizations and plot developments promise
more.

FEMALE CATHOLICS ON THE ROAD

Like Hassler in *A Green Journey*, Kit Reed employs a journey motif
in her novel of change, *Catholic Girls* (1987), and the vision of reconciliation by a female author is interestingly different from that presented by
her male counterparts. The plot relates the picaresque adventures of three
Catholic college graduates, Georgia, Mickey, and Kath, now in their
forties and engaged in a rescue mission to retrieve a fourth college
roommate Ag (Agnes Mary) from an unfortunate romantic liaison. The
story of these four women invokes the familiar pattern of the college-
friends-face-life Bildungsroman with the added twist that at the time when
the characters have reached maturity and the Bildungsroman traditionally
ends, these "Catholic girls" face an unexpected life challenge in the loss

of innocence in the postconciliar Church. At the beginning of the novel, Georgia reflects on her experience of the postconciliar Church:

> Protest rattled every window in the monolith; untidy doubt blundered in and set up housekeeping in the lobby, where it had been making itself at home ever since. People either tried to pretend it wasn't crouching there or else they acknowledged the mess and learned to live with it, or they checked everything and left.[10]

All the principals discover leakage in their neat Catholic life raft. Georgia, raised to believe in the perpetuity of marriage, is troubled by the increasing divorces among friends and relatives, and Mickey is distraught because she can no longer preserve the family values to which she has dutifully devoted her entire life. Both women are astounded to discover that their college friend Kath is recently divorced and living with a man twenty years her junior because, Kath explains, the rigidity of Church marriage law places her in a relational limbo, condemned to twenty years as a member of the "Catholic Singles" while waiting for her former husband to die. The novel's central question is posed by Mickey who asks Georgia, "Do you ever get the idea the whole world is going in the opposite direction?"—a question Georgia answers with a simple, "Yes" (p. 265).

Mickey asks her question near the end of the novel as the group, now at their Florida destination, prepares for early morning Sunday Mass. It is during that liturgy that Georgia resolves some of her conflicts. First, she separates the essence of the worship experience from its external manifestations:

> It was a good thing she wasn't in this for the aesthetic experience, she thought, because except in abbeys and some college chapels and certain urban churches, the aesthetics were almost always terrible. (pp. 265–66)

So she asks the obvious and crucial question, "Why was she in this?" Georgia suddenly understands that the apparent paradox of her inability to achieve her ideals, magnified by her friends' similar failings, actually confirms the presence of a larger context for human experience. In light of the disorder the women experience, Georgia concludes that this simply indicates that people are "human, frail, fallible in ways that made it clear" that there are "larger powers at work" (p. 252).

Attending Mass, Georgia realizes, is an act that transcends the aesthetic experience (or lack of it) but that reinforces her commitment to the Church as a symbol of those "larger powers." Georgia finally understands the source of the tension she has been experiencing throughout the novel when the sudden association with her college roommates brought to consciousness the system in which they had been nurtured:

> she understood what she was tugging against: the ethic, or truth or ultimately mystical belief that what you did in this life had consequences beyond the temporal. Whatever you did, for better or worse you were writing on eternity. Which explained why she was here. She was here, she thought, because she absolutely had to be. (p. 266)

It *is* a different world today, Reed admits, but in Georgia's resolution she attempts to identify the nature of the religious experience itself rather than focus solely on the ecclesiastical questions that seem to occupy writers with their emphasis on the lives of priests. Interestingly, Reed affirms traditional Catholicism but without the bias toward the past that caricatures modernity in McInerny's fiction or generates the sentimental nostalgia of Kennedy or Hassler.

In focusing on Georgia's story and effectively dramatizing her character, Reed's methodology indicates an important aspect of faith and fiction that it is well to keep in mind. It is not the function of the novelist to reconcile all the divergent forces in the contemporary Church. Fiction is not polemic nor was meant to be. The novel is essentially human drama. As Walker Percy has commented, "people and the fixes they're in" is the subject of fiction, and the novelist attends to the needs of those people in his or her work.[11] Reed's attention to Georgia Kendall not only produces effective fiction, it also models contemporary theological understanding of religious experience.

Reed's authorial perspective in *Catholic Girls* is also strikingly consonant with contemporary theological method. The central shift in theological focus during the past twenty-five years has been to reflect on the human situation in light of theological imperatives to arrive at meaning. The pattern of Reed's fiction reflects this modern emphasis. It is through Georgia's life experiences, reflected on in light of her Catholic past, that she comes to a new awareness of her faith. By focusing on the human dilemma instead of the ecclesial situation, and by fidelity to her characters, Reed manages to conciliate the claims of traditional Catholicism for Georgia Kendall in believable and viable fictional framework; Georgia reconciles herself to the postconciliar world through an affirmation of her spiritual ethos. Like most older Catholics whose values have been formed in the preconciliar Church, Georgia looks for security not in new liturgical expression but in the ultimate reality that transcends the cultural moment. A similar authorial perspective informs two novels by Caryl Rivers.

VIRGINS NO LONGER

In two novels, Rivers presents the experiences of three young Catholics formed in the traditional Church (*Virgins*, 1982) and examines their lives in a changed world only fourteen years later (*Girls Forever Brave and True*, 1986). Ostensibly the story of Constance Wepplener and Peg Morrison, seniors at Immaculate Heart High School in 1957, the principals must also include Peg's neighbor and faithful companion Sean McCaffrey. The friends comprise a triumvirate whose experiences typify American Catholic adolescence of the 1950's.

Virgins is a comic novel, and Rivers manages to recreate the Catholic 1950's for anyone with memories of adolescence during that era. From Sean's Illuminated Map of Sin, "imprinted on his brain cells," which enabled him to neck with Peg "for two hours and still stay in the state of grace," through the "Marylike" fashions designed to preserve female modesty in dress with high necklines and long sleeves and skirts, *Virgins* smiles benignly on "the way we were" in those pre-60's days when the practice of Catholicism involved an earnest effort to comply with its various strictures, an effect that was so totally accepted, it was, in a sense, effortless. The novel points out that the American Catholic culture, as experienced by young people growing to maturity in the 1950's, did not really change; it disappeared. As the narrator, an older Peg Morrison, remarks at the end of the 1957 school year,

> I didn't know it then, but in saying goodbye to Immaculate Heart, I was saying goodbye to a world that in a few short years would simply cease to exist. I would not have believed it then, because that world seemed timeless, stretched out beneath the sun as eternally as the Eternal City itself. But the Church we knew . . . was the last gasp of another age, the remnants of an immigrant religion of mysteries and miracles, saints and visions. It would be swept away by winds that had already begun to stir.[12]

One problem with Rivers' presentation is that in the adolescent world of *Virgins* the Church is principally experienced in terms of its constraining objective code of sexual morality. While this perspective is consonant with that of the adolescent protagonists in that novel, Rivers offers no other view of the Church, and in the culture of sexual license in *Girls Forever*

Brave and True, Catholicism seems much more an anachronistic shared history among the characters than a faith expression that might inform lived experience.

However, in this apparent limitation of vision, Rivers reflects a significant aspect of the change in Catholic culture. For many young Catholics who experienced the Church as an early formative influence but whose adolescent crisis of identity formation occurred during the ascendancy of the Sentimental Love Ethic that dominated American culture in the 60's and 70's, Catholicism's import is limited to a "remembrance of things past." Speaking for many of her generation, the journalist Anna Quindlen has commented:

> We are cultural Catholics . . . Catholicism is to us now not so much a system of beliefs or a set of laws but a shared history. It is not so much our faith as our past.[13]

While the phenomenon of "cradle Catholics" who eventually abandon the practice of their religion is certainly nothing new, Quindlen points to an important difference in the lives of those who were nurtured in the preconciliar era but had no real adult experience of the Church. She does not deny belief so much as admit confusion and remarks that unlike her Jewish friends who sometimes go back to orthodoxy, she cannot go home again. As a character in another novel points out, "The forge which forged us has been dismantled."[14]

However, although no one in *Girls Forever Brave and True* is going to Mass, much less novenas or benediction, and while the novel reflects the sexual license of the 60's and 70's and includes Sean McCaffrey's decision to leave the priesthood, Rivers indirectly points to what might be termed "the survival of American Catholicism" in that inimical culture. For in spite of the absence of specific references to Catholic philosophic principles or characters who adhere to their faith and seek to make it viable in contemporary society, Rivers' novel presents important values that inform contemporary life and provide a link to the Catholic past.

In an essay on her Catholic education, "The Belles of St. Mary's," Jeanne Schinto described a transition from past to present not unlike that reflected in Rivers' fiction. Schinto explained: "In the end, I see I chose to secularize what I was taught at St. Mary's, and in a changing world, these principles and techniques have served me well."[15] Similarly, *Girls Forever Brave and True* is a sequel to *Virgins*, not in terms of a liberation from the Catholic past, but in the application of values developed in that Catholic past to modern situations, values that transcend the cultural manifestations of specific religious observance. The institutional Church may lack currency in the secular world of *Girls Forever Brave and True*, but a Catholic presence is enfleshed in the values of Rivers' protagonists.

The primary value in *Girls Forever Brave and True* is the human person, not as an autonomous entity freed from repressive constraints as the culture of the times would dictate, but as a person in relationship, both with the self and with others and, by implication, with God as well. Reed's emphasis is on human experience as an indicator of meaning; Rivers expands that perspective to emphasize the importance of psychological wholeness as a primary value in the development of the human person.

Virgins ends with Constance denying her ambitions for college and a career by marrying right after high school graduation, with Sean entering the seminary, and with Peg going off to college to prepare for her dreamed-of career as a journalist. Although there are suggestions that Sean has been "tracked" into the priesthood by the plans of a domineering father and his own need for that father's recognition, it is only in the second novel, when he experiences a crisis in his vocation, that the earlier situation is fully explicated. Con's early marriage is also more fully explained in the second novel as the result of a desire to escape a home life dominated by her abusive alcoholic father. Only Peg Morrison, the much-loved child, fulfills her dreams, and at the beginning of the second novel is returning to the United States after years as a foreign correspondent, having won the Pulitzer Prize she had always dreamed of. Peg's return precipitates a crisis for Sean. They had been lovers before his ordination, and the renewal of their relationship eventually leads to bed, causing him to reevaluate his priesthood.

It is obviously a soap opera plot, but what rescues *Girls Forever Brave and True* from triviality is Rivers' nuanced development of her characters' decisions. Unlike Kennedy's heroic celibate Thomas Kinsella, Sean McCaffrey leaves the priesthood for marriage, but the latter character is developed more fully and with greater attention to interior qualities than Kennedy's glossy priest–hero. The fact that Sean's initial choice of priesthood was hardly a free act is reinforced in scenes with his father and older brother in this novel. Moreover, in spite of his overwhelming attraction to Peg Morrison, Sean does not immediately abandon his vocation, but discusses his difficulty with another priest and has a long conversation with a professional counselor at the Catholic institute in which he works. His ultimate decision to leave the priesthood is less a comment on that vocation than on the negative forces in his life that originally impelled him to seek ordination. Rivers never diminishes the priesthood or gets on a soap box about the requirement for clerical celibacy. Her portraits of priests include Sean's fellow curate Brian Byrne who, despite conflicts, makes an informed decision to remain in the priesthood.

In the reconciliation achieved by her principal characters, Rivers projects a shift in the center of significance in the modern world. The difference between the Catholic Past reflected in *Virgins* and the postconciliar Church of *Girls Forever Brave and True* is exemplified in the differences between the personal reconciliations achieved by the characters in those novels as opposed to those in *Connolly's Life* and *Leave of Absence*. Rivers' Constance and McInerny's Vera are paradigmatic of the differences in vision. Both women separate from their husbands and both choose to continue their marriages. As we have seen, Vera reluctantly returns to Edward, resigned to the permanence of their relationship by the decree of Church law. McInerny considers no other issues in their separation, and Vera's fidelity to her marriage vows is clearly depicted as more important than her human feelings.

Constance leaves her husband Lee because he beats her in a drunken rage, a singular incident in their fourteen years of marriage but one that immediately reminds her of past experiences with her alcoholic father. After they separate, Lee seeks counseling, but Constance, with no intention of ever resuming their life together, concentrates on her career and eventually develops a relationship with another man. However, their children provide Lee and Constance with some contact and opportunities for discussion, and she gradually begins to appreciate her husband's growing self-awareness and is able to make peace with the aspect of herself that condemned him, less because of one violent incident than because of her memory of her father. In reconciling with her husband, Constance reconciles with her past as well.

The theme that develops through both *Virgins* and *Girls Forever Brave and True* is not simply that our actions have consequences but that those actions are often not freely chosen but are limited by what has been done to us in the past. In this context, Sean's decision to leave the priesthood is as positive as Constance's decision to allow her husband to return. Rivers extends the limited moral framework McInerny projects, a moral perspective that dehumanizes his characters as Catholicism's rigid application of objective codes did in the past.

However, *Girls Forever Brave and True*, although it complements and extends Reed's emphasis on human experience as a source of truth, never connects psychological wholeness with holiness. In Rivers' fiction, Catholicism is a pleasant anachronism, a part of a shared history; the institutional Church is scarcely relevant to the present. In theme, Rivers' two novels reflect both the title and thesis of Kennedy's commentary on the postconciliar world of Catholicism, *Tomorrow's Catholics/ Yesterday's Church* (1988), as Rivers' protagonists find "their center of gravity in America at large rather than within the handsomely fenced churchyard of ecclesiastical structure."[16] This correlates with the "secular city" model of Christian presence in which the Church's absence is considered evidence of the fulfillment of its mission.[17] *Tomorrow's Catholics/Yesterday's Church*, however, is not so optimistic, insisting that the Church's intransigence in the work of renewing its institutional structures accounts for its increasing irrelevance in the secular city.

The fiction of Kit Reed and Caryl Rivers provides a watershed in this study. As writers in subsequent chapters eschew simple nostalgia for the old paradigm or a reductive antagonism directed at its persistence and focus more intently on the human person in conflict, they will, almost paradoxically, offer a broader perspective on the current Catholic moment and the situation of the Church in the modern world.

NOTES

1. Ralph McInerny, *The Priest* (New York: Harper and Row, 1973), p. 529.

2. Ralph McInerny, *Connolly's Life* (New York: Atheneum, 1983), p. 188.

3. Ralph McInerny, *Her Death of Cold* (New York: The Vanguard Press, 1977), pp. 27–28.

4. Ralph McInerny, *Leave of Absence* (New York: Atheneum, 1986), p. 202.

5. Eugene Kennedy, *Father's Day* (New York: Pocket Books, 1981), pp. 6 and 174.

6. The Irish hegemony in American Catholicism, well documented in Jay Dolan's *The American Catholic Experience* (see especially pp. 143–44), supports a reading of the Kinsellas as a microcosm of Catholic experience in the United States.

7. Eugene Kennedy, *The Now and Future Church* (New York: Doubleday and Company, Inc., 1984), p. 67.

8. Jon Hassler, *North of Hope* (New York: Ballantine Books, 1990), p. 442.

9. Andrew Greeley, "The Catholic Novels of Jon Hassler," *America* (November 17, 1990), p. 367. For Greeley on the celibacy issue, see his *Confessions of a Parish Priest*, Chapter 5 "Celibacy and Sexuality," pp. 107–32.

10. Kit Reed, *Catholic Girls* (New York: Ivy Books, 1987), p. 117.

11. Walker Percy, "Reflections on the Novelist's Characters and the Language," *U.S. Catholic Historian* 6 (Spring/Summer 1987), 144.

12. Caryl Rivers, *Virgins* (New York: Pocket Books, 1984), p. 274.

13. Anna Quindlen, *The New York Times* (June 18, 1986), p. C12.

14. Sharon Sheehe Stark, *A Wrestling Season* (New York: William Morrow and Company, 1987), p. 230.

15. Jeanne Schinto, "The Belles of St. Mary's: Reflections on a Catholic Education," *The Boston Globe* (February 2, 1986), p. 50.

16. Eugene Kennedy, *Tomorrow's Catholics/Yesterday's Church: The Two Cultures of American Catholicism* (New York: Harper and Row, 1988), p. 24.

17. Richard John Neuhaus, *The Catholic Moment: The Paradox of the Church in the Postmodern World* (San Francisco: Harper and Row, 1987), p. 19.

6

Alternative Visions

And cast the Kingdome old
Into another mold.

Andrew Marvell

The poet Andrew Marvell, commemorating the Puritan Revolution in
England in the seventeenth century, rightly understood that the old form
of monarchy would never again exist. When Charles II eventually assumed the throne eleven years later, he could not wield the absolute power
of his predecessors; his role was redefined by the constitutional government that had deposed his father and governed England during the
interregnum. Undoubtedly, there were those who imagined that the reign
of Charles II would replicate the monarchical rule with which they were
familiar, and it would be many years before the new mode of Constitutional monarchy was established as the norm for rule in the hearts and
minds of the country's citizens.

American Catholics are experiencing a similar transitional process in
their concept of church. In the years since the Second Vatican Council, it
has become apparent that Catholicism's confrontation with modernity
involves a radical shift in consciousness. Renewal cannot be accomplished
simply with a change to vernacular ritual and a demythologized calendar
of saints. The past twenty-five years in American Catholicism can be seen
as analogous to the interregnum between the reigns of Charles I and
Charles II in England. The "Kingdome old" of triumphal Catholicism is

being cast "into another mold." Just as the reign of Charles II involved a different concept of governance than that which guided his father, contemporary Catholicism involves an experience of church that is different from that of the past.

Clearly a paradigm shift is indicated, but for the new paradigm to emerge, there must first be the awareness of anomaly, some recognition that the old paradigm is not working.[1] It is in light of this principle of paradigm shift that the preponderance of fiction that obsesses about the institution—implicitly or explicitly longing for a restoration of a valorized Catholic past or simply mourning its loss—is unhelpful. The contemporary American fiction of the Catholic experience discussed so far in this book reflects a strong emotional attachment to the classical paradigm and a tendency to exalt its virtues, and such fiction has little prophetic value. It mirrors the current discontent but offers no illumination, no ability to perceive an emerging paradigm.

Less prevalent is American fiction that recognizes anomaly and highlights the inadequacy of the old paradigm and its residual effects in the present. The novels in this chapter provide such an "alternative vision," one that transcends a nostalgia for past certitude or a mourning for that loss. This fiction recognizes the signs that indicate that the old paradigm no longer suffices and some form of renewal is necessary for the continued life and growth of the Church. Several novels published during the past twenty years provide this vision of anomaly.

ALL THAT GLITTERS . . .

The title of Elizabeth Cullinan's novel of Irish American family life *House of Gold* (1970) literally refers to the draperies and other ornaments with which the Devlin family home was decorated several years earlier to celebrate a golden wedding anniversary in the family. In the course of the novel, these gold accessories take on a metaphoric significance, as Cullinan indicates how the Devlin family home is an emblem of the controlling *raison d'être* that governed the home, the ideology of the Golden Age of Catholicism in America. Ultimately, the reader comes to understand the enormous physical and psychological cost in maintaining the "house of gold." Thus, the Catholic culture of the 30's, 40's, and 50's that McInerny and Kennedy idealize is presented from a different vantage point in Cullinan's novel.

House of Gold tells the story of the passing of Julia Devlin, an Irish Catholic matriarch totally committed to religion and family. Of Julia's nine children, four become religious (two priests, two nuns), and as the six surviving children gather at her deathbed, the Devlins initially seem like the model Catholic family. Gradually the atmosphere changes as Cullinan develops her characters.

There is something bizarre in the veneration of the family religious. Phillip, the surviving family priest, is addressed as "Father" by his brothers and sisters and is deferred to in all decisions, although he is clearly not the most competent family member nor has he had any direct responsibility for the household. The two nuns are treated as honored guests, leaving all the household responsibilities to their sister Elizabeth and her two daughters. Until very recently Elizabeth and her family had lived in the Devlin home so she could care for her mother, and Elizabeth's husband is a demoralized man. Having spent his married life dominated by his wife's family, his only comforts are drink and playing the horses, both of which he must indulge secretly, like a mischievous adolescent. In Claire, the wife of the second youngest son, Tom, Cullinan provides a contrast to the Devlin family and an instrument for explaining the increasingly discomforting atmosphere in this house of gold.

The exuberance of Claire's two young sons contrasts with the excessively ordered behavior of the rest of the family. And her recognition of their needs in this constraining situation is markedly different than her husband's concern for propriety and decorum, the Devlin ruling passion. Claire gets insight into the family when she discovers Julia's handwritten attempt at autobiography (a project instigated by one of her nun-daughters) called "The Story of a Mother." In Julia's turgid account of her life, Claire notices that the mother records only

> the clear lines and brilliant colors of the surfaces, tragedy and triumph and nothing in between, nothing but the bold sweep of events past all that was day to day or moment to moment, past boredom, irritation, triviality, past doubt and disorder and the effort to understand.[2]

And Claire marvels, "What unshakable belief you'd need if you were to eliminate all that, belief in yourself and in True Life" (p. 169). But as a more recent member of this family, Claire also recognizes that in the effort to live "True Life" the Devlins had repressed its more mundane manifestations. To deny boredom, irritation, triviality, doubt and disorder will not eliminate them from life. So ultimately the source of the disquieting atmosphere one senses in the house of gold is its repression of the human, the suppression of any expression of emotion among family members, and the lack of self-awareness that comes from reliance on pious platitudes for meaning. This is exemplified in the pattern of Elizabeth's thinking when she is faced with the inescapable truth about her life:

> God was good. God was just and He was merciful. She had given the better part of her life to her mother and her mother's house, and God wouldn't let all that go to waste. He'd see to it that she got her second chance and when it came she'd be ready . . . Elizabeth's lips began to move in the aspiration that had gotten her through so many other times of trouble: *Jesus, Mary and Joseph, I place all my trust in Thee; Jesus, Mary and Joseph, I place all my trust in Thee; Jesus, Mary and Joseph, I place all my trust in Thee.* (p. 96)

Cullinan's *House of Gold*, with its portrait of repression, contrasts with the idealization of the Golden Age of Catholicism so marked in the fiction of Ralph McInerny. But McInerny reveals more than he intends, for it is clear that the repression of human feeling at the heart of the Devlin household is also at the heart of the perspective that informs *Leave of Absence*. The latter novel ends without resolution for Andrea and with Vera apparently bound for life to a man to whom she is indifferent. Against the dangers of moral relativism, McInerny posits a slavish adherence to rules and principles. Vera apparently resumes her marriage solely because of her recognition of the perpetuity of the sacramental bond, without regard for the question of the human relationship that such a bond symbolizes, the community of love it should represent.

In a similar way, Eugene Kennedy's novel *Father's Day* raises the issue of the importance of the emotional life but fails to deal with that issue, substituting nostalgia and sentiment for character development. The novel ends with Thomas Kinsella apparently continuing to exploit Maria Moore's commitment to him by maintaining the relationship for his own convenience. Certainly, the issue of the claims of human love raised in the novel is never again addressed, must less resolved. The patriarchal aspects of the Church of the Golden Age are thus reflected in the character of Thomas Kinsella, Kennedy's modern golden boy.

There has been a vast cultural shift in American life and values reflected in the differences between the 1950 popularity of Henry Morton Robinson's *The Cardinal* and Andrew Greeley's deliberate (and successful) attempt to replicate that popularity with his 1980 *The Cardinal Sins*.[3] Robinson's novel depicts a Catholic ideology consonant with that of Cullinan's Devlin family, a cultural expression of the Immigrant American Church in which human feeling was always subservient to the rule of law, the emphasis on the primacy of authority so characteristic of devotional

Catholicism. The perspective inherent in *The Cardinal Sins* (and other fiction of that ilk, discussed in Chapters 4 and 5) reductively suggests that simply removing authority is a sufficient solution to the vast problem of renewing Catholicism in the modern world. From this perspective, Alfred Alcorn's *The Pull of the Earth* (1985) is instructive.

A CATHOLIC TRAGEDY

The Pull of the Earth is set on a small New England family farm in the 1950's. Janet Vaughn, an Irish Catholic married to a Protestant many years her senior, longs for a child but has miscarried several times. Her husband's recent heart attack has limited his ability to work the farm, so he takes on a somewhat disreputable hired hand, Lucien Quirk. In a subsequent accident, Hedley Vaughn suffers another, more serious, heart attack and is hospitalized for some time. Janet and Lucien, united in their joint effort to manage the farm, eventually become lovers, for Janet discovers that the fear of sin and judgment is not a sufficient deterrent to the expression of her human needs.

> But there was more than the pleasure of it. Indeed, the pleasure of it signaled its deeper significance. That, embryonic at first, had unfolded with time to a dreadful and thrilling realization as obvious as the flesh of her own body: she wanted a child.[4]

Soon pregnant, Janet must face the consequences of her choice when Hedley is released from the hospital and Lucien begs her to run away with him. Resolved to remain with her husband, Janet imagines the sacramental confession she would honestly make:

> Bless me, Father, for I have sinned. I have betrayed my husband, my family, and my God. But understand that my sin sprang as much from necessity and circumstance as from weakness or willfulness and that I will sin no more. (p. 200)

She decides against seeking absolution, not out of any fear of an unforgiving God but because of her perception of the inability of the Church's representative to understand her sin.

> She didn't trust him to see the complexity of her situation, how others were going to suffer. What did he know of life? A sin is a sin, he would intone, holding tight his purse of grace. (p. 202)

Ultimately, Janet is reconciled through the Church, but both she and Lucien Quirk die tragically near the end of the novel. Their deaths are the enactment of Janet's earlier realization: "The Church was right: out of sin came chaos the road to ruin, her ruin, his ruin" (p. 196).

In this tragic tale of misguided lovers, Alcorn reinforces traditional Catholic values but depicts the institutional Church as ineffectual in presenting those values in a viable social context. Janet Vaughn, in her rural isolation, is emblematic of the individual Catholic of the 1950's, alienated by the supernaturalistic theology that pervaded the preconciliar Church. Her awareness that the label "sin" is affixed to her relationship with Lucien Quirk has little meaning other than to engender a guilt she willingly embraces if the affair will enable her to bear a child; "She would risk the essential blasphemy of women who, in having children, provide the only real resurrection of the flesh" (p. 173).

Janet Vaughn's decision is reminiscent of that of Twain's Huckleberry Finn who, in expressing a willingness to "go to hell" rather than betray his black companion Jim, highlights the inability of the social norm to account for human experience.[5] Twain's novel, set in the years before the Civil War but published in 1884, is analogous to Alcorn's narrative, set in the preconciliar 1950's. Twain expects his readers to understand Huck's choice as a recognition of the fact that human experience did not correspond to the accepted belief that blacks were chattel. Similarly, Janet Vaughn's experience in *The Pull of the Earth* highlights the inadequacy of a preconciliar, act-centered morality that focused on guilt and punishment rather than adult decision making.

The destruction that ensues in the novel is less the direct result of Janet's adultery than of the protagonists' inability to deal with their passions within a viable moral framework. It is the distance between the Church's theological formulations and the experience of its members that Alcorn depicts as a harbinger of the need for renewal. The preconciliar world of *The Pull of the Earth* reinforces Cullinan's vision of the dark side of Catholicism's Golden Age. The authoritarian emphasis on sin and guilt so characteristic of the devotional Catholicism that had sustained the Immigrant Church was rapidly losing currency in the 1950's among the more educated second- and third-generation Catholics who were becoming assimilated into mainstream American culture.

It is important to note, however, that neither Cullinan nor Alcorn urge the reductive abolition of authority. Their novels point to the need to bridge the distance between law and life. Both *House of Gold* and *The Pull of the Earth* are important texts for an appreciation of the shift in theological emphasis promoted by the Second Vatican Council, an understanding of life's experiences in light of the gospel message rather than an application of static precept to life's situations. The need for this transition in theological and pastoral emphasis is reflected in Robert Benard's *A Catholic Education* (1982), a novel that highlights the ideological differences between Catholic Past and American Present.

BEYOND THE CLASSROOM

Superficially, Benard's *A Catholic Education* might seem to be simply a protest novel against traditional Catholicism. It is the story of Nicholas Manion, the only son of affluent, devout Catholic parents. A bright student and natural leader, Nicholas is the golden boy of American Catholicism who in the preconciliar Church was often tracked into the priesthood. And in the late 1950's when Nicholas is in high school this is precisely what happens to him. At the age of eighteen he finds himself in a Jesuit novitiate and truly believes he has answered a call from God.

Unexpectedly, he finds the novitiate routine constraining and feels alienated from his fellow aspirants. He is attracted to a second-year novice, a Yale graduate who seems to share his intellectual and social interests. This "particular friendship" ends in the situation that religious superiors always feared when proscribing such relationships. Nicholas responds to a physical attraction for his senior and realizes that the sense of specialness and separateness he had always felt was not evidence of a vocation to the priesthood but a sign of his homosexual orientation. But unlike Patricia Nell Warren's *The Fancy Dancer*, Benard's novel does not attempt to exalt the gay lifestyle with a reductive depiction of a homophobic Church. Rather, in the comparison between the "Catholic education" of Nicholas and his father Thomas, Benard highlights essential differences in outlook and formation that mark the shift to postconciliar American Catholicism.

For Thomas Manion, Nicholas' strong-willed and independent father, the Church is a philosophical as well as ideological center in his life.

Reverence for authority was no sentimental contrivance, mere middle-aged inertia, but a bulwark against chaos, a means of measuring what was in a man's power and what was not.[6]

Thomas' faith reflects the muscularity of devotional Catholicism, the bulwark of the "brick and mortar" age when the Church built churches and schools throughout America. Nicholas, formed by that faith, is nevertheless a child of change. More conscious of his own moral power, Nicholas has no need to see authority as the "bulwark against chaos" that Thomas envisions. So in spite of his adherence to the tenets of the Baltimore Catechism and his acceptance of Church authority, Nicholas' confrontation with traditional Catholicism in the novitiate discomforts him. At first he thinks it is just a matter of his disdain for anachronistic rules:

> Training heroes for God in the sixteenth century was one thing. But the rules handed down from generation to generation now bore little relation to the real future they faced. (p. 175)

But, Benard insists, the difficulty is deeper. Never before had Nicholas had to confront the difference between the implicit belief in the primacy of self he had absorbed from modern American culture and traditional Catholic practices of submission to authority. Raised as a Catholic in post-World War II America, Nicholas discovers that his religion is at odds with the secular culture's emphasis on individual self-determination. Both American and Catholic, Nicholas experiences a conflict between the two identities in the isolation of the novitiate where life is based on the Catholicism of sixteenth-century Europe.

The difference between Thomas and Nicholas in their attitude toward authority is illustrative of the shift in consciousness that the Church must consider in articulating its truth in the contemporary world. As Nicholas' novitiate experience emphasizes, Catholicism's renewal is not simply a matter of updating the Church. The paradigm of preconciliar Catholicism was more responsive to the world of sixteenth-century Europe than twentieth-century America. In having Nicholas leave the Jesuits but not the Church, Benard makes a careful distinction between the doctrinal truths of Catholicism and their expression in a particular cultural context. Nicholas believes and accepts the fundamental doctrinal positions of the Church but is suddenly confronted by the fact that official teaching would condemn him to a life of unwilling celibacy.

Nicholas Manion's story, like that of Janet Vaughn, is one of lost innocence. This is exemplified in the consciousness that both Nicholas and Janet share, an awareness that the Baltimore Catechism's definitions are insufficient support for the complexities of human experience. Unlike Christopher Durang, however, whose *Sister Mary Ignatius Tells It All* focuses exclusively on the faults of the past, Benard attempts a reformulation of "a Catholic education" in a manner more consonant with contemporary understanding yet faithful to Catholic heritage. Nicholas, having abandoned his aspiration to the priesthood and conscious that his homosexual orientation may eventually cause him to formally separate from the Church, nevertheless affirms the value of his formation:

> What point was there to religious education, to its sweeping heuristic drive, if you could not face the truth? . . . If he had discovered that the Faith was friable, he knew in his bones that he could never be content with unbelief. (pp. 274–75)

Benard's novel highlights the fact that the individual's relationship with God is a mystery. According to this text, an authentic Catholic education is not limited to those years spent in parochial school classrooms but should apply to the entire process of formation that supports Catholics in living out their relationship to God. At one time in history, Catholic schools provided an appropriate and effective forum for such a Catholic education, one that served Thomas Manion well. But Nicholas Manion discovers that the authoritarianism that guided his father and led him to the novitiate masked rather than revealed his true self.

Moreover, he must face the possibility that living authentically for him may mean acting in ways the Church clearly labels sinful. In his efforts to deal with that dilemma, Nicholas questions the image of God presented by the Church:

> How could you sin if you were true to yourself?
> Could God, having made him, now refuse to love him? Surely, if He meant anything at all, He had to be more than a supreme accountant toting up "faults" on an infinite set of *culpa* beads. (p. 248)

A Catholic Education also reveals a particular danger for American Catholics. As they moved progressively into the cultural mainstream following World War II, their concept of religion was strongly affected by the primacy of individualism in American life. Benard affirms this for Nicholas with the advice of his Jesuit mentor who comments on the young man's leaving both the community and, perhaps, the Church with the advice, "We've all got to scramble to salvation as best we can. Finally, it's all a matter between us and God" (p. 262). The priest's words echo in the novel's finale when Nicholas' ultimate disappointment is in the discovery of the fact that the institution cannot be responsive to his developing self-awareness with concomitant change.

Susan Cahill's *Earth Angels* (1978) is a similar story of one young woman's experience of preconciliar Catholic education and her venture into religious life in the late 60's. And like Nicholas Manion, Cahill's heroine Martha Girlinghausen finds herself lost in postconciliar Catholicism when she experiences the institution mired in the inability to transcend the old paradigm. As the Mother General tells the young nun during her exit interview: "You're not for us—you're the kind who is concerned with becoming rather than being. Religious life is about being."[7].

What both *A Catholic Education* and *Earth Angels* emphasize is the fact that true renewal requires an imaginative change, an ability to question basic presuppositions in the light of contradictory evidence and envision alternatives. That this change has not been accomplished in contemporary Catholicism is reflected in a variety of novels that focus on the institutional dimension of the postconciliar Church.

THE POWER AND THE POLITICS

Predictably, the "season of discontent" following Vatican II led to critiques of the institutional Church in fiction as well as nonfiction. The privileging of American individualism was the hallmark of the cultural revolution known as The Sixties, so it is hardly surprising that Catholicism's hierarchical organization would be inimical to the *Zeitgeist*. One response was the fiction of passionate intensity informed by antagonism to the entire structure of authority in Catholicism. One commentator archly refers to "the sacerdotal school of American Catholic novelists whose New Frontier is sex."[8] In fact, the common denominator in the sacerdotal school of Kavanaugh, Carroll, Kienzle, and Greeley is not a fixation on the sexual but commitment to portraying Church authority as the central villain in their novels.

While it is undeniable that the Church in America during the Golden Age of the 30's, 40's, and 50's was rigidly authoritarian, the facile denigration of authority among members of the sacerdotal school is more indicative of a reaction to the past than any response to the present. In this fiction, the alternative to authority is an adolescent fantasy of pure solipsism. Carroll's Michael Maguire challenges the authority of Cardinal Spellman and resorts instead to the certitude of the self. Kavanaugh's Ted Santek similarly challenges his fictional Bishop, arguing for an end to the discipline of clerical celibacy solely on the basis of his own sexual needs. And Greeley completely disestablishes the institutional Church with his separatist Church of the Ryan clan and its idealized cleric and hierarch, Blackie Ryan and Sean Cronin.

The poet W. H. Auden has commented that the identification of fantasy is always an attempt to avoid one's own suffering.[9] The fantasy of independence from external authority characteristic of fiction by the sacerdotal school reduces all the ills of Catholicism to the abuse of power by the hierarchy and avoids the really difficult issues of the proper use of authority in a Christian context. Another group of writers offers a more nuanced critique of the problem with authority in the Church, providing an alternative vision of ecclesiastical power and institutional structures that, like the fiction of Cullinan, Alcorn, Benard, and Cahill, illuminates the nature of the problem and further indicates that the new paradigm of Catholicism has not yet emerged.

URBAN REDIVIVUS

J. F. Powers, principally a writer of short stories, has produced only two novels in his long career, but *Morte D'Urban* (1962) and *Wheat That Springeth Green* (1988), separated by more than a quarter of a century, are texts that imaginatively register the changes in American Catholic culture. The parallels between the portraits of the preconciliar Church and the postconciliar Church in these novels indicate the persistence of old patterns within the renewed institution.

The elegiac *Morte D'Urban* (1962) identified the need for renewal but it also presaged postconciliar confusion. The protagonist of that novel, Father Urban Roche, having absorbed a secular value system, returned to the gospel imperative only to oversee the disintegration of his religious community, a group that had prospered because of his entrepreneurial gifts. Powers presents Urban not as some unique opportunistic priest but as a sincere individual who has been seduced by the Church's own version of the American dream of progress and prosperity.

Through his story of Father Urban, Powers also presents his vision of the American Catholic Church in the 1950's. Its success in American industrial society, a Church both urban and urbane, was achieved at the cost of absorbing the values of that society at the expense of the gospel of Jesus. The danger, as Powers points out, was that the absolute denial of any degree of secularization necessary for the preservation of innocence left the Church defenseless against those inevitable influences. Thus, when Urban is suddenly faced with the self-knowledge that renders his way of life unacceptable, he has no alternative model of faith expression available other than the insular piety of the more phlegmatic members of his community. In the absence of a new paradigm to give meaning to a renewed spiritual life in the modern world, the reformed Urban can only watch over the slow deterioration of his order.

In the basically good world that literature assumes, recognition and reformation would palliate catastrophe. That Urban's world is destroyed as a direct result of his reformation is an ironic indication of the fact that there is no new paradigm available. That same type of ironic vision undercuts the symbol of hope in the title of Powers' second novel, *Wheat That Springeth Green* (1988).

In this postconciliar novel, Powers again tells the story of one individual priest, Joe Hackett, who, like Urban Roche, experiences what James Joyce would term an "epiphany," a moment of seeing clearly that results in a life change. The novel begins with a very young Joe Hackett and proceeds episodically through various adventures in his life to a dramatic change indicated by the very last word of the text. During his preparation for the priesthood, Joe experiences a tension caused by an impulse toward personal spirituality that is at odds with the pragmatism of seminary life in which spirituality is marginalized and sometimes openly derided. Joe survives as an idealist, but not even his own classmates support his aspirations. At his first Mass, he objects to being ordered by the pastor to personally take up a special collection designed to exploit the sentiment of the occasion. Ultimately, he is trapped into complying through his classmate Toohey's collusion. Toohey's advice to Joe is for him to "grow up."

Joe grows up. At the center of the novel is a forty-four year old pastor who eats too much and drinks too much and is principally concerned with the merits of his newly constructed rectory and its revolutionary concept in office arrangement—a triumph for Joe who not only conceived the idea of the rectory office space but persuaded the Archbishop to allow him to build the rectory before the new church building, contrary to diocesan policy. The arrival of his first curate involves Joe in the details of purchasing new furniture for office and bedroom.

It is 1968 but Joe, ordained in the 50's is a priest of the old Church, principally attentive to details of building and finance. In fact, the rectory building that pervades Joe's (and the reader's) consciousness throughout the novel is clearly a metaphor of Church Past, Golden Age ideology that still exerts its influence despite the theological renewal of the Second Vatican Council. Joe Hackett, educated in the preconciliar age, responds to the turbulence in the postconciliar Church in typical Counter-Reformation style. In Joe's parish, clericalism has become entrenched; his rectory is a bastion erected against the encroachments of the world. And Joe Hackett, as the ordinariness of his name implies, is a company man. Joe suspects that the Chancery is an industrial park but does not identify his own role in middle management. The Church is not simply allied with secular values as in *Morte D'Urban*; it is thoroughly based in commodity exchange, and religion's essential functions have been superseded by secular institutions in this postconciliar novel.

Both salvation and its attendant iconography are offered by the Great Badger, "the discount house with a heart," a full-service store whose central symbol is more than coincidentally reminiscent of the traditional Catholic image of the Sacred Heart of Jesus.

> The Great Badger itself, a forty-foot idol—its enlarged, exposed, red neon heart beating faintly in the sunlight that morning—sat upon its hunkers in the middle of the parking lot and waved a paw at cars going by.[10]

The Badger gives priority to the employment of the elderly and the handicapped and even promises its customers help in the hereafter by cancelling any debts incurred by the deceased and allowing the beneficiaries to keep the merchandise. In the novel, the Badger actually does more good for people than Father Hackett, pastor of the local Catholic Church.

Another symbol of secular society's usurpation of the role of the Church is an omnipresent weather ball that presides over Joe's suburban town. It changes color to indicate its predictions, and everyone knows the rhyme they must recite to interpret its color code (p. 102). The weather ball is the object toward which people continually turn their attention, for it provides the sense of security that comes with the knowledge of impending weather. It is the axis of everything in a natural world lacking any impulse toward transcendence.

In his early years, Joe Hackett was trying to decide between two vocations—to become either a priest or a businessman (his father was the owner of a prosperous coal company). Powers shows us that Joe chose the former and by mid-life has become the latter. Throughout the novel Joe's principal activity is shopping, and he is seen interacting with parishioners mainly about financial matters, either explaining his innovative financial system to new parishioners or trying to collect from other parishioners who have been delinquent in their payments.

Like Urban, Joe Hackett is a well-meaning individual unaware of the conflicts in his life. Seemingly oblivious to his own secularization, Joe doggedly clings to the outward forms of clerical identity. Although the central clerics in this novel are always "Joe" and "Bill" to the reader, Joe insists on the proper forms of address from lay people. And when his curate arrives in overalls, Joe insists that he exchange his jeans for suitable black trousers. Powers indicates that at some level Joe is dimly aware of his own compromises, and this is confirmed at the end of the novel. Just before the final section that chronicles Joe's conversion, the paunchy, alcoholic, and materialistic pastor thinks

> that the separation of Church and Dreck was a matter of life and death for the world, that the Church was the one force in the world with a chance to save it (but first, "Physician, heal thyself!"). (p. 316)

And he does. Joe quietly requests a transfer to a notoriously poor inner-city parish, Holy Cross, whose pastor has recently been hospitalized. The final line of the book is revealing. The owner of the Great Badger, Dave Brock, has shown up late for Joe's farewell party just as the priest is leaving, "and when Dave called after him, 'Where is it you're stationed now—Holy . . . Faith?' Joe shook his head and kept going, calling back, '*Cross*' " (p. 335).

The combination of "faith" and "cross" in the final line of this text suggests that the climax of Powers' novel is effectively glossed by a passage in the Epistle to the Philippians:

> For many, as I have often told you, and now tell you in tears, conduct themselves as enemies of the cross of Christ. Their end is destruction. Their God is their stomach; their glory is in their "shame." Their minds are occupied with earthly things. But our citizenship is in heaven, and from it we await a savior, our Lord, Jesus Christ. (3:18–19)

Paul's words indicate the nature of Joe's conversion and suggest that for Powers radical personal conversion is the way to further the Kingdom of God in the world.

The finality of death in the title of Powers' earlier novel has been replaced by an image of hope. Like sprouting wheat, the individual person contains within him or her self the seeds of new life. Grace does not "build on nature" in the old supernaturalist schema but interpenetrates nature in Powers' postconciliar text. Powers' contemporary vision challenges Catholicism to look beyond the externals of change to its essence. To borrow another Powers title, the Catholic Church must learn how to be "the presence of grace" in the modern world.

Ultimately, however, *Wheat That Springeth Green* offers a view of a postconciliar Church that is changed rather than improved. Joe Hackett's renewal is personal and clearly idiosyncratic. It excludes his suburban parishioners, leaving them, it seems, to the ministrations of the Great Badger and the guidance of the weather ball. In spite of the fact that Powers depicts priest and Church synechdocally, conversion is effected solely on the personal level. The chancery remains an industrial park and the seminary a training center for middle management.

However, although *Wheat That Springeth Green* offers no corporate form of conversion, it is, nonetheless, important in the process of transition to a new paradigm. Kuhn notes that "the sense of malfunction" is prerequisite to change. Powers' vision of the Church highlights the institutional malfunction in the post-Vatican II Church and leads to hope only if the Council is considered the beginning of a process of transition. If Vatican II is considered a *fait accompli*, then *Wheat That Springeth Green* offers hope for Joe Hackett alone, because it depicts an institutional Church sliding into irrelevance.

RESISTING TEMPTATION

Peter Drucker's *The Temptation To Do Good* (1984) similarly provides a vision of the conflicts inherent in a temporal institution that seeks to represent a transcendent reality. Like Ralph McInerny's *Gate of Heaven*, Drucker's novel focuses on a crisis at a Catholic college, but while McInerny's vision leads to a resolution in favor of traditional lawful authority at the expense of the modern managerial cleric, Father Hoyt, Drucker's is a more nuanced examination of the issues of authority and power in a religious context. *The Temptation To Do Good* does not reject the Father Hoyts of the Church; it attempts to explain their dilemma. In his fiction, Drucker, a corporate management specialist, raises important questions about the nature of Catholic higher education in America, indeed about the nature of the Church's institutional life itself.

Drucker's title refers to the action of Father Heinz Zimmerman, the President of the fictional midwestern St. Jerome University, which he has elevated from a "cow college" to a major American research institution. When Zimmerman obeys his pastoral instincts and tries to find alternative employment for a terminated faculty member, he finds himself embroiled in controversy with the department chairman and other university officials. The President has inadvertently circumvented proper channels of authority by indulging his temptation to do good. He discovers that his role as priest is limited by his position as a modern university President, albeit a Catholic university President.

As Father Zimmerman's Bishop later explains, there is an inherent contradiction in the establishment of a religious institution according to a secular model. Although the first President of St. Jerome had the motto *Ad majorem Dei gloriam* chiseled over the portal of the Administration Building, the science departments at the school are joined "in the worship of the golden calf and the brazen pursuit of consulting assignments in industry, research contracts from business and corporation fellowships," and that is how it must be if St. Jerome is to be a competitive institution of higher education in the United States.[11] If, as the Bishop insists, the pursuit of knowledge in the modern world is an essentially secular activity, are Catholic universities as anachronistic as St. Jerome's neo-Gothic architecture? That is certainly one question Drucker's fiction raises.

In the novel, the local Bishop points out that "all of us in the American Catholic Church" have always assumed that we have Catholic colleges and universities to teach Catholic students Catholic values (p. 43). According to this Bishop, the actual reason for the establishment of Catholic colleges was because the Immigrant Church of the first half of this century viewed American higher education as distinctly Protestant and anti-Catholic. Without Catholic institutions, it was feared that Catholics would have had no access to secular learning (p. 43). Since that is no longer a viable premise in America, it seems logical that such institutions no longer have that initial mission. Not only are Catholic colleges and universities a vestige of the Immigrant Church in America, they are also suffering from the conflict between the secular goals of education and the Church's mission in the world. The brazen pursuit of fellowships and research dollars mitigates against a focus on gospel values.

Later in the novel, Drucker connects the academic conflict to the entire institutional structure. When the Bishop tries to dissuade his secretary from seeking a pastoral assignment by pointing out the young priest's exemplary executive ability, the secretary explains that in choosing the priesthood, he had assumed he was choosing a life of pastoral service. If he discovers that he is to be an executive, the secretary tells his Bishop that he would rather work in his father's business:

> With all due respect for you and your great office, if I have to be an executive, I see more scope and a greater contribution for me in a business than in the Church. Here it's all rules and regulations and paperwork. The main task is to preserve, to prevent change, discourage innovation, and not go in for experiments. (p. 151)

The question of which "father" one is ultimately serving, whether in the academy or the chancery, is the critical one raised by this novel. The book ends with the Bishop reflecting on the irony of the fact that having knowingly sacrificed the well-intentioned and innocent Father Zimmerman to avoid unpleasantness at St. Jerome University, he is being rewarded with elevation to the rank of Archbishop.

Drucker seeks to highlight the inherent contradiction in a system in which a priest's executive and managerial talents are measured by exclusively secular values. Father Zimmerman's temptation to do good, to find suitable employment for the faculty member he has been forced to fire, results in his own dismissal and disgrace, whereas the Bishop is rewarded for his decision to sacrifice Father Zimmerman on the altar of expediency. Drucker never disparages the cleric-as-manager but suggests that secular management skills in the Church should be in service of a Catholic Christian vision.

The Temptation To Do Good highlights the reductive perspective in McInerny's *Gate of Heaven*. In the latter novel, order is restored with the defeat of the clerical college President, Father Hoyt, who is attempting to strengthen the educational level of his religious community's college. As Drucker's fictional presentation of a similar crisis indicates, it is as simplistic to paint Father Hoyt as the villain as it would be to depict him as a hero. In any supposedly Catholic system, when doing good is considered a temptation, something certainly is amiss.

SOMETHING AMISS IN ROME

The basis of Walter Murphy's enormously popular *Vicar of Christ* (1979) is a similar concern with the nature of ecclesiastical authority. Although Murphy's focus is on the Papacy, he shares Drucker's interest in the tensions between the secular and the spiritual dimensions of ecclesiastical authority. There are remarkable similarities between Murphy's "vicar of Christ," Declan Walsh, and James Carroll's "prince of peace," Michael Maguire, similarities that highlight the radical differences between the perspectives of these two novelists.

Like Michael Maguire, Declan Walsh is a war hero who later embraces pacifism. Both authors envision their heroes as martyrs to their pacifist ideals. However, Maguire, the quintessential activist priest, dies alienated from the Church, while Declan Walsh becomes the first American Pope and is assassinated because of his uncompromising vision of the gospel imperative. Yet in spite of the sensationalist nature of his plot, Murphy offers more insight into the nature of ecclesiastical authority than the reductively antiauthoritarian James Carroll.

Despite the fact that Murphy presents an unbelievable plot line (Chief Justice of the U.S. Supreme Court becomes first American Pope), his portrait of Declan Walsh is a study in the human conflict inherent in the urge to power, especially when that power is ecclesiastical. Like Drucker's *The Temptation To Do Good*, Murphy's *Vicar of Christ* provides an opportunity for reflection about the use and abuse of power in the Church without the passionate intensity that marks the sacerdotal school. Murphy's Declan Walsh offers a positive view of Catholic unrest and ecclesiastical turmoil, a view that would be praised by Nicholas Manion and Martha Girlinghausen:

> The Church, . . . along with all of western society, is in chaos. But why not look on this chaos as an opportunity rather than as a menace, a challenge rather than a threat? People aren't rejecting religion or God so much as they're looking for new answers that fit new problems. The old catechism's approach doesn't help. These people are yearning, not rejecting. It's only when we question accepted facts and values that we progress.[12]

Murphy's central concern is the underlying attitude toward power and authority that should inform the decisions of the Vicar of Christ. The key to this attitude is in Declan Walsh's description of himself as Pope near the end of the novel:

> Perhaps we see ourself, in a much less exalted way than Christ, as stumbling down a road, burdened with the cross of humanity on our back, yet pushed by a divine energy the meaning of which we do not totally comprehend and the power of which we do not even know how to use effectively. (p. 716)

As Murphy emphasizes in his subsequent novel of the papacy during World War II, *The Roman Enigma* (1981), he is principally concerned with misuses of power that support the institution against the Good News.[13] However, Murphy, like Carroll, attempts to illuminate systemic corruption through the creation of one heroic individual who challenges the status quo. What both novelists share is a bias in favor of patriarchy. In his character Declan Walsh, who wields power as autocratically as any Renaissance monarch, Murphy privileges the system, ignoring the fact that fallible human nature is often corrupted by the trappings of power and prestige that are so very much a part of that system.

Malachi Martin's *The Final Conclave* (1978) goes a step further in asserting that the monarchical structure of the Papacy itself is in need of reform. When Martin's agenda is finally presented near the end of his novel, he would have the Church survive by divesting itself of all financial and political involvements that mitigate against its proclamation of the message of Christ. Ultimately, however, *The Final Conclave* simplistically seeks to institutionalize the urge to self-abnegation. Unlike John Gregory Dunne's Des Spellacy or Powers' Joe Hackett, Martin's Pope does not simply personally withdraw from the secular world; he withdraws the entire Church, dismantling the institutional structure and thereby returning Catholicism to its roots in testamental times.

Thus, what appears to be a radically innovative restructuring of the Church is, in fact, yet another retreat to some imagined Golden Age of Church Past. This is less a nostalgia for the immediate past than a misreading of Christian history, for *The Final Conclave* reflects a commitment to what scholars call "the myth of Christian beginnings," a reductive belief that the New Testament represents a pure Christianity that has been diluted throughout the centuries.[14] This retreat to early Christianity is also central to the two postconciliar novels in Morris West's Papal trilogy.

West's Papal trilogy reflects the dramatic changes in the perception of the Papacy during the past three decades as the effects of the Second Vatican Council were felt in American Catholicism. *The Shoes of the Fisherman* (1963), published two years before the Council concluded, presents a populist Pope, the Russian Kiril I, nominated in conclave by a Curial Cardinal who explains the need for a pastoral Pope to a colleague:

> Who cares about theology except the theologians? We [the Curia] are necessary, but less important than we think. The Church is Christ— Christ and the people. And all the people want to know is whether or not there is a God, and what is His relation with them, and how they can get back to Him when they stray.[15]

Kiril I, clearly modeled on John XXIII and a product of the optimism his personality generated, proceeds to become a conduit for discussions between the U.S.S.R. and the United States, and the novel ends not only with the promise that the Church will lead people to God, but that it will be instrumental in effecting world peace. *The Shoes of the Fisherman* undoubtedly remained on the best seller lists because it reflected America's romance with preconciliar Catholicism and encapsulated a common hope that the planned renewal of the Church would have far-reaching effects in the social and political realm.

Eighteen years later, West's *The Clowns of God* (1981) presents a bleaker picture of authority. It is the story of a visionary Pope who is dethroned by the Curia because of his discomforting prophecy of an imminent Second Coming but who becomes, in the course of the novel, a second Peter, invested with authority by a mysterious stranger who is revealed as the Christ. The image of the Vatican is now of a structure beyond redemption; the Church will live on only in its new pilgrim form. Like the vision of Malachi Martin, West's fiction is retrogressive, presenting a fantasy of obliterating 1900 years of Christian history and returning to an ideal of testamental times.

West's third novel, *Lazarus* (1990), is more wish-fulfillment fantasy than prophecy as an authoritarian Pope committed to the establishment of worldwide orthodoxy experiences a radical conversion, repents of his autocratic rule, and plans to govern in a new spirit. West accounts for his two earlier attempts at restructuring the Vatican in fiction by mentioning in *Lazarus* that Kiril I's commitment to his public role in *The Shoes of the Fisherman* had allowed the Curia to strengthen the institutional dimension, and the visionary Jean Marie Barette of *The Clowns of God* remains in his self-exile; the Curia is apparently unaffected by the mysterious stranger in that novel. The reigning Pontiff is Leo XIV, a conservative, absolutist Pope determined to purify Church teaching and pastoral practice. The good hierarch is Cardinal Anton Drexel, a cleric who is the benevolent leader of a small community of the mentally impaired. Drexel plays Kent to Leo's Lear, as he is banished for his appeal for a more compassionate Papal rule but later is called upon to instruct the converted Leo in more appropriate forms of leadership.

The catalyst for this change of heart is Leo's heart surgery, a bypass operation that results in a change in ecclesial perspective as well. Unfortunately, Leo seems to be converted to the Sentimental Love Ethic, and the novel's model for a structure of authority for the universal Church is Cardinal Drexel's small community of mentally impaired people. Leo never has to demonstrate any ability to rule the Church according to his new principles, for the benevolent Pope is soon assassinated, another Christ martyred by the religious hegemony. While West's presentation is rather simplistic, the similarity in the papal novels of Murphy, Martin, and West clearly reflects dissatisfaction with Catholicism's feudal structure of authority.

Religion develops in a cultural matrix, and the Judaic–Christian understanding of its relationship with Transcendence was articulated in the language of the master–slave relationship common to that culture's perception of ultimate power. Although the central message of the New Testament is the intimacy of the Divine–human encounter, the feudal culture in which Christianity developed tended to reinforce the competitive model of power relations. Today, at a time when democratic ideals make possible an understanding of the Divine–human encounter that is consonant with Jesus' radical definition of that relationship, it is important to identify the ways in which we are still bound by the power model.

This is most obvious in one mode of popular fiction that transcends authorial allegiance to the past or present. Liberal or conservative, the quintessential expression of the fiction obsessed with the institutional Church is the political thriller. McInerny's *The Noonday Devil* (1985) and Eugene Kennedy's *Fixes* (1989) are paradigmatic of this type of fiction of Catholic experience. *The Noonday Devil* recounts the efforts of the KGB to infiltrate the American hierarchy, a McCarthyite vision of the post-conciliary Church. Kennedy's *Fixes* is the liberal version of this trope, the CIA-supported assassination of a Pope and the attempt to fix the subsequent election of his successor. Although Kennedy sets his action in an indeterminate future, the resemblance to the situation involving the death of Pope John Paul I and the election of John Paul II is unmistakable. Whether the thriller is an attempt to cater to reactionary fears of change or to indict both the institutional Church and the American government, the vision is one of power relations as a model for religious experience.

Of the novels in this chapter, *The Shoes of the Fisherman*, published in 1963 before the completion of the Second Vatican Council, is notable for its optimistic vision. Clearly, the alternative vision of the other fiction chronicles a perception of anomaly in the preconciliar model of Catholicism as well as an awareness of the fact that the postconciliar Church has not yet developed a viable new paradigm. While the Immigrant Church flourished under an authoritarian hierarchy, when Catholics came of age in American society, they absorbed the dominant ethos of individualism. Whether or not Catholicism develops a new paradigm, it is becoming obvious that hierarchical authority is deemed increasingly anachronistic in contemporary society. It is the spirit of individualism that is beginning to write the Catholic story in the United States, both in fiction and nonfiction.

NOTES

1. Thomas Kuhn, *The Structure of Scientific Revolutions* (Chicago: University of Chicago Press, 1970), especially p. 52, "Discovery commences with the awareness of anomaly. . . ."

2. Elizabeth Cullinan, *House of Gold* (Boston: Houghton Mifflin Company, 1970), p. 169.

3. The creative evolution of Andrew Greeley's *The Cardinal Sins* (New York: Warner Books, 1981) is recounted by Greeley in *Confessions of a Parish Priest* (New York: Pocket Books, 1987), pp. 487–90.

4. Alfred Alcorn, *The Pull of the Earth* (Boston: Houghton Mifflin Company, 1985), p. 173.

5. Mark Twain, *The Adventures of Huckleberry Finn* (1884 reprint, n.p.: Grosset and Dunlap, 1918). Huck's decision, "All right, then, I'll go to hell" (p. 297) is the moral climax of the novel, the center of Chapter XXXI "You Can't Pray a Lie."

6. Robert Benard, *A Catholic Education* (New York: Holt, Rinehart and Winston, 1982), p. 18.

7. Susan Cahill, *Earth Angels: Portraits from Childhood and Youth* (1976; reprint, Harrington Park, New Jersey: Ampersand Associates, 1988), p. 209.

8. Michael Gallagher, "A Passion for the Papacy: A Conversation with Novelist Walter F. Murphy," *National Catholic Reporter* (February 5, 1988), p. 9.

9. W. H. Auden, "The Guilty Vicarage," *The Dyer's Hand and Other Essays* (1948; reprint, New York: Random House, 1968), p. 24.

10. J. F. Powers, *Wheat That Springeth Green* (New York: Alfred A. Knopf, 1988), p. 60.

11. Peter F. Drucker, *The Temptation To Do Good* (New York: Harper and Row, 1984), p. 81.

12. Walter F. Murphy, *Vicar of Christ* (New York: Ballantine Books, 1979), p. 256.

13. Murphy, as quoted by Gallagher, p. 10.

14. Richard John Neuhaus, *The Catholic Moment: The Paradox of the Church in the Postmodern World* (San Francisco: Harper and Row, 1987), p. 11.

15. Morris West, *The Shoes of the Fisherman* (1963; reprint, New York: Pocket Books, 1974), p. 7.

7

Visions of Individualism

For every man alone thinkes he hath got
To be a Phoenix, and that there can bee
None of that kinde, of which he is, but hee.

John Donne

As John Donne's lines from 1611 indicate, individualism is neither exclusively American nor predominantly a contemporary trait. However, it is America's ruling passion, as Robert Bellah and his colleagues point out in their study, *Habits of the Heart*.[1] Individualism rather than equality has been the controlling theme of life in the United States throughout history. As long as American Catholicism insulated itself, it was protected from the contradiction between its monarchical organization and the ruling passion of the secular society within which it existed in the United States. But even without the impetus of the Second Vatican Council, Catholicism would have faced a crisis in the 60's and 70's as the spirit of individualism reached its zenith in American political and social life.

Hence, the Council's attempt at renewal, opening the windows of Catholicism at the very moment when the winds of individualism in this country had reached hurricane velocity, seems to have occasioned a radical disestablishment of the institutional Church among Catholics in the United States. The leveling influence of the cultural revolution begun in the 1960's produced a trend in American Catholicism remarkably similar to the tenor of change in Protestantism in early nineteenth-century America, as described in Bellah's study, when sermons "became less doctrinal and more emotional and sentimental. . . . Religion, like the family, was a place of love and acceptance in an otherwise harsh and competitive society."[2] In both instances, a stable and hierarchical order *seems* to remain in place, but the predominant emphasis is on individual self-determination.

As postconciliar Catholicism absorbed American culture and flourished in ecumenical endeavors, it also assimilated the ethos of individualism dominant in American Christianity. Paul Shannon, the returning veteran of World War II in Robert Byrne's novel *Once A Catholic* (1970), reflects this shift in emphasis in his insistence that his younger brother be transferred from the local Catholic school, where superstition is more pervasive than scholarship, and enrolled in the public high school. When his mother complains that the pastor would object, Paul proclaims that "we have to put Tommy ahead of Father Grundy."[3] In postconciliar Catholicism, "Mrs. Grundy," the symbol in literature of propriety and repression, provides the name for the traditional American Catholic authoritarian pastor.[4]

Contemporary commentators applaud the new pluralism that the Second Vatican Council ushered in, yet seem unmindful of the lessons of American history. For, as Bellah points out, when individualism becomes predominant, community frequently comes from the "empathetic sharing of feelings" rather than from the demands of a tradition.[5] Moreover, as individualism erodes the communal spiritual life, churches tend to "reproduce the middle-class, suburban world that they serve," as the Protestant theologian Langdon Gilkey has remarked in discussing the development of mainline Protestant churches in America.[6] The American Catholic tradition of isolationism is perhaps responsible for the failure to heed the warnings of the Protestant experience, for if authoritarianism was the preconciliar model of American Catholicism, individualism is rapidly becoming its postconciliar counterpart. Always prioritized in mainstream American culture, individualism has become the virtue of preference among many commentators on American Catholicism.

Both Andrew Greeley and Eugene Kennedy reinforce their antagonism to institutionalism with an enthusiastic support of Catholic individualism. In *How To Save the Catholic Church*, Greeley and his coauthor Mary Greeley Durkin exalt "The Rise of Selective Catholicism" in the title of their first chapter and seem to regard individualism as the quintessential Christian virtue as they conclude:

The Second Vatican Council, the encyclical [*Humanae Vitae*], and the dawn of "Catholicism on One's Own Terms" seem to have combined to produce a new generation of Catholics who are admirable by almost any Christian standard.[7]

Similarly, in prose that borders on the hagiographic, Kennedy describes his "Culture Two" Catholics as the only possible future for the Church:

> They reflect, unself-consciously, the sacramental thrust of Catholicism at its best, that is Catholicism in love with art rather than law, Catholicism at home in the world instead of embattled with it, Catholicism as the agent of freedom, rather than only of control, for all that is profoundly human.[8]

The celebration of pluralism in Catholicism in the 1960's was understandable in view of the excessive triumphalism of the Immigrant Church in America. Father Grundy needed to be deposed. But those who hail the advent of pluralism fail to consider the history of religion in American society. Father Grundy's insistence on the priority of hierarchy separated Catholics from the dominant privatization of religion in America. But postconciliar Catholics in the United States seem to have assimilated well; a 1978 Gallup poll found that eighty percent of Americans, Catholics included, agreed that "an individual should arrive at his or her own religious beliefs independent of any churches or synagogues."[9] However, there are indications that American Catholics, freed from the rule of Father Grundy, are in danger of simply replicating the Protestant experience.

A 1987 *New York Times Magazine* article on "Being Catholic in America" provides a case in point. Author Joseph Berger identifies the pertinent issue:

> With authority so central a precept in Catholicism, the ferment among articulate Catholics steeped in the logic and habits of democracy poses one of the most profound dilemmas the Vatican faces.[10]

Berger's model contemporary Catholic, a dentist from Greenwich, Connecticut, "struggles with the Beatitudes' emphasis on being meek and humble 'in a world that reinforces people who are otherwise' " (p. 64). In this modern Catholic's reading of Scripture, the countercultural sayings of Jesus are in need of revision. Rather than the Word challenging the world, here the world challenges the Word. This marks the shift from a concept of church that enters into the world culturally and socially in order to influence it, to one of religious privatism that focuses on the spirituality of the individual, a personal ethos derived solely from his or her individual experience of the world.

As the article continues, this active Catholic, a member of her parish's liturgy committee, explains her concept of the Eucharist:

I don't know that I believe in the blood and body of Christ. . . . For me it's people communing together and sharing a meal and sharing some time together.[11]

This classic illustration of community based on the empathetic sharing of feelings to the exclusion of the demands of tradition is unsettling.

While the work of James Fowler emphasizes the importance of independent thinking in the development of a mature faith life, there is the danger that tradition and scholarship may be countered solely with personal opinion unless the Church can meet what Gilkey describes as the major political requirement of the moment: "to direct the process [of ecclesiastical change] so as to remain loyal to the deepest levels of tradition and yet also to be open to experiment with new and creative forms."[12] As Gilkey points out, this necessitates "some reasoned understanding of what authentic Catholicism *is* in order to realize legitimate goals" for the future.[13]

The myopic adulation of selective Catholicism tends to ignore its explicit dismissal of tradition and its claims. Without a grounding in a tradition of shared meanings, religion becomes simply an expression of a secular ethical ideal and loses the dimension of a relationship to Another—who, for Christians, is the Christ—as well as the challenge of self-transcendence inherent in that relationship.

The trend toward privatization of religion among Catholics is readily apparent in the differences between the fiction of Kit Reed and Caryl Rivers discussed in Chapter 5. For Reed's Georgia Kendall the confrontation with modern culture is experienced in a larger context. Regardless of the inadequacy of the institutional Church in meeting the needs of modern Catholics, herself included, Georgia expresses confidence in its emphasis on the priority of the supernatural. Rivers' novels reflect the influence of the cultural revolution of the 60's. The preconciliar Catholicism of *Virgins* is depicted principally in the comical experiences of adolescents in the late 50's, a focus on the absurdities occasioned by attempting to deal with modernity through authoritarianism. In the postconciliar world of *Girls Forever Brave and True*, memories of those absurdities comprise a shared history among the protagonists, and it is the empathetic sharing of feelings that produces community for Peg, Con, and Sean rather than the demands of tradition. There is no rejection of Catholicism; it is simply subordinated to the individual.

The result of the progressive privatization of Catholicism is exemplified in contemporary American fiction in the work of David Plante and Andre Dubus. Theirs is not a mourning for a lost Catholic past, nor do they exhibit anger at an intransigent institution. Their fiction reflects an assertion of Catholic identity conveyed with comfortingly traditional images and orthodox diction. In light of so much unrest in fiction, the Catholic atmosphere in the fiction of Plante and Dubus may seem less troubling at first reading than it appears on closer examination. Ultimately, though, the notion of Catholicism in the work of both writers is disquietingly idiosyncratic.

GODLESS CATHOLICISM

Readers of Plante's prior fiction are somewhat prepared for *The Catholic* (1986), a brief novel narrated by Daniel Francoeur whose family's story is told in Plante's Francoeur trilogy, *The Family* (1978), *The Country* (1981), and *The Woods* (1982). Plante's fiction seems to have a closer affiliation with *cinema verite* than the novel, as the trilogy recounts various episodes in the life of this French Canadian family in Rhode Island with little attention to the meaning of those events. These apparently autobiographical novels seem to belong more to the genre of diary than novel, more of a catharsis for the author than fiction addressed to readers. Indeed, Plante has commented that he does not write "for what I have to say—I believe I have nothing to say."[14]

In *The Catholic* Daniel is twenty-five and teaching in Boston. He is, however, both personally and professionally unsettled. The first-person narrative, reflecting Daniel's confusion and uncertainty, adds an elliptical quality to this novel. The central event of the narrative is Daniel's liaison with Henry, a young man he has picked up in a local bar. And Daniel's comment on that liaison not only connects it to the technique in the earlier novels but reveals the authorial perspective that informs Plante's fiction:

> As a Catholic, I felt my childhood had, in a way that seemed simultaneously concrete and elusive, been like that night I'd spent with Henry: there was no explaining it, there was only experiencing it, like some strange conversion, to have any sense of it.[15]

That sense of the concrete and elusive, so central to Daniel's perception of the world, is also the fictional matrix of Plante's novels. In the trilogy, Plante's narrative energies are used in service of enabling the reader to experience Daniel's childhood—sights and sounds are faithfully depicted— and in *The Catholic* Plante writes graphically of the sexual encounter

between Henry and Daniel in a prolonged narrative sequence that dominates the book. But with no attempt to provide a sense of meaningfulness
to those experiences, no "fiction" imposed on the raw material of life,
Plante's narratives have an elusive quality that is somewhat disconcerting.
In the conventions of prose, the reader expects there to be some order
imposed on the flux of events.

Moreover, the opening phrase "As a Catholic" suggests that Daniel's
weltanschauung derives from his religious affiliation, and Plante offers
similarly vague associations between faith, religion, and Daniel's erotic
preoccupations. Daniel describes his sexual longing for Henry, for example, as analogous to a search for faith:

> He meant everything to me, he had to mean everything, and my faith
> in the idea of such meaning was all the faith I had. (p. 146)

Ironically, Daniel seems intent on keeping this desire unfulfilled. Although
he complains of unrequited love throughout the narrative, his friends point
out that it is Daniel himself who is aloof and unwilling to develop a
relationship with Henry. A friend advises, "Don't you see that there is no
basis, none at all, to loving someone except in a relationship, however
complex, however massively complex, it is?" (p. 110)

But for Daniel, Henry cannot be a flesh and blood sexual partner, only
some mysterious ideal:

> There was nothing I could do but ask myself where such desire came
> from. Where did such awareness, never to be fulfilled, come from:
> Why was there such a sense of promise in us, if the promise would
> never be kept? (p. 148)

In seeking only the ecstasy of sexual union while refusing any relationship
with the other person and suggesting that such a perspective is somehow
linked to his Catholic heritage, Daniel Francoeur reflects the "magical"
thinking that pervaded preconciliar theology. Plante presents Daniel as
somehow condemned by Catholicism to an uncompromising dualism
between body and spirit. At the beach with Henry, Daniel thinks, "I did
not really like to be out in athletic America, but always wished I were in
my small Catholic room, which was quiet" (p. 65).

The novel ends with Daniel alone in his small Catholic room awaiting
some revelatory experience with "a longing for the illuminating idea that
precedes all thought, and perhaps all feeling—an idea that we know is the

center of all true thinking and feeling" (p. 150). As he expresses his philosophy of life:

As a totally intentional person, your greatest intention is to keep yourself open to such ideas, to take such risks. Nothing will enter. But it will. Everything will enter. (p. 150)

If this sounds vaguely like a secular version of prayer, that seems to be what Plante intends. In an essay explaining how his Catholicism and writing intersect, Plante presented his rather idiosyncratic notion of Catholicism with the comment that "it is because I am a Catholic that I believe in grace, but I am also an atheist and do not at all believe in God."[16] Because he also expresses "a loathing for anything spiritualist," one longs to ask for a definition of grace. That definition may be indicated by the references to Walt Whitman in the text of *The Catholic* where Daniel idealizes the romantic author of "Song of Myself." In the character of Daniel Francoeur, Plante projects a belief in the self as the source for the transcendent experiences traditionally associated with the Divine, and the novels of the Francoeur trilogy thus become his sacred texts.

The Catholic presents a protagonist who is so totally self-enclosed in his concern for awaiting the graced moment that he has little relational capacity. The reader might be tempted to conclude that Daniel has been warped by his Catholic heritage, yet Plante's essay makes it clear that Daniel's quietism represents some type of aesthetic and religious ideal for the author, a personal notion of Catholicism. Catholicism imprints only an ontological, not an empirical, identity according to Plante's revisionist theology, and that identity is self-reflexive, having no relationship to the reality Catholics customarily denote as God. Whatever lies on the other side of silence remains obscure for Daniel; as the novel ends, he is awaiting his revelation.

Plante, a product of Jesuit education, has reformulated traditional theological concepts to inform a private notion of the world. He affirms the concept of grace because it is consonant with his experience as a novelist. The fact that the process of writing is often surprisingly revelatory confirms the action of grace for him. Ironically, David Plante's reworking of his religious heritage to correlate with and reinforce his personal life experience is not dissimilar in process to Berger's modern Catholic dentist's reformation of Scripture and sacraments in an effort to personalize religion. Both individuals affirm only those religious values that are consonant with their personal life experience.

Andre Dubus provides another example of the revision of Catholicism to accord with personal experience. Interestingly, Dubus offers such a conventionally Catholic atmosphere in his fiction that his individualistic moral perspective can easily go unnoticed. So rare is the American male writer who does not express anger or disappointment in relation to Catholicism that Dubus can appear to be a Catholic writer of the old didactic school. But in art as in life, appearances are often deceiving.

SEMPER CATHOLIC

Superficially, the Catholic experience in Dubus' fiction may seem more allied to that depicted by Ralph McInerny than that of David Plante. Characters in a Dubus story are frequently Catholic, talk earnestly of sin and guilt, and are concerned with the sacramental life in a manner more consonant with the 1940's than the 1980's. But this is no encomium to the Golden Age, for Catholics in the fiction of Dubus compartmentalize their faith, and Catholicism, though pervasive, is presented as so pristine as to be incompatible with authentic human experience.

Paradigmatic of Dubus' fictional representation of Catholicism is his novella *Voices from the Moon* (1984). The story begins with Richie Stowe who is twelve and wants to be a priest. He goes to daily Mass, a celebration Dubus unfailingly depicts rather anachronistically with the imagery of preconciliar Catholic piety:

> Father Oberti was approaching the Consecration and Richie waited for the miracle, then watched it, nearly breathless, and prayed My Lord and my God to the white Host elevated in Father Oberti's hands, and softly struck his breast.[17]

Richie is upset because his divorced father is planning to marry Brenda, his older brother's former wife. He worries about the fact that "It will be very hard to be a Catholic in our house" (p. 5). In light of this comment, it is surprising to discover that Richie's father Greg enters the narrative as a good man, hardworking and reliable, an excellent father who would never interfere with his son's life. So Richie's concern for the planned marriage as a threat to his own faith life is almost incongruous, except in light of the peculiar version of Catholicism that permeates Dubus' fiction. It is a religious expression limited solely to the world of innocence.

In Dubus' fiction, love is the greatest virtue and its corruption the only sin. Catholicism, seemingly a positive force, is reserved for the innocence of untested love. In *Voices from the Moon*, Richie is the only member of the Stowe family who is a practicing Catholic, but he is also the only member of the family who has not yet had an opportunity to fail at love. When we meet the rest of Richie's family, we discover a curious group of well-intentioned but weak people searching for happiness in a totally secular milieu, as though their weakness has separated them from their religious heritage. At the end of the story Richie is lying on the grass in the company of a girl to whom he is attracted. In view of the complicated lives of his family members, the reader wonders if Richie's plans for the priesthood will survive this first love. Dubus' ending suggests that puberty may bring a loss of innocence that will separate Richie from this pristine Church as it has the other members of his family.

Another story of adolescence, "Sorrowful Mysteries," depicts a young Cajun, Gerry Fontenot, assimilating his Catholicism, as he begins to understand racism in his perception of a condemned black man as a type of the suffering Christ. But the story ends while Gerry is still in college, his love yet untested. A subsequent story, "Deaths at Sea," depicts an older Gerry who further develops his understanding of the destructiveness of racist attitudes, but he is still an onlooker in the action, a passive viewer of others' pain.

In "The Pretty Girl," the divorced and jaded Polly contrasts herself to her sister Margaret who at seventeen is still a regular communicant, neither drinks nor smokes, is "certainly a virgin," and jogs regularly.

> She [Margaret] was dark and pretty, but Polly thought all that virtue had left its mark on her face, and it would never be the sort that makes men change their lives.[18]

Similarly, Catholicism, although pure, does not have the vital energy "that makes men" change their lives. Quite the reverse. The highest degree of perfection is attained by those who transcend the limitations of "all that virtue." This is most evident in Dubus' contrast between Catholicism and love in "A Father's Story," a narrative from *The Last Worthless Evening* (1986), that was chosen to end the 1988 edition of *Selected Stories* as though it is the capstone of Dubus' authorial vision.

Luke Ripley, the fifty-four year old narrator of "A Father's Story" is a daily communicant. His wife left him some years earlier, and Ripley lives alone, simply and, apparently, peacefully. Initially he seems the exception to Dubus' association of the practice of Catholicism with untested, virginal love, but Luke Ripley's story is not only consonant with Dubus' prior fiction, it most fully reveals his indebtedness to the Sentimental Love Ethic for his definition of love.

Receiving the Eucharist each day, Luke Ripley has

a feeling that I am thankful I have not lost in the forty-eight years since my first Communion. At its center is excitement, spreading out from it is the peace of certainty. Or the certainty of peace.[19]

That peace is disturbed during a visit from his twenty-year-old daughter, Jennifer. One rainy night, driving home alone after an evening with friends, Jennifer accidentally hits someone and continues home without stopping. She wakes her father, and he goes out to investigate. Finding the victim, Luke cannot determine whether the man is dead or alive, but he realizes that in not stopping for the priest or calling for an ambulance to meet him at the scene of the accident, he had already decided what to do. He returns home and tells Jennifer that the man is dead, although it is clear that Luke himself is not sure whether the man he abandoned on the road was dead or alive.

The next morning he takes her damaged car to Mass, driving it into a tree before anyone can notice the already smashed fender. When the priest, alarmed by Luke's apparently careless driving, suggests he rest rather than attend Mass, Luke unself-consciously responds, "No, I want to receive" (p. 178). Amazingly, Dubus presents Luke's abandonment of the man in the road (who, because of the rain, is not found until twenty-four hours later) and protection of his daughter as virtuous. Luke's love for his daughter has been tested and found acceptable; he comes to an awareness of a more mature peace beyond that offered by his religious practices.

I do not feel the peace I once did, not with God, nor the earth, or anyone on it. I have begun to prefer this state, to remember with fondness the other one as a period of peace I neither earned nor deserved. (p. 179)

In an imagined dialogue with God, Luke argues that he would do it again, that God may have sacrificed his Son but he never had a daughter, and Luke asserts, "if You had, You could not have borne her passion" (p. 179). There is no indication that Dubus intends Luke Ripley as an unreliable narrator, no suggestion that he wants to shock the reader by the fact of Luke's having abandoned a possibly still living man and gone to Mass in order to obliterate evidence of the accident. The love between fathers and daughters is a strong theme in Dubus' work, suggesting that indeed he expects readers to admire this father for having saved his daughter the ordeal of a police inquiry.

While love may seem to be the moral center of Dubus' fiction, the definition of love is idiosyncratic. Ultimately, the moral center of Dubus' fiction, as in Plante's, is the isolated individual self. The process of privatization is apparent in the central preoccupations in Dubus' fiction—failed marriages and the strong bonds between parents and children, not surprising from the father of six children, a veteran of three marriages. But even more central is Dubus' five-and-a-half years' experience as a Marine, for the behavior of his characters is best understood in light of Marine idealism: being out in front, even at the risk of peril, protecting and saving one another.[20] Hence, Luke personally saves his daughter at the expense of the "enemy," the man in the road who is a threat to her happiness. The father in "Killings" executes his son's murderer, even though the latter is already indicted and awaiting trial, and Polly kills her abusive and threatening former husband in "The Pretty Girl," without any attempt to resolve her dilemma through recourse to the law.

This apparent depiction of ordinary life in terms of combat is meliorated by an absence of a true enemy. The first half of "The Pretty Girl" is narrated by Polly's husband, a narrative strategy that presents him to the reader as a pathetically limited man whose obsession with his former wife derives from an understandable, if irrational, response to an entire constellation of events in his life. The murder of the killer in "Killings" is carried out with prolonged contact between the executioner and his victim, enabling the reader to identify the young man as a frightened human being confronting his death rather than a crazed killer.

This strong empathetic strain in Dubus' prose could serve to remind us of the sinfulness that leads to subsequent sin were it not for the relativism of the moral perspective in which the extreme actions of the protagonists are unfailingly presented (and implicitly approved) as the natural effects of experiencing love. As one reviewer commented, rather than confront the moral problems in his fiction, Dubus "prefers to let them dissolve in the amniotic fluid of his empathy."[21]

Thus, in spite of the conservative ambience of Dubus' fiction, its moral world is the natural extension of contemporary liberal Christianity in which "community and attachment come not from the demands of a tradition, but from the empathetic sharing of feelings among therapeutically attuned selves."[22] Rescued from obeisance to "Father Grundy," American Catholics are prey to the authority of unbridled autonomy. From these examples of its manifestations in fiction, the contemporary impulse toward exaltation of Catholic individualism is incredibly myopic. The fiction of Plante and Dubus presages the primary distortion of individualism—Catholicism formulated with no operative paradigm, no shared meanings. However, there is an "alternative vision" that derives from

American individualism, a vision that has produced the contemporary confessional novel of Catholic experience.

WRITING ONE'S LIFE

The autobiographical novel has a long history, and it is particularly suited to the writer who seeks to establish meaning within his or her own life. As Paul Theroux said of his autobiographical novel *My Secret History* (1989), "it has released me, freed me of the past by understanding it."[23] It is Theroux's novel and two novels by Larry Woiwode that provide insight into the contemporary Catholic moment.

Fiction provides writers with a forum for subjecting experience to the medium of imagination in order to discern meaning, and both Theroux and Woiwode have publicly referred to the autobiographical elements in their fiction. Both writers are of an age; they grew up in the preconciliar 50's and left the Church during their college years in the cataclysmic 60's. What is particularly fascinating is that, unlike Plante and Dubus who have fashioned their own version of Catholicism, Theroux and Woiwode, who write of only "Catholicism Lost," help provide a context for exploring the possibility of "Catholicism Found." In varying ways, both writers help gloss Paul Tillich's principles of cultural change, a process that is helpful in understanding Catholicism's recent past.

PROCESS OF CHANGE

Tillich's interpretation of the history of Christianity is especially instructive for contemporary Catholicism not only because Tillich was also responding to the collapse of supernaturalism but because he sees the *felix culpa* in revolutionary change. Originally formulated as a way of describing the process of change known historically as the Protestant Reformation, Tillich's categories can be applied to any description of the effect of religion in the life of an individual, a group, or an entire culture.

Tillich's theory of cultural change is principally identified by his use of three words derived from Greek.[24] His three key words are *theonomy*, *heteronomy*, and *autonomy*, which, from their Greek roots, refer respectively to "Divine rule," "foreign rule," and "self-rule." For Tillich, and any religious person, the ideal state is, of course, *theonomy* (Divine rule). However, Tillich points out that religions can often harden into repressive structures, so that the individual members are living under *heteronomy* (foreign rule). Then, he argues, the assertion of *autonomy* (self-rule) is inevitable. The assertion of autonomy, according to this schema, was at the root of the Reformation and, it now seems clear, is central to postconciliar Catholicism. Happily, Tillich's is a cyclical process, and he envisions an eventual return to theonomy. This process is aptly illustrated in the life of an individual in Theroux's autobiographical novel *My Secret History* (1989).

LEAVING THE WEDDING

My Secret History tells the story of Andre Parent from his altar boy days in 1956 through 1984, and in that span of years Parent's story offers insight into the current dilemma for American Catholics. The 1956 segment of *My Secret History*, "Altar Boy," recounts Andrew Parent's experiences as a youth in the preconciliar Church and vividly fictionalizes the experience of heteronomy. Religion is the domain of God and most of the adults in his life, especially the Pastor, an autocrat whose absolute rule is reflected in the capitalized title by which he is always designated. Andre enters the sanctum of adult religion through his role as altar boy.

It is in serving Mass that the boy encounters an alternative model of religion, Father Furty, a priest about whom there are whispers of scandal (he is rumored to be an alcoholic). Furty is an open-hearted, gentle man from whom Andre absorbs a less juridical Catholicism: "I had stopped feeling that I was probably going to Hell, and I sensed that I would most likely end up in Purgatory."[25]

The rule among altar servers is that serving three funerals earns the boy a wedding, an event that promises a monetary reward from the celebrants, and Andre is working toward his first wedding while also becoming fast friends with Father Furty. Soon Andre is thinking of becoming a priest; his acquaintance with Father Furty has shown him that "you could be a priest and still have a wonderful time" (p. 72).

Father Furty unexpectedly dies, and Andre feels impelled toward priesthood in imitation of his mentor. However, in an interview with the Pastor, the fifteen-year-old discovers that a vocation will entail denying the ebullient Furty and conforming himself to the model preferred by the Pastor. As the disconcerting interview ends, the Pastor reminds Andre that he has finally earned his wedding; Father Furty's funeral had been the third one the boy had served.

But Andre never serves that wedding. Having earned it through the death of Father Furty, whose memory he is being asked to abjure, the boy reacts by symbolically rejecting the Pastor and the Church he represents. Preparing to serve the long-sought wedding, Andre arrives at the church but cannot bring himself to enter:

Then I walked away and was aware in those seconds that my life had
just begun—like a wheel slipping off an axle and rolling alone, and
already it was spinning faster. I thought: A wedding is just a happy
funeral. (p. 92)

There is irony in the fact that the festive table-sharing at a wedding feast
is characteristic of Jesus and his movement in the gospels. Andre's
wedding symbolizes to him the cost of belonging to the Triumphal Church
of the Golden Age whose representative is the Pastor, a Church that would
cast out Father Furty.

Andre Parent's interview with the Pastor is evocative of Stephen
Dedalus' famous interview with the Rector in James Joyce's *A Portrait of
the Artist as a Young Man*. In both novels, the subject of the interview is
the boy's vocation to the priesthood, and it is the stifling atmosphere of
repression that leads to both young men's eventual *non serviam*. In both
works, it is not relationship with the Divine that is being rejected, but the
protagonist's experience of the heteronomous world of religion.

Like Stephen Dedalus, Andre Parent eventually finds his vocation as a
writer. Rejecting the seminary, Andre works his way through college in
this episodic novel, and, in the spirit of the 60's, goes to Africa as a Peace
Corps volunteer. It is clear from the novel that it is not pure self-interest
that leads Andre to eschew priesthood, but, like Nicholas Manion in *A
Catholic Education*, Andrew understands that priesthood demands a distortion of his very self. Autonomy (self-rule) is impossible in a heteronomous world, and that is the world the Pastor represents.

However, the novel also makes it clear that a self-enclosed autonomy
has limits. Freed from the repressive force of his authoritarian Church,
Andre Parent spends the next eight years principally indulging his libido.
The balance of *My Secret History* is devoted to the exercise of autonomy
writ large. Even his eventual marriage provides only a brief interlude of
monogamy, for the final section of the novel depicts the now well-estab-
lished writer shuttling across the Atlantic between wife and mistress.

Near the end of the novel, Andre has an experience that recalls to him
the religion of his youth, and there are intimations of a longing for a
reconnection to the Divine. While traveling in India with his mistress,
Andre and the woman go white-water rafting on the Ganges accompanied
by several Indians. The party discovers a badly decomposed body, and the
Indians insist on giving it proper burial. Watching the reverence with
which the Indians complete the burial rite, Andre thinks, "In a world of
ambiguity and cross-purposes this was indisputably a good deed" (p. 440).
And suddenly, for the first time in twenty-eight years, he recalls his days

as an altar boy serving Mass and concludes: "It was the first sign I had ever had that I might find my way back to believing" (p. 440). Andre Parent has exhausted the possibilities of self-enclosed autonomy and now yearns for a way to reintegrate his life.

In a way, *My Secret History* is *our* secret history, the story of contemporary Catholicism. In "Altar Boy," the young Andre Parent sees the heteronomous face of 50's Catholicism personified in the Pastor who conveys a similarly heteronomous image of God to the boy who realizes that

> I had modeled God on the Pastor—God's glare, and God's scowling
> face, and even his paleness and his white upswept hair; and both God
> and the Pastor had narrow Irish mouths that they held slightly open
> to show doubt or scorn or self-importance. (p. 80)

And the Pastor also affects the boy's conception of the Church, which he envisions as a sparsely populated building, "a tiny boxlike thing with a stumpy steeple and very few pews; it was hard to enter and uncomfortable inside, which was why most of us were outside" (p. 90).

Theroux's "Altar Boy" serves as a companion to all the fiction of alternative visions discussed in Chapter 6, novels that highlight the reductiveness in idolizing the American Catholic past. Following World War II, the authoritarian Irish-American Church was increasingly experienced as oppressive rather than life-giving. The structure that served the Immigrant Church so well was not suited to its children. In Benard's *A Catholic Education*, Thomas Manion, a child of immigrant America, perceives ecclesiastical authority as liberating. His son Nicholas perceives it as repressive and destructive.

Nicholas Manion faces an uncertain future at the end of *A Catholic Education*, and the story of Andre Parent in Theroux's *My Secret History* provides one example of that future. Having left the Church, Andre Parent relies solely on the self, a stage that Tillich indicates is the natural result of having liberated oneself from heteronomy. But Theroux's novel highlights the reductiveness in idealizing autonomy, as is a current habit. Andre's extended adventures as an autonomous self are unsatisfying for him in spite of his professional success. In Tillich's model, there is a natural movement toward theonomy, and American fiction of Catholic experience has now begun to reflect this movement. Near the end of Theroux's novel, Andre Parent reflects on his reverent response to the Indian burial rite he had witnessed, "the first sign I had ever had that I might find my way back to believing" (p. 400).

In *My Secret History*, Theroux charts the process of a sloughing off of the claims of repressive religion (heteronomy), the vitality in a newly discovered independence (autonomy), its eventual dissipation, and the incipient longing for relationship with the Divine (theonomy).[26] Larry Woiwode makes the need for authentic religious experience more explicit in his novels of the Neumiller family, *Beyond the Bedroom Wall* (1975) and *Born Brothers* (1988).

BEYOND THE INSTITUTION

The positive aspects of preconciliar Catholicism are reflected in the life of Charles Neumiller's parents (married in 1939) and paternal grandparents. There is nothing ostentatious or pietistic about the faith life of these simple farm people, and when Charles' mother Alpha considers converting to Catholicism (following five years of instruction), it is apparent that hers is a mature faith choice, reflecting a deep spirituality.

But the secure world is shattered when Alpha dies while attempting to give birth to her fifth child. Woiwode brilliantly depicts the deterioration of the family's life with no mother in the home. The unsought autonomy resulting from his mother's death eventually leads Charles to a personally appropriated autonomy when he is older:

> I had come to the conclusion that there were no absolutes, at least not for me. The only truth that was valid was the truth that originated in me, without presuppositions, and all I needed was the time to prove that.[27]

Religion, Charles' last security, is abandoned.

The fragility of a life of pure autonomy is reflected in Charles' eventual slide into alcoholism with the resultant disintegration of his own family and his promising career. His crisis, displayed more than explained in the novels, is similar to that experienced by Susan Chace's protagonist Cecilia O'Rourke in *Intimacy* (1989). This first novel, which recounts the efforts of a woman to survive her past, highlights the double bind that affects many "born Catholics" like Charles Neumiller.

Catholicism represents not only a repressive past but an ethical ideal and a source of security, something that is suggested in the narrative of Charles Neumiller but explicit in Cecilia's fantasy. In her deteriorating mental state, Cecilia fantasizes the presence of Father Dwyer, a young priest she vaguely knew in her childhood, a man who died at the age of thirty-five. Like Charles Neumiller, Cecilia O'Rourke becomes an alcoholic, and Father Dwyer represents both her residual conscience and a lost ideal self. She associates him with the guilt of the morning after, and, in speaking to his image, she addresses the Church he represents to her: "you chose that inconclusive time before dawn, when the morning headache is still building, to remind me just how important was your grip on me."[28] The priest personifies the authoritarian heritage that Cecilia has abandoned but without which she is unanchored. Like Charles who must believe that the Church is the source of his problems, Cecilia berates the phantom priest for "how much wine you made me drink before you let me sleep" (p. 81).

At the end of *Intimacy*, Cecilia O'Rourke is struggling to maintain a precarious psychological balance, supported by analysts and exercise (both secular substitutions for the Divine), but in Woiwode's fiction Charles Neumiller is depicted as having returned to the God of his youth. His redemption is effected by his renewed commitment to Christianity in an unnamed denomination, an experience author Woiwode shares with his protagonist. In an interview Woiwode revealed that he left the Roman Catholic Church in 1961 while a college student and is currently a member of the Orthodox Presbyterian Church. The final comment of that interview suggests that he, like Charles Neumiller, lives a spiritual life, attempting to discern God's will in all things. Woiwode speaks of a central question that has haunted him since his college years and still continues to obsess him. "The more words I build up, the more I find myself asking that question—Is this serving God?"[29]

Fiction, therefore, offers Catholicism two different visions of American individualism. The first, represented by the fiction of Plante and Dubus, is ostentatiously "Catholic," clinging to the name in an assertion of autonomy that does not simply reject heteronomy but appropriates its codes. The second model is one of personal process, as seen in the fiction of Theroux, Woiwode, and Chace. It is a developmental model that can lead an individual to Fowler's Stage 4 faith and beyond, to a personally appropriated religious expression most consonant with the individual's experience of the Divine. Ironically, Catholicism is frequently abandoned in this model. This fiction, which focuses on the search for a true religious self, is, not surprisingly, most evident in women's fiction, the subject of the next chapter.

I say not surprisingly because the historical convergence of the Women's Movement and the renewal of Catholicism would lend some inevitability to the phenomenon of fiction about the American Catholic experience authored by women. Feminism provided an impetus for self-reflection, and the changes in the Church directed that reflection to the question of religious identity. The search for an authentic spirituality, so much a part of Charles Neumiller's story, informs the "prophetic vision" of women writers.

NOTES

1. Robert N. Bellah et al., *Habits of the Heart: Individualism and Commitment in American Life* (New York: Harper and Row Perennial Library, 1985), p. vii.
2. Bellah et al., p. 223.
3. Robert Byrne, *Once A Catholic* (New York: Pinnacle Books, 1970), p. 208.
4. *The Harper Handbook to Literature*, comps. Northrop Frye, Sheridan Baker, and George Perkins (New York: Harper and Row, 1985), provides the identification of Mrs. Grundy: "In Thomas Morton's melodrama *Speed the Plough* (1798), a character who never appears. She is the neighbor of Dame Ashfield, who constantly asks, 'What will Mrs. Grundy say?' She thus represents the cream of propriety and snobbish disapproval." In the Victorian era, "Mrs. Grundy" became a symbol of the censor and thus of repression, usually sexual repression, for the sake of propriety.
5. Bellah et al., p. 232.
6. Langdon Gilkey, *Catholicism Confronts Modernity* (New York: The Seabury Press, 1975), p. 14.
7. Andrew Greeley and Mary Greeley Durkin, *How to Save the Catholic Church* (New York: Viking, 1984), p. 17.
8. Eugene Kennedy, *Tomorrow's Catholics/Yesterday's Church: The Two Cultures of American Catholicism* (New York: Harper and Row, 1988), p. 25.
9. Reported in Bellah et al., p. 228.
10. Joseph Berger, "Being Catholic in America," *The New York Times Magazine* (August 23, 1987), p. 25.
11. Ibid., p. 64.
12. Gilkey, pp. 6–7.
13. Ibid., p. 7; italics are his.
14. David Plante, "Rising to Grace," *Boston College Magazine* (Summer 1989), p. 35.
15. David Plante, *The Catholic* (New York: Atheneum, 1986), p. 72.
16. Plante, "Rising to Grace," p. 35.
17. Andre Dubus, *Voices from the Moon* (Boston: David R. Godine, 1984), p. 9.
18. Andre Dubus, "The Pretty Girl," *The Last Worthless Evening* (Boston: David R. Godine, 1986), p. 24.
19. Andre Dubus, "A Father's Story," *The Last Worthless Evening*, p. 165.
20. Bruce Weber, "Andre Dubus's Hard-Luck Stories," *The New York Times Magazine* (November 20, 1988), p. 110.
21. Eva Hoffman, "Taking a Chance on Pathos," *The New York Times Book Review* (November 6, 1988), p. 7.
22. Bellah et al., p. 232.
23. Quoted by Holcomb B. Noble, "A Novel Gives You a Second Chance," *The New York Times Book Review* (June 4, 1989), p. 28.
24. Paul Tillich, *A History of Christian Thought*, ed. Carl E. Braaten (New York: Simon and Schuster, 1968), pp. 320–23. Tillich's theory is inextricably tied to the specialized use of these three terms, but I have tried to avoid relying on them in the subsequent discussion to avoid obfuscation.
25. Paul Theroux, *My Secret History* (New York: G. P. Putnam's Sons, 1989), p. 54.

26. Another writer whose work is tangential to the fiction discussed here is Robert Stone who, though he does not specifically focus on the Catholic story, nevertheless provides a suggestion of the longing for theonomy in the culture at large. In spite of the violence that characterizes his fiction, Stone depicts the yearning for authentic spirituality, especially in the characters of Sister Justin in *A Flag for Sunrise* (New York: Ballantine Books, 1981) and Lu Anne Bourgeois in *Children of Light* (New York: Ballantine Books, 1986).

27. Larry Woiwode, *Born Brothers* (New York: Farrar, Straus and Giroux, 1988), p. 13.

28. Susan Chace, *Intimacy* (New York: Random House, 1989), p. 79.

29. Quoted by Joseph A. Cincotti, "God's Work and the Novelist's," *The New York Times Book Review* (December 17, 1989), p. 7.

8

Prophetic Vision: The Spiritual Quest

She says, "But in contentment I still feel
The need of some imperishable bliss."

Wallace Stevens

The speaker in Wallace Stevens' "Sunday Morning" reflects the dissatisfaction with a self-enclosed autonomy indicated in Paul Theroux's *My
Secret History* and the novels of Larry Woiwode discussed in the preceding chapter. It is especially interesting that Stevens' narrator is a woman,
for the pattern of spiritual development reflected in Paul Tillich's principles of cyclical change is most evident in women's fiction of American
Catholic experience. Traditions of the past as well as contemporary events
have combined to provide American women writers with a distinct angle
of vision.

Vision is conditioned by the experience of the agent, as is evident in the
well-known scene in Shakespeare's *The Tempest* when Prospero's innocent daughter Miranda, seeing other human beings for the first time,
exclaims, "O brave new world / That has such people in't!" (V.i.183) to
which her more experienced father responds, "Tis new to thee." The
comments of Shakespeare's cynical father and naive daughter reflect the
manner in which their vision has been conditioned by their respective life
experiences. So it is not surprising that there are gender-specific differences in postconciliar fiction of American Catholicism, for the historical
and contemporary experience of women differs from that of men.

Among writers of fiction, males most commonly project a sense of loss in relation to Catholicism, as has been apparent in the literature discussed in this book. Their typical narrative stance is encapsulated in the "visions of experience," an expression of grief occasioned by the loss of certitude and stability that the preconciliar Church provided. Even fiction of passionate intensity, which reacts against the authoritarianism of preconciliar Catholicism, is redolent with nostalgia for the social presence of the Church, as is evident in the fiction of Andrew Greeley and James Carroll. The title of Walker Percy's last novel, *The Thanatos Syndrome*, is emblematic of the male vision of American Catholicism.

There is another narrative stance in this fiction, one which results in a literature of promise rather than a literature of loss, and it is found in fiction that reflects the need for "some imperishable bliss." This fiction is thoroughly grounded in the natural world yet explores the interpenetration of the Divine and the human. This fiction tends to be less institutionally oriented, locating meaning in human relationships rather than in institutional preoccupations, as has been evident in the novels of Kit Reed and Caryl Rivers (see Chapter 5).

A major shift in contemporary theology is to approach truth from life rather than from dogma, and this emphasis on human relationships in fiction provides an important occasion for theological reflection. The novels of Theroux and Woiwode discussed in Chapter 7 demonstrate the fact that this perspective is not exclusively gender-specific, but it is clearly more dominant among women writers, as the fiction in this chapter will illustrate. A constellation of cultural conditions provides women with a unique angle of vision and a narrative model for the expression of their vision.

For women writers, the story of Catholicism is not the saga of the institution because historically women have been marginalized by the Church. They did not identify with its patriarchal structure in the same way as men. However, their very lack of status within the institutional Church provides women with a more perceptive angle of vision in the dynamics of paradigm change. Thomas Kuhn highlights the fact that it is those with the least invested in the old paradigm who are most able to envision the new. This is usually facilitated by two circumstances:

Invariably their attention has been intensely concentrated upon the crisis-provoking problems; usually, in addition, they are men [sic] so young or so new to the crisis-ridden field that practice has committed them less deeply than most of their contemporaries to the world view and rules determined by the old paradigm.[1]

Women's traditional marginalization within Catholicism has separated them from the dominant patriarchy in terms of vocation and office, but that exclusion enables them to be less obsessed with the "world view and rules" of the old paradigm, the dominant pattern in fiction authored by males. In addition, the Women's Movement has intensely concentrated women's attention on issues of identity and personal development.

So it is not surprising that women, marginalized in the institutional Church, would not exhibit grief at the loss of preconciliar certitude or its world of male privilege. Due principally to the convergence of the Women's Movement with postconciliar Catholicism, many American Catholic women experienced the Church within a larger context, as they were inspired to explore all aspects of their lives in society. Religious questions became part of the overall quest for individual self-definition.

Catholic women in the United States are uniquely suited to this task. Their less central role in liturgy and ecclesiastical life has been a *felix culpa*, as it were, because their separate but unequal status has empowered them. In speaking of the Catholic education of women, the novelist Mary Gordon mentions that "The very sexual segregation spared you from a lower place in the hierarchy run by males." And she adds: "I think paradoxically that this gave young women a kind of strength and a notion that other women were important."[2] The other women that Catholic girls looked to as role models were, of course, nuns, "the largest group of professional Christian women in the world," as Sara Maitland points out in her study of women and Christianity.[3]

Moreover, as Carol Gilligan has demonstrated, women's distinct vision is rooted not only in their cultural subordination but in the substance of their moral vision. Briefly, one might describe the differences between male and female perspectives as the morality of rights, with an emphasis on separation (male) as opposed to the morality of responsibility with an emphasis on relationship (female).[4] Especially pertinent to this study of fiction is Gilligan's methodology, an empirical observation of women's voices, their narratives of personal experience. For, as Gilligan points out, "the way people talk about their lives is of significance, . . . the language they use and the connections they make reveal the world that they see and in which they act."[5] The differences Gilligan observes in the voices of males and females are analogous to the differences I observe in their fiction of Catholic experience.

The male emphasis on separation is reflected in fiction in the predominance of the loner as hero—James Carroll's Michael Maguire, Philip Deaver's Martin Wolfe, Andre Dubus' Luke Ripley, Walter Murphy's Declan Walsh, Walker Percy's Tom More, David Plante's Daniel

Francoeur, and Paul Theroux's Andre Parent. Compare all of this fiction to the work of the three female writers whose work has already been discussed in this book. Both Kit Reed and Caryl Rivers depict protagonists embedded in relationships: Georgia Kendall and her two college class-mates involved in the rescue of a fourth friend and Rivers' Peg, Con, and Sean as they attempt to bridge the conciliar chasm in life and love. Even Sister Carol Anne O'Marie, writing in the detective mode in which the loner is *de rigueur*, provides Sister Mary Helen with an investigative team, her companions in crime Sister Eileen and Sister Anne.

From a political vantage point, one might expect the Women's Move-ment to produce a simplistic imaging of the Church as symbolic of the oppression that the liberated female has transcended, but this response is not normative. Susan Cahill's *Earth Angels* (1976) and Margaret Wander Bonanno's *Ember Days* (1980) both depict women whose personal devel-opment leaves them critical of the hierarchical Church, but these novels are far more nuanced than the fiction of passionate intensity discussed in Chapter 3. In both *Earth Angels* and *Ember Days* there is less emphasis on the oppressive nature of institutional Catholicism than on its inability to change as quickly as the enlightened heroines. In Kathleen Rockwell Lawrence's *Maud Gone* (1986), the Catholic past is even less oppressive but quite irrelevant to the modern heroine. Lawrence's Maud, like Rivers' Peg Morrison, envisions her Catholic past as irrevocably "gone" and of little interest to the contemporary woman.

However, a more prevalent theme in women's fiction of Catholicism is the search for "some imperishable bliss," a movement beyond personal liberation to a renewed spirituality, and this is the fiction of prophetic vision. I use the term "prophetic" not to characterize a literature that describes the future but for one that calls us from the isolation of autonomy to reflect on the ground of our being. The Old Testament prophets who reminded Israel of their covenantal relationship with Yahweh were, to use Tillich's principle, recalling them to theonomy, to a right relationship with their Creator and Lord. And the fiction in this chapter provides a model for similar theological reflection, a call to re-imagine one's relationship to self and God.

Mary Daly writes of a "prophetic knowing" that is characteristic of the Women's Movement, a knowledge pointing beyond "things as they are." She uses the metaphor of the Fall to explain this dynamic:

This will be a Fall from false innocence into a new kind of adulthood. Unlike the old adulthood that required the arresting of growth, this demands a growing that is ever continuing, never completed.[6]

Such narratives of awakening are common to initiation stories, and it is not surprising that the convergence of the Women's Movement with postconciliar American Catholicism has produced fiction that illustrates Daly's dynamic. As described by one of the characters in Mary Gordon's *The Company of Women*, this prophetic vision is not gender-specific but is part of "the central human struggle to place oneself in relation to the absolute."[7]

For this is also a fiction consonant with the major shift in contemporary theology to approach truth from life rather than dogma. Hans Küng has asserted that the only productive contemporary theology is one

> which has laid aside the still widespread denominational ghetto mentality and is capable of blending the greatest possible tolerance toward those outside the Church, toward what is universally religious, toward the simply human, with the task of elaborating what is specifically Christian.[8]

It is in stressing what is "universally religious" in the context of the "simply human" that women's fiction of American Catholic experience transcends the "denominational ghetto mentality" and achieves its prophetic vision. Essentially disenfranchised from the institution, the American Catholic woman is more easily able to identify the lineaments of the new paradigm as it emerges. Miranda-like, women writers whose fiction concerns American Catholic experience are most able to see the reasons to hope for a brave new world for church and to indicate its dimensions.

Jeanne Schinto's short story "Before Sewing One Must Cut" (1988), mentioned at the opening of this book, provides an illustration of the way the experience of Church takes on metaphoric significance in this prophetic vision. Ostensibly about one young woman, this narrative also reflects a common experience among postconciliar American Catholics. The story is narrated by a nameless adolescent female whose father has recently died, and who, in consequence, has been offered an after-school job as receptionist in the parish rectory. The year is 1968, and one of the three parish priests is vocal in his opposition to the Vietnam War, a position not shared by many of the blue-collar parishioners nor by the pastor and senior associate. The antiwar priest is the only one in whom the narrator can consider confiding, but even he, she comes to realize, is "just an altar boy who had grown up."[9]

The young narrator's disillusionment with the Church in the course of the story is something she herself does not quite understand; she plans a return to the practice of her religion at some vague future date. Schinto presents this dissatisfaction with religion as symptomatic of a larger consciousness shift occasioned by the death of the girl's father, a loss of innocence with which the adolescent is attempting to cope. Thematically, this is a story of the distress of unsought autonomy—whether that autonomous state is precipitated by the death of a parent, an inglorious and unjust war, or the collapse of a paternalistic Church.

Although the story's title, from Jacques Maritain, is explicit in its image of gain from loss, a gloss of its meaning is provided in the text when the narrator finds an unfinished letter belonging to one of the priests and feels the words could have been written to her.[10] Though they indeed would be applicable to the girl's pain at the loss of her father, they are applicable as well to Catholics who sense a loss in their experience of Church:

> I pray you will trust your instincts and lean into this. That you will permit it to cut you, heal you, and cut you again. That you will stare at it into its own center. And that you will accept the faith that you will find there. (p. 55)

Growth involves pain, Schinto's narrator learns. In this story of the inevitability of loss in the process of life development, disillusionment with the Church becomes a component in the larger human experience of loss of innocence. As the narrator has lost a parent, she also loses the model of Church-as-parent, a loss that, Schinto indicates, is not hers alone.

For feminists, the experience of Catholicism provides an important symbol for fiction. Barbara White's study of adolescent fiction, *Growing Up Female*, makes the point that the novel is grounded in realism, so it is difficult to accurately depict females triumphing over patriarchal structures in a society in which women are still dominated by those forms. Indeed, there is a tendency to retreat to fantasy literature in order to present such victories.[11] However, the Catholic Church provides an image of patriarchy (or heteronomy, to use Tillich's term) that, coincidentally, many people are struggling with in the real world. Hence, the experience of Catholicism for women writers of fiction provides a metaphor for the exploration of larger questions of personal development and human dignity.

An archetypical example of such women's fiction is Sara Maitland's *Virgin Territory* (1984), the work of a British writer but a novel that is so illustrative of the conflation of feminism and Catholicism that it bears notice in this study. Although it is the story of an American nun who leaves her convent, Maitland's fiction has no relationship to the "I leapt over the wall" genre of antireligious propaganda. Rather, the novel's focus is one woman's growth through self-knowledge.

ANNA'S AWAKENING

The novel begins with the rape of a U.S. nun missioned in a small South American country. Because of a complex political situation, the rapist is never apprehended, but there is some assurance that this violent act poses no threat to the small community of sisters, and within several weeks everyone seems to have readjusted except for Sister Anna. She was neither the victim nor the witness to the assault, yet she is having a psychological breakdown that is somehow related to this incident. She is sent back to the Motherhouse in upstate New York to recuperate, but her condition worsens, and she is assigned to study in London, a vague mission designed to give her a year of rest and reflection.

While Anna is in London, inner voices she calls "the Fathers" become more forceful, and she fears for her sanity. Ultimately, she realizes that the reason the rape had precipitated her breakdown was because she had entered religious life to preserve her safe world.

The purpose of the Fathers is to protect the daughters. Of the man to protect his woman. That was their justification for everything. That was what the whole deal was. If they weren't going to do it, if they could not do it, then who needed them?[12]

Anna discovers that the Fathers are a part of herself; they reflect her submission and refusal to challenge life:

She wanted to tell them that they had only the power she had given them, only the power that a social structure and years of experience had given them. (p. 97)

Finally, the reader learns the source of Anna's haunting Fathers. Throughout the novel she refers to a motherless but idyllic childhood. Her widowed father was much admired by relatives and friends for the way he managed his extensive business interests and raised his five small daughters alone. As Anna explores the voices of the Fathers in her consciousness, she realizes that her father was not the model parent of her memory but had succeeded in his difficult task by being authoritarian and domineering. Because pleasing this overbearing parent was Anna's only source of self-esteem, she internalized his voice when she entered religious life, a choice conditioned by her father's earnest Catholicism and interest in a possible vocation for one of his daughters.

Psychologically, the Fathers were Anna's way of continuing as her father's daughter; they would be domineering but protective in exchange for her obedience. Anna had chosen submission to insure her safety, creating the oppressive power herself. The random violence of the attack in South America was the first intrusion on her security, frightening Anna who now felt the Fathers had capriciously abandoned her.

> I have been a good child of the Fathers for thirty-six years . . . and what have I got out of it? You don't deal straight do you? What have you given me? Dear God, I've done my bit, haven't I? (p. 189)

In an ultimate revelation, she recognizes that the Fathers are a projection of her own fears of autonomy:

> Your voices are mine. You have no more power over me than the power I have given you. And I have given you a lot of power, the power of my fears and frailties, my weakness, my stupidities, my evasions and dishonesties. (p. 189)

Aware that gaining freedom from this internalized oppressive force of law and guilt will not be an easy process, Anna nevertheless recognizes the fact that the very strength of the Fathers is her own strength. What has been assigned to a coercive force can be reappropriated.

At the very end of the novel, Anna recalls that her great fear had been that without the protection of the Fathers she would deteriorate and die. Now she senses that this has been a lie and that in destroying the power of the Fathers and dealing with her fears of vulnerability she will ultimately "see God and live" (p. 197).

Maitland suggests that authentic faith is the province of the self-actualized, and the task of freeing oneself from inner compulsions and dependencies is essential to growth. This, of course, correlates with Fowler's pattern of faith development, but Maitland's novel also has affinities with the delineation of female spirituality in Madonna Kolbenschlag's *Kiss Sleeping Beauty Good-bye.* In her study of feminist spirituality, Kolbenschlag highlights the correlations between personal and cultural development, pointing out that

> the contemporary transformation in the spirituality of women is a sign and symbol of . . . [a] greater metamorphosis in the religious experience of humanity.[13]

Women's fiction of Catholic experience reflects this metamorphosis.

Kolbenschlag employs Tillich's cyclical process to chart what she terms the "triptychal development of the spiritual personality," citing another pattern described by Teilhard de Chardin, a pattern more applicable to individual development.[14] His "laws of inner unification" parallel Tillich's stages of cultural change and are especially useful in observing the pattern of women's fiction of American Catholic experience.

In de Chardin's pattern of spiritual development, the first stage is the unification of the self within our own selves, a pattern comparable to the achievement of autonomy and prominent in *Virgin Territory*. This is followed by a pattern of union of our own being with other beings who are our equals, a dynamic of affiliation that Gilligan identifies as especially characteristic of women's relational behavior. Finally, there is an approach to a relationship with the Divine in the subordination of personal life to a greater power.

Three novels by Mary Gordon provide an anatomy of the process of change delineated by de Chardin: *Final Payments* offers a vision of inner unification; *The Company of Women* is about the nature of affiliation and its importance; and *Men and Angels* indicates the need for a relationship with the Absolute to achieve full humanity. Although this process is often conflated in fiction, other novels of Catholic experience by women writers reflect this pattern, as I will indicate using Gordon's first three novels as exemplary of the individual stages of spiritual development.

CHOOSING LIFE

What we might term the classic contemporary novel of American women's experience of Catholicism is the novel of initiation or awakening. It is a fiction that recognizes the power of external oppression but also suggests that the truly dangerous coercion is the power of one's own compulsions and dependencies. This is the vision novels like Gordon's *Final Payments* and Sonia Gernes' *The Way to Saint Ives* share with Maitland's *Virgin Territory*.

Final Payments (1978) begins with the death of Isabel Moore's father, an invalid she has nursed for the past eleven of her thirty years. So when Isabel remarks at the opening of the novel, "After they lowered his body, I would have to invent an existence for myself," the reader is led to look forward to another Miranda learning about the brave new world, an innocent girl in search of womanly experience.[15] And so it seems as Isabel buys fashionable clothes at Bloomingdale's, experiments with makeup, secures a job, sleeps with her best friend's husband, and seems to find happiness in an affair with a married man. Farewell good little Catholic girl; hello secular world.

Isabel's new life is short-lived. Crisis occurs when she is devastated by a public confrontation with her lover's wife, a scene that serves as a catalyst for Isabel's realization of what sustained her during those eleven years of drudgery, what she has lost in her brave new world.

> I was the good daughter. I took care of my father. I had nothing to fear. Faces were open to me, for mine, they believed, was the face of a saint. . . . As the daughter of my father I walked in goodness. I was clothed in the white garment of my goodness, visibly a subject of the Kingdom of God. (p. 230)

She concludes, "As the daughter of my father I lived always in sanctuary. Think of the appeal of sanctuary, the pure shelter," a statement that makes the analogy between the protection offered by Isabel's medievalist father and that of a patriarchal Church irresistible (p. 230). And Isabel's lover makes the parallel explicit in his anger at her withdrawal:

> You're a coward. That's all you are, with your Catholic school virtue, and your pat little heart, and your sense of morals like a gold watch you won in Catechism class. (p. 243)

In her effort to regain that sense of personal goodness, Isabel retreats to the home of the abhorrent Margaret, an elderly spinster (once the family housekeeper) who embodies all the negative features of parochial and triumphal thinking. Isabel plans to devote herself to Margaret as she once served her invalid father. Fortunately, this self-destructive activity is short-lived. During an argument with the elderly woman, Isabel experiences a moment of insight when she counters Margaret's claim to be only a "poor woman" with the rejoinder, "The poor you have always with you," thinking at the same time:

> It is one of the marvels of a Catholic education that the impulse of a few words can bring whole narratives to light with an immediacy and a clarity that are utterly absorbing. (p. 288)

Like Sister Anna, Isabel recognizes that the coercive power she needs to be liberated from is not the Church so much as her own need for its assurance of innocence and virtue, the safe haven represented by the pietistic Margaret:

It came to me that life was monstrous: what you loved you were always in danger of losing. The greatest love meant only, finally, the greatest danger. That was life; life was monstrous.

But it was life I wanted. Not Margaret. (p. 294)

In Isabel's personal story, Gordon has analogously indicated the nature of the change in American Catholicism. The Church that preserved innocence fostered dependency in its members. The loss of that haven is discomforting, but, as Gordon's fiction indicates, it is ultimately more satisfying to live a life-enhancing rather than a life-denying spirituality.

Note that Isabel's ultimate realization of her theology of life comes from her Catholic education. Characteristic of the female vision of American Catholicism is a refusal to either glory in or condemn the past but to note its strengths as well as its weaknesses. There is no reductive identification of the Church with oppression, but a realization that the situation is far more complex. Gordon's focus on a spirituality of the human as a counter to the excessive supernaturalism of the past is the emphasis in this fiction. The parallel between the personal and ecclesial is also explicit in Sonia Gernes' novel of awakening, *The Way to St. Ives* (1982).

Gernes' novel tells of Rosie Deane, whose story, like that of Isabel Moore, begins with a funeral. When Rosie's older brother suddenly dies of a heart attack, she is forty-one and alone for the first time in her life. Only a year earlier, in a disagreement with her brother Jack, she had discovered how her mother had used her adolescent "spells" as a means of control, depriving her of normal patterns of social development. Now alone, Rosie notices the expressions of pity among her neighbors in the small Minnesota town and, motivated to demonstrate her competence in living alone, she gradually begins a new life.

As Rosie risks change, she also notices change in the local Catholic Church to which she is devoted, and, like Isabel Moore, she must confront the loss of innocence and the complexity of life's disorder. She is devastated to learn that one of the nuns is planning to leave the convent. With that news comes the collapse of the structure she had unconsciously used for support in her aloneness.

She felt a sense of loss, of betrayal, of secret wrongdoing in what the nun had told her. If priests got married, if nuns did not keep their vows, then nothing was steady; none of the things they taught you could be counted on. All the rules that had kept her world solid began to shudder, and Rosie wanted to clutch at what she felt was slipping away.[16]

In Rosie's thoughts Gernes encapsulates the sense of loss felt by Catholics for whom the Church was a stable vessel, well anchored in the chaotic seas of life. Rosie's ability to cope with this loss of stability seems directly related to a distinctively female perspective.

Women's moral sense involves the reconciliation of competing demands for affiliation. Thus, Rosie's acquaintance with the nun and the latter's request for help provide Rosie with a means for ameliorating her sense of loss. Responding to the nun's need for assistance helps Rosie overcome her initial shock, and by the time they have completed a shopping expedition together, the sheltered little Catholic girl in Rosie has been replaced by a forward-looking woman who is actively assisting a fellow human being in the process of change.

In spite of this victory and her growing self-confidence, Rosie is unable to deal with her discovery of the fact that Ray, a newcomer who has gently courted her and finally asked her to marry him, is a married man whose wife is comatose in a distant nursing home. Devastated by the news of Ray's living wife and angered by his duplicity, Rosie is almost suicidal in her despair. Finally, with the help of the parish priest, she comes to recognize that her anger is not against the man who deceived her but is the final payment she must make to be liberated:

> It had not occurred to her that she would need to forgive the Rosie who spent twenty years waiting for life, who had always chosen safety, and was always willing to submit. (p. 263)

Gernes' novel reinforces Gordon's focus on liberation from the internal compulsions as the necessary prelude to any true autonomy. By using a situation so reminiscent of *Jane Eyre* (the heroine in love with a man unable to marry because of a still-living wife) Gernes emphasizes the modern "monstrous life" to which Rosie, like Isabel, willingly commits herself. There is no destructive fire to obliterate the madwoman in the attic in this fiction. Ray's wife does not die; there is no "happily ever after." Rosie puts aside safety for human experience and growth.

Gernes goes well beyond Gordon in relating Rosie's personal liberation to that of other characters who are seeking to reconcile their personal faith with the demands of religion. In addition to the departure of Sister Carol Anne from religious life, Gernes depicts a young priest resolving his personal conflict by remaining in the priesthood. Both choices are presented as mature decisions based on the individual's sense of personal responsibility, and the tone of the fiction is markedly tolerant. There is no suggestion of the institutional Church as villain. The novel's moral center is in the individual choices characters make in negotiating the claims of life. Isabel Moore and Rosie Deane had remained home with demanding parents in order to preserve their self-concept as good Catholic girls. As James Fowler records, leaving home is often a metaphor for growth in faith, and that is apparent in these novels which indicate metaphorically how the discomfort of unsought autonomy, often characteristic of postconciliar Catholicism, can be a source of growth.

SINGULAR LIVES TOGETHER

Tillich's theory of cultural change does not discriminate within the stage of autonomy, but in Teilhard de Chardin's "laws of inner unification," there is a point at which the autonomous self seeks relationships of equality with similar autonomous selves. If this is indeed an essential part of the spiritual journey, women would seem to be well suited to this passage. As Gilligan's important study of women's moral development shows, affiliation with others is more generally primary for women who are socialized to show concern for relationships and responsibilities.[17]

And this pattern of affiliation is consistently present in fiction of Catholic experience authored by women, as is very evident in the novels discussed earlier in this book. Relationships are central to the development of Sister Anna, Isabel Moore, and Rosie Deane; they foster their awakening to a new consciousness of themselves in the world. But in Gordon's second novel, *The Company of Women*, the dynamic of affiliation is brought into even sharper focus.

The Company of Women (1980) is perhaps more successful in what it attempts than in what it achieves. It is ostensibly the story of a group of five Catholic women whose common life consists of their devotion to a strong-minded and domineering priest, Father Cyprian. The focal character, however, is Felicitas, the daughter of Charlotte, a widowed member of the group of five. She is "fathered" by Cyprian with a rigorous education worthy, he imagines, of her fine mind. Reflecting pre-Vatican II dualism, it is an eduction in the exclusive virtue of reason.

As Felicitas enters adolescence, she develops disdain for this company of women and their obeisance to the priest. She thinks to herself:

> The lives of the women she loved were bankrupt. She was tired of their efforts to live the lives of bankrupts, making do with God and each other, purchasing the icon of a man, a tyrant, who had won their veneration not through honorableness but through fear, who stood

out on the landscape not for his distinction but because it was a desert.
(p. 98)

And she is determined that she will not join the company of women:

> She would not give up the comradeship of fellows to be the youngest
> of the brood hens circled around the dying cock whose struts they
> reverenced. She would not do it. (p. 99)

But scarcely has her college registration been processed than Felicitas
becomes involved with her political science professor, Robert Cavendish,
a self-important autocrat who is a far less benevolent dictator than the
priest. Felicitas romanticizes their relationship with religious imagery, at
one point suggesting to her mother that she might let her hair grow—the
better to wipe Robert's feet with. When she moves into Robert's apartment
and finds two other women also in residence, she identifies this small
harem as a type of the Mystical Body of Christ. In fact, Gordon eventually
points to a truth in this analogy, but not as Felicitas had originally thought
in her deification of Robert. Instead, as the fragile Felicitas finds herself
increasingly dominated by the boorish Robert and eventually pregnant as
well, it is this alternative company of women that provides her initial
support. The other women in the apartment offer her solace, and Felicitas
comes to understand not only her connection with these women but her
separateness as well. Finally she returns to her original "company" to await
the birth of her child.

Felicitas' rejection of her mother's pattern of relationship only to
replicate it in the secular Sixties, indicates the need for self-knowledge as
essential to growth. In Felicitas' brave new world, she too deifies a male
tyrant. As she thinks much later

> I wonder what abuse a woman has to go through at the hands of a
> man before she gives up the inward flicker of delight, like the click
> and flame of a cheap cigarette lighter, at being chosen? Where did
> we learn that definition of honor? As long as it is there, we are never
> really independent. (p. 261)

The final section of the novel takes place eight years later and is
composed of first-person monologues by each member of the company,
now including Felicitas' daughter, Linda. It is 1977, and as each character
reflects on life, including the fourteen years since the novel began, we
realize that Felicitas was raised in the preconciliar world, and Linda is a

child of new awareness. Their names signify this revolution. Not for Felicitas' child the Latin name from the canon of the Mass; Linda's name is specifically chosen for its ordinariness (p. 253).

Cyprian's reflections reveal that, like Isabel Moore in Gordon's first novel, the priest has discovered his error in ignoring the claims of the human. In spite of his years as a priest, he only comes to a sense of the meaning of the Incarnation at the end of the novel, in "the enduring promise of plain human love."

And I understood the incarnation for, I believe, the first time: Christ took on flesh for love, because the flesh is lovable. (p. 285)

Cyprian's realization that "the source of all error is the failure of charity" (p. 282) is reinforced in the lines from Auden's "The Common Life" that serve as the novel's epigraph and conclude:

though truth and love
can never really differ, when they seem to
the subaltern should be truth.

It is in this common life, in the relationally oriented patterns of this company of women, that this truth emerges. Not in isolation but in affiliation does truth emerge for each individual in this novel. That same emphasis on the importance of personal conversion and self-knowledge is at the heart of a very different novel, Valerie Martin's *A Recent Martyr* (1985). As in Gordon's fiction, this liberation comes through affiliation.

Martin's is a more symbolic vision. The novel is set in New Orleans during a time of social deterioration, a degeneration reflected in the life of the narrator, Emma Miller. Emma is married and the mother of a young daughter, but her principal relationship is with Pascal Toussaint. She is his mistress, and he progressively dominates her consciousness as their relationship develops. As Pascal becomes increasingly brutal and sadistic, Emma finds herself both craving his violence and fearing her attraction to it.

Through Pascal, Emma comes to know Claire D'Anjou. Claire is a novice on "leave." She had disturbed her Carmelite superiors with her spiritual excesses and was asked to take some time in the world to test her vocation. Pascal is challenged to try to corrupt Claire, and eventually she and Emma meet. Dramatic circumstances bring them into closer contact.

During an outbreak of plague, the section of the city both Claire and Emma live in is quarantined, and a friendship develops between the two women. Emma admires Claire's passion for God, comparing it to her own passion for Pascal, a passion she regards as evidence of her own corrupt nature. But it is also apparent to the reader that Claire's spiritual drive is not an ideal; it is based on a fear of intimacy and a rejection of her own humanity. Eventually, Claire's year of probation comes to an end, and she plans to return to the cloister. On her way back, she is brutally murdered in a vicious and apparently random attack.

The novel ends with Emma, who has narrated the entire story, concluding that Claire, though dead, is now an inescapable part of her life. Through her relationship with Claire, Emma has become convinced of her own essential goodness and is provided with the strength to end her relationship with Pascal. Yet despite her refusal to be with him, Emma admits to his persistent presence in her dreams.

Martin has written a story of good and evil; both Claire and Pascal are polarities of Emma's psyche. The deteriorating city of New Orleans parallels the degenerate Emma who, allowing Pascal to dominate her, derives her self-concept from his corruption. Claire's virtue provides Emma with a needed reminder of her own goodness, and, in affiliation with Claire, Emma is empowered to enact her authentic self. In Claire's sanctification of her avoidance of intimacy, Martin offers an important caveat. Supernaturalism commits people to a destructive spirituality that is essentially anti-Christian in its denial of value in the human. Claire's death in the novel is less the destruction of good by evil than the symbolic consequence of her life-denying spirituality.

The locus of meaning in this fiction is Emma who has identified her capacity for evil and chosen to repress it in favor of her potential for goodness. Her comment that ends the novel points to a recognition of this precarious balance as the essence of the human condition:

> The future holds a simple promise. We are well below sea level, and inundation is inevitable. We are content, for now, to have our heads above water.[18]

A sense of precarious balance is also at the heart of Sharon Sheehe Stark's *A Wrestling Season* (1987), a family novel of reconciliation through affiliation. Although located in rural Pennsylvania rather than New Orleans, the novel's central character Louise Kleeve is barely able to keep her head above water, though figuratively rather than literally. The chaos in the Kleeve household is both physical and psychological, and Louise longs for order and peace. This is symbolized in her art, sculptures she creates from photographs. Successful in forming other groups, Louise is consistently unable to capture her own family perfectly ("I want it whole, not pieced. Is that too much to ask?").[19] The story of the Kleeve family takes its title from son Michael's high school wrestling season, the time-span of the novel.

During this wrestling season Louise's childhood friend comes to visit, Frances Jane, nicknamed Frank and known in religion as Sister Innocent. Frank is experiencing her own mid-life crisis as she questions the viability of religious life in the modern world, and the women eventually realize that their conflicts are similar. As Frank explains, their convent school bred them for yearning, not possession:

> We grew up on the numinous. They filled our heads with incense and visions, taught us to pray in an ancient language. . . . Joy's a drug, I think, of the sort that keeps coming back on you, flaring up for no reason at all except that we live and love what we can, at hideous risk, as fierce as we're able, all of it so tenuous and absurd because . . . (p. 315)

"Because God is with us?" Louise asks hesitantly. To which Frank responds, "Amen" (pp. 315–16). Both women begin to accept their own spirituality.

Michael completes his wrestling season, but there is no fairy tale ending; he is pinned in the championship match. Frank returns to her convent, and Louise finally completes her family sculpture, now willingly patching rather than insisting on perfection. Each woman is resigned to "the unclassed middle of things, which is where most of us plod on, with the vigor and bewilderment and occasional transcendence of the not-yet-saved" (p. 344). At the end of the novel Louise writes a conciliatory letter to her alienated sister-in-law, explaining the reconciliation she has effected with her past:

> However true it is that we can't go back to Lackawanna, it is truer yet that we cannot safely disengage. Despite that our interests and visions diverge perhaps indefinitely and the generations grow more distinct, this branch from that, we all are nonetheless attached at ground level, fed from the same roots. (p. 345)

For Louise Kleeve those roots are a graced human nature, something she has been forced to articulate in her wrestling with the exigencies of life. Although she has tended to avoid the Church because "The forge that forged her had been dismantled" (p. 230), Louise is led to identify the

Divine within the human, the single city inhabited by both God and men, and is thus reconciled with the spiritual self she had exiled.

The Company of Women, *A Recent Martyr*, and *A Wrestling Season* are disparate novels from a formal literary perspective, yet they share an incarnational vision that values the graced nature of the human person in existential reality, in the wrestling season of human efforts to find meaning in life. In all three novels, characters achieve their self-awareness through the process of affiliation with others. This fiction points to the inadequacy of the supernaturalistic paradigm and the need for a theological perspective that validates the human in the context of relationship with the Divine. It looks forward to the emergence of a new paradigm that embodies the interpenetration of the Divine and the human. This interpenetration is a theme of a final group of novels.

THE NEED FOR GOD

In Gordon's third novel *Men and Angels* (1985), Catholicism is notable in its absence, yet this text is best understood as another variation on a theme central to Gordon's previous novels—what is the nature of love and how is it achieved? In eliminating the ambience of Catholicism in *Men and Angels*, Gordon raises the more fundamental issue of the value of religion in the modern world apart from any denominational context. In *The Company of Women*, Father Cyprian had concluded that "The source of all error is the failure of charity" (p. 282), and Gordon makes this the focus of her third novel, its title an allusion to 1 Corinthians 13.

Men and Angels tells the story of two women, Anne Foster and Laura Post, through a narrative that focuses on each one successively in alternating chapters. Gordon's technique allows the reader to know more about Anne and Laura than they know about each other, and this is central to the achievement of meaning in the novel. Anne Foster is a professional art historian, wife of a college professor, and mother of two young children. Her husband is spending the academic year in France, but she has just contracted to write the catalogue for an important exhibition and remains in New England with the children. Anne needs reliable household help, and Laura Post, referred by an academic acquaintance, seems ideal. But from the narrative focus on Laura, the reader knows that under that competent exterior Laura is a pathetic, love-starved woman whose docile demeanor masks a virulent religious mania.

As the novel develops, Anne's politeness convinces Laura that the woman accepts and loves her, while Anne becomes progressively uncomfortable with Laura as the latter's obsessive nature begins to surface. In spite of her sense that Laura craves love, Anne finds herself unable to transcend her inexplicable dislike.

> But every day that Laura lived beside her in the house, she disliked her more. Some days, even the simplest civilities were grueling to her. Yet every time she turned away from Laura, she felt Laura's yearning, like a furnace left on in a summer house. She knew that Laura craved love. But the best Anne could do was to keep from being cruel.[20]

Gradually, the reader's sympathy shifts. When the narrative focuses on Laura, her dismal past is revealed, a past that includes extreme psychological abuse from her parents and the religious leaders she later turned to for solace. She has been unloved and exploited all her life. Yet Anne, who will admit at the end of the novel, "I have always been beloved. I have never been alone" (p. 231), is unable to offer Laura even kindness. Gordon's fiction indicates that although sociologists suggest that abused children become abusive adults, children who are loved as Anne has been, will not thereby be loving adults. *Caritas* is only possible from participation in the Divine. The totally secular but well-intentioned Anne Foster has no human resources sufficient to allow her to offer Laura the love she craves.

Finally, Anne fires Laura, and the latter commits suicide immediately afterward, identifying Anne with the mother who had always rejected her, the mother she had tried so hard to please all her life. After Laura's death one of the other characters in the novel remarks to Anne how sad it is that Laura, who had read the gospels over and over, had missed the fact that she was greatly beloved, adding:

> Of course it is never enough, the love of God. It is always insufficient for the human heart. It can't keep us from despair as well as the most ordinary kindness from a stranger. The love of God means nothing to a heart that is starved of human love. (p. 231)

This has been a concern for Gordon in all her novels. In *Final Payments*, she had cited Auden's famous lines from "September 1, 1939":

> For the error bred in the bone
> Of each woman and each man
> Craves what it cannot have

Not universal love
But to be loved alone.

In *Men and Angels*, the Pentecostal groups to which Laura was attracted had failed to provide that love, indeed they exploited her compulsion to please. But the secular Anne Foster is equally unable to extend love even though she recognizes Laura's need. Gordon risked subverting her own fiction, for the reader ultimately finds no significant admirable character in this story. Neither "men," the purely secular, nor "angels," the excessively spiritualized, are sufficient for human life; only *caritas* would have saved Laura, a love that overcomes the unlovely. With the destruction of life in *Men and Angels*, Gordon points to the need for relationship with Transcendence in the contemporary world, the relationship that must serve as the basis for authentic religious communities.

In a novel of urban ethnic life, Francine Prose depicts people attempting to come to terms with the mystery at the heart of human existence. Her *Household Saints* (1986) not only affirms the fact that the spiritual dimension of life cannot be dispensed with but asserts that, if repressed, it will be perverted. *Household Saints* is the story of Italian Catholic ethnic life, a novel of domestic realism that is pervaded with the aura of mystery.

In the circumstances of the marriage of Joseph Santangelo to Catherine Falconetti, Prose highlights the mystery that is central to human love. Joseph wins Catherine from her father in a poker game, a whimsical bet that no one takes seriously and Joseph has no intention of collecting. But Catherine and Joseph are soon wed, and the card game becomes part of neighborhood folklore.

The newlyweds live above the family butcher shop with Joseph's widowed mother, and the old Mrs. Santangelo's kitchen is adorned with shrines to her favorite saints, complete with votive lights. Catherine, rejecting the supernaturalism of her religious heritage, prefers to decorate with houseplants. During Catherine's first pregnancy, she happens to enter the butcher shop when Joseph is killing a Thanksgiving turkey, violating a superstitious proscription, and old Mrs. Santangelo predicts a stillbirth. Catherine is distraught, half-believing the superstition she knows better than to credit, and she begs for a reprieve. The Santangelo women begin a campaign to invoke the "household saints," Mrs. Santangelo's favorites, to protect Catherine's unborn child. Despite their efforts, the child is stillborn exactly as the older woman had originally predicted, and Catherine succumbs to a deep depression.

Catherine Santangelo's stillborn baby causes a loss of faith, a faith she thought she had repudiated long ago. Catherine had given up religious

observance along with other superstitions of the old country but had
continued to live with the implicit notion that we inhabit an inherently
benevolent universe. That innocence is lost with the death of her child;
she senses a power in the old woman's superstitions against which she had
been powerless. She could not protect her child.

As the weeks extend into months, Catherine's depression deepens, and
her once carefully tended houseplants wither as she does. But on Easter
morning she awakens to the fragrance of flowers in bloom; all her plants
are thriving and the flowering ones are blossoming—a miracle. Catherine
is renewed by this example of benevolent Divine intervention and returns
to health and sanity. Joseph tells her there was no miracle; he had been
tending her plants, replacing those that were beyond his ministrations. She
just had not noticed until that moment. So renewed is Catherine that she
does not even object to Joseph's natural explanation of her miracle. In this
Easter tale, Prose highlights the transcendent dimension of human relationships. Catherine is healed; does it matter that the plants were restored
with human assistance? Is Joseph's love for Catherine the real miracle, a
reflection of Divine love?

That same Easter morning, old Mrs. Santangelo dies and Catherine
conceives another child. During this pregnancy, Catherine is resolved to
be American and modern; no saints or superstitions. She converts her
deceased mother-in-law's bedroom into a nursery, removing the heavy
old-fashioned furniture and with it, she imagines, an old-fashioned view
of the world: "First the crucifix came down off the wall" to be followed
by rosaries, pictures of San Gennaro and of the Holy Family.[21] During this
pregnancy, Catherine is checked at the hospital "like a true American
woman" and buys modern books about childbearing and childrearing
(p. 114). Protected now by the charms of modern American health care,
Catherine is soon delivered of a healthy daughter who is named Theresa.

With this blessing on her endeavors, Catherine continues her quest for
happiness through reliance on modernity:

> Mrs. Santangelo, with her spitting three times and making the sign
> of the horns, was no more fervent and ritualistic than Catherine with
> her one-cup-per-load of Ivory Snow. (p. 114)

Prose points out that Catherine has not rejected the sacred, she has
sacralized the secular:

> It was obvious to her that the search for newer and stronger detergents
> was part of the same blessed science which had arranged Theresa's

safe arrival into the world, equally obvious that America and its
science had already served the Santangelos better than any old
country saints. (p. 114)

But in spite of the direction of Catherine's devotion, her child insists on
orthodox religious expression. She happily goes off to Mass with neighbors, and although Catherine enrolls her in public school, Theresa winds
up at the parochial school every day until Catherine relents and allows her
to attend permanently. Although Catherine is determined to counter this
religious influence by stressing Santa at Christmas and marshmallow eggs
from the Bunny at Easter, Theresa begins transforming her bedroom with
Mrs. Santangelo's old things; the crucifix and the pictures of Jesus and the
Holy Family are returned to the walls.

In the eighth grade when she wins a copy of *The Story of a Soul*, the
autobiography of St. Theresa, the Little Flower, in a school essay contest,
Theresa Santangelo's future is sealed. She will become a Carmelite. But
Joseph will not permit her to enter the convent and is adamant in that
decision. When Theresa tries a hunger strike to force him to change his
mind but weakens and breaks her fast, she becomes disheartened and
agrees to go to college instead of Carmel.

Deciding that God has rejected her because she did not maintain her
fast, Theresa begins a campaign to win God over by showing him she can
live the "Little Way" in the world. The parallel between Catherine trying
to assuage the saints to protect her unborn child, and Theresa trying to gain
God's approval through self-sacrifice is apparent. Both envision the
supernatural and the natural world radically divided with the only value
in the supernatural. For both mother and daughter the ruling power is
capricious rather than benevolent. Despite her conventional expressions
of faith, Theresa's spirituality is as distorted as her mother's.

Eventually Theresa drifts into psychosis and is institutionalized. She
dies at the age of twenty, and because all the neighbors are especially sorry
for the Santangelos and decide to spare no expense and send roses,
Theresa's wake seems yet another miracle. The masses of roses recall the
traditional intervention of the Little Flower, and the stories of Theresa's
saintliness become part of the neighborhood folklore. Like the "miracle
of the plants" that renewed Catherine, Theresa's roses have a human
source in the generosity of friends. So, too, the stories of her goodness that
now circulate in the neighborhood are narratives designed to give meaning
to such a brief and apparently wasted life and to provide comfort for her
parents in the loss of their only child.

When Theresa's parents are informed of her death, they are told, "If

Theresa had lived in another era, they might have called her a saint."
Joseph is annoyed and responds that if they had had lithium in Jesus' day
there would not have been any saints (p. 221). But Prose intends no
reductive debunking of the supernatural in this tale. As the novel continues
with the miracle of Theresa's roses and the folklore that develops in the
neighborhood, Prose indicates how much the Divine is part of the ordinary,
and the human is impregnated by the supernatural. Jacob wrestled with an
angel, but the transformation of thinking in the twentieth century reveals
that we actually wrestle with ourselves to allow the presence of God to be
revealed in our midst.

In her story of three generations of Santangelo women, Prose highlights
the fact that human existence includes mystery, a mystery that is denied
at our own peril. Old Mrs. Santangelo's mixture of religion and pious
superstition was a result of the impulse to impregnate the natural with the
sacred, a corrective to the prevailing emphasis on the supernatural.
Catherine's attempt to repudiate religion and Theresa's obsession with the
spiritual are extremes. Neither woman is ever liberated from her inner
compulsions—Catherine's to deny the Divine, Theresa's to deny the
human.

But the story of Theresa Santangelo offers an additional insight. The
effort to live a contemporary spiritual life according to the pious practices
of an earlier era is destructive. As with Claire D'Anjou in *A Recent Martyr*,
Theresa's anachronistic spirituality is not life giving, and its adherent
cannot survive. Our world is interpenetrated with a sense of the sacred,
Prose tells us in *Household Saints*. We need to reconcile ourselves to that
reality and attend to the claims of the holy, developing religious practices
and structures consonant with those claims.

In a very different novel, A. G. Mojtabai similarly points to the need
for relationship with Transcendence, and she illustrates the inability of
organized religion to foster that relationship in the modern world. The
novel's title, *Ordinary Time* (1989) refers to the season of the liturgical
year described by the local priest as "the longest, and hardest," and the
irony of the title is revealed in the question he then asks: "But, why hard?
When the message—*the reign of God is already in your midst*—is so
simple. . . ."[22] And it should be even simpler in Durance, Texas, the
fictional location of this novel, a town full of "holy stuff," as the newcomer
Val terms it. In Durance, Christianity is everywhere—on billboards and
walls, over the radio, "even the traffic signs are scribbled over: YIELD—
TO JESUS, STOP—SIN" (p. 43).

But *Ordinary Time* is a novel of people longing for imperishable bliss,
and the novel cites the inability of organized religion to support that

longing. Mojtabai's locale, the wasteland of rural Texas, mirrors the
contemporary world she depicts. The local Catholic priest, Father Gilvary,
is pastor of St. Jude's Church ("intercessor for those in desperate straits,
patron saint of lost causes" [p. 187]), and he is in somewhat desperate
straits himself as he faces impending blindness with a spiritual aridity that
matches the landscape. Unable to cope with his crisis, he is trying simply
to endure:

> There is nothing in him but the longing to pray, sharp as a thorn. He
> offers it up. He says simply, as he answered *adsum* to that first roll
> call, "I'm here." Asks: "Be with me now." (p. 219)

Durance, Texas is on the plains, and that is one of the difficult things
about living in faith, according to this novel. Mountaintop experiences are
more thrilling, easier for the maintenance of faith. As a local Pentecostal
preacher pleads when he tries to raise a recently deceased member of his
congregation:

> I've walked around this mountain long enough, Lord. Let me stand
> on the mountaintop. Just once. It's been so long, Lord. (p. 177)

But Brother Shad does not reach the mountaintop, and his church is unable
to alleviate the pain of Henrietta, owner of the Three Square Meals
restaurant, an aging woman suffering from incredible loneliness:

> There are times, small hours of the night, when she'll reach for the
> phone and dial the weather to hear a voice, any human voice. And
> there are times when she goes clear beyond feeling, beyond tears
> even. Those are the worst times of all. (pp. 28–29)

She has lost a husband and infant daughter and is completely alone except
for her customers and her "church home," Rooftree Pentecostal Church,
where she has been saved most recently. Henrietta's simple-mindedness
and garish makeup and dress make her seem ludicrous, but she is the
novel's counterpart to Father Gilvary—another individual seeking spiritual solace and suffering from institutional religion's inability to provide
that support.

While the novel's Pentecostals focus on mountaintop experiences, the
emotional high that will disguise the emptiness, institutional Catholicism's
contemporary relevance is derided in Father Gilvary's dismissal of his
diocese's agenda:

Diocesan Development Fund, new buildings, the latest wheelings and dealings in real estate, the list of approved altar wines. (pp. 69–70)

He is tired of always raising the objection, always asking, "Why do we never talk about prayer?" He knows that image is everything in this modern Church:

Young Jim [the vicar general] is considered a model priest—his twenty-some-inch waist a real boost to vocations in the chancery view. (p. 70)

A. G. Mojtabai shares with Gordon and Prose a commitment to the centrality of mystery in our midst, a source of consolation in this "hard place," and she illustrates the limitations of organized religion's attempts to meet this need. In all three novels, the seekers of faith are lost. Laura Post is driven to suicide in *Men and Angels*, and Theresa Santangelo retreats to psychosis and eventually dies in *Household Saints*. In *Ordinary Time* this destructiveness is reflected in the character of a mysterious foundling known as Cleat. The adolescent is Durance's silent evangelist who distributes written reminders of the Kingdom in response to an ambiguous voice that directs him. While there is some question as to whether this is authentic spirituality or delusion, it is undeniable that Cleat is a confused adolescent in need of human understanding and solace. He never receives the love he needs and is eventually borne away in the most violent episode in the book. His name and nickname encapsulate the central issue in all three novels.

Cleat was baptized "Cletus," and Father Gilvary wonders, "Who but a Catholic—a Catholic of the old school—would burden a child with such a name?" (p. 181). The orphan has been brought up by pious Baptist parents, and now, with his call to evangelize, seems to represent the complete spectrum of organized religion in Durance. And his nickname reflects the purpose of religion in the world; a "cleat"—an object to give strength or support. But the strength and support Cleat offers in his evangelistic activity is rejected, and the boy himself is abused by the violence of the stranger Val. Although Father Gilvary keeps muttering the line from Luke that "The Kingdom of God is in your midst" (17:21), the novel more accurately reflects Matthew 11:12, "From the days of John the Baptist until now, the kingdom of heaven suffers violence, and the violent are taking it by force."

In all three novels, *Men and Angels*, *Household Saints*, and *Ordinary*

Time, the seekers of faith are represented as dysfunctional in the modern world and destroyed by their longing. In spite of the yearning for a relationship with the Divine within the human heart, Gordon, Prose, and Mojtabai present a fictional world in which that yearning is frustrated, principally because of the failure of any institutional religion to meet the needs of those thirsting for God. This prophetic vision of individuals searching for God in the modern world naturally leads to an examination of the role of the Church in that quest.

NOTES

1. Thomas Kuhn, *The Structure of Scientific Revolutions* (Chicago: University of Chicago Press, 1970), p. 144.

2. As quoted by Peter Occhiogrosso, ed., *Once a Catholic* (Boston: Houghton Mifflin Company, 1987), pp. 70–71.

3. Sara Maitland, *A Map of the New Country: Women and Christianity* (London: Routledge and Kegan Paul, 1983), p. 49. Like Maitland, I will use the term "nun" even though it may not be strictly accurate in some instances for several reasons. First, the distinction between religious women in solemn vows (nuns) and those in simple vows (sisters) is not ordinarily known, and the female members of religious communities are popularly known as "nuns." In addition, the term "sisters" has developed in a specific secular context among feminists that is valuable and important, and the alternative "religious women" is equally unacceptable because it carries the connotation that women who have not made canonical vows are somehow less "religious."

4. Carol Gilligan, *In a Different Voice: Psychological Theory and Women's Development* (Cambridge and London: Harvard University Press, 1982), p. 8. Gilligan's entire first chapter "Women's Place in Man's Life Cycle" (pp. 5–23) is an explication of this important distinction.

5. Ibid., p. 2.

6. Mary Daly, *Beyond God the Father: Toward a Philosophy of Women's Liberation* (Boston: Beacon Press, 1973), p. 67.

7. Mary Gordon, *The Company of Women* (New York: Ballantine Books, 1980), p. 266.

8. Hans Küng, *Theology for the Third Millennium*, trans. Peter Heinegg (New York: Doubleday and Company, Inc., 1988), p. 200.

9. Jeanne Schinto, *Shadow Bands* (Princeton, Ontario Review Press, 1988), p. 45.

10. In a personal letter, Jeanne Schinto advised me that she took her title from Jacques Maritain, *Creative Intuition in Art and Poetry* (New York: Pantheon Books, 1953), p. 44.

11. Barbara A. White, *Growing Up Female: Adolescent Girlhood in American Fiction* (Westport, Connecticut: Greenwood Press, 1985), p. 185.

12. Sara Maitland, *Virgin Territory* (New York: Beaufort Books, 1984), p. 96.

13. Madonna Kolbenschlag, *Kiss Sleeping Beauty Good-Bye: Breaking the Spell of Feminine Myths and Models* (New York: Doubleday and Company, Inc., 1979), pp. 26–27.

14. Ibid., pp. 167–68.

15. Mary Gordon, *Final Payments* (New York: Random House, 1978), p. 5.

16. Sonia Gernes, *The Way to St. Ives* (New York: Charles Scribner's Sons, 1982), p. 151.

17. Gilligan, see especially Chapter 6, "Visions of Maturity" (pp. 151–74) for an extended discussion of this concept.

18. Valerie Martin, *A Recent Martyr* (Boston: Houghton Mifflin Company, 1987), p. 204.

19. Sharon Sheehe Stark, *A Wrestling Season* (New York: William Morrow and Company, 1987), p. 157.

20. Mary Gordon, *Men and Angels* (New York: Random House, 1985), p. 158.

21. Francine Prose, *Household Saints* (Boston: G. K. Hall, 1986), p. 110.

22. A. G. Mojtabai, *Ordinary Time* (New York: Doubleday and Company, Inc., 1989), p. 34; ellipsis in text.

9

Prophetic Vision: As We Are Now

Wandering between two worlds, one dead,
The other powerless to be born. . . .

Matthew Arnold

The search for a new paradigm for religious experience in the modern world is not solely the province of Catholicism. It is commonly agreed that postconciliar Catholicism is engaged in the very struggle that has occupied the rest of Christianity for the past 200 years. It is the perception that mainline Protestantism has failed to effectively confront modernity that has directed theologians like Langdon Gilkey and Richard John Neuhaus to turn to Catholicism as "the possible source or matrix for a creative modern Christianity."[1] Unfortunately, although American fiction of Catholic experience indicates that the mourning for the old paradigm has subsided, there is little indication that contemporary Catholicism has had much more success in confronting modernity than mainline Protestantism. From the perspective of contemporary fiction, the new paradigm is still "powerless to be born."

As the fiction in the preceding chapters indicates, postconciliar Catholicism struggles between two worlds: an exhausted paradigm to which it desperately clings and the new paradigm that must be envisioned in light of "what is permanent, essential, and validly traditional in Catholic life."[2] In Mary Gordon's fourth novel, issues of this struggle are highlighted, and her perspective is enhanced by the work of several writers of prophetic vision whose fiction moves beyond the process of faith development to confront the limitations of American Catholicism as it "wanders between two worlds." These writers depict individuals in the process of personal growth encountering a contemporary Church bereft of meaning.

ANOTHER SIDE

Among Catholicism's traditional strengths, Gilkey identifies "the unity and substantiality of the *people* as community,"[3] and that is the prime emphasis in Gordon's fourth novel, *The Other Side* (1989). This is a family saga concerned with four generations of the Irish-American MacNamaras as they await the death of the family matriarch, Ellen. Gordon's concentration is on the immigrant first generation, Ellen and Vincent, and their grandchildren, Daniel and Camille, the competent adult members of the family who are searching for a faith expression consonant with their experience of the modern world.

The cousins seem a rather contrived symbol of fragmented modernity in this novel. Both suffer from ruined marriages, and they share a legal practice specializing in divorce. Yet Gordon takes pains to show that ignoring religious observance does not obviate the need to address questions of faith. As Dan reflects on the differences between his grandparents, he concludes that the "faith of our fathers" is "probably a hoax but one the world did not seem better off without."[4] He expresses his own faith as a belief in human frailty and is motivated by a compassion for all those who suffer because of that frailty (pp. 349–50). Camille similarly locates her faith in the human dimension. For her the strongest bonds are relational, and Gordon emphasizes how an ethic of care evolves from Cam's intelligent reflection on life experience in light of those bonds. Facing the question of whether or not to abandon her sterile marriage for a more permanent liaison with her lover Ira, Cam reflects on her personal and professional experience of the unreliability of sexual love and its deceptive powers.

> Suppose Cam moved out of her house, dismantled the structure of several lives, and in a year found herself out of love? Or found that Ira was. It happened all the time: Cam had handled hundreds of divorces; it was the most commonplace story in the world. (p. 381)

Significantly, there are no priests in *The Other Side*. *Final Payments* began with Isabel's remark that "My father's house was full of priests," and in that novel Gordon imaged the priest in Father Mulcahy, kindly but muddled, escaping his postconciliar confusion and loneliness with the aid of alcohol. Father Cyprian in *The Company of Women* is depicted as capable of growth and understanding but only apart from his religious community and other institutional affiliations, living in remote retirement among the company of women. The institutional Church's presence in *The Other Side* is supplied by Sister Otile Ryan who, unlike her male counterparts in religion, does not build but dismantles.

Faced with a typical Catholic religious community's crisis—dwindling membership, expensive physical plant—Sister Otile has transformed her community's motherhouse into a home for the aged and for battered wives seeking shelter with their children. To make the elaborate mansion more functional, she replaces marble with Formica and covers parquet floors with linoleum "like a sansculotte dismantling a chateau" (p. 12). To the critical Camille who disapproves of the loss of beauty, Otile remarks,

> Look around you, Camille. People are happy here. They're living their lives without worrying all day about where they live. That's something. They're a hell of a lot happier than the people who lived here when this place was a shrine to its own woodwork. (pp. 12–13)

The implications are clear. Can the Church dismantle the edifice to meet human needs—or has it become "a shrine to its own woodwork"? Will there be no modern paradigm for Catholicism simply because the institution is occupied with the preservation of archaic edifices, figuratively as well as literally? By indirection, Gordon's novel poses such challenging questions to the Church.

In *The Other Side*, the moral matrix for the third-generation Irish-Americans is not Catholicism but the strength of familial bonds. Attempting to decide whether or not to abandon her loveless marriage, Cam consults Sister Otile who encourages separation. When Cam counters that such a situation would hurt her grandfather ("He'd be heartbroken if I left Bob and moved in with a man who'd been divorced twice"), Otile persists, "You could marry Ira. Go for three." Camille ironically responds, "Thanks, Otile. I love it when you're worldly" (p. 380). If there was little solace for Catholics in preconciliar conservatism, Gordon depicts a distressing lack of moral substance in postconciliar liberalism.

Men and Angels clearly expressed a need for *caritas* in human life, and one wonders if Gordon's frustration with Catholicism's lingering "between two worlds" provides the vision in *The Other Side,* a belief in the ability of the individual to achieve self-transcendence apart from any denominational context. In the wake of her earlier novels, Gordon's comments on Catholicism focused on the positive aspects of the past for her as both a woman and a writer.[5] But an essay in *The Atlantic* reflects the emphasis on the ethical strength of the individual that pervades *The Other Side*. Writing about the abortion issue, Gordon uses her obvious talent with language to suggest that the central problem in this controversy is a lack of confidence in women's ability to make the best possible choices.[6] As Gordon's past work makes clear, this position evolved from her attempt to place the Church in the modern world.

This fourth novel provides Gordon's fullest vision of the current Catholic moment. She images the decline of the devotional Catholicism of the Immigrant Church in the aged Vincent MacNamara and depicts the limitations of the contemporary Church in the mindless enthusiasm of Vincent's Charismatic daughter Theresa and the moral relativism of the liberal Sister Otile. In the vacuum left by the decline of a strong Catholic presence, Vincent's grandchildren, Daniel and Camille, attempt to resolve their personal moral dilemmas.

In the contrast between the generations, Gordon implicitly points to an important fact about the Immigrant Church in America that is often overlooked in the valorization of the past. The undeniable vigor of Golden Age Catholicism was due in large measure to the congruence of specific social and religious factors of that age. It was the immigrant experience that profoundly shaped the local Catholic parish in the United States, both socially and theologically.[7] Religion was an anchor in the new world for various Catholic ethnic groups, a means of forging an American identity while still retaining a sense of personal heritage. These cultural Catholics did not necessarily frequent the sacraments (indeed, in the beginning they hardly ever did), but a strong devotional Catholicism developed from this focus on the parish as the center of neighborhood life. Vincent MacNamara is a child of the Golden Age, and his faith expression is a vestige of that culture.

With the gradual disappearance of ethnic neighborhoods and the full assimilation of the Daniel and Camille MacNamaras into the American mainstream, the abandonment of formal ties to the Church is understandable. (Indeed, the Church itself hastened this process with the Vatican II disestablishment of devotional Catholicism.) The grandchildren of immigrants no longer have a need for that locus of identity. But the need for moral guidance remains for Daniel and Camille in Gordon's *The Other Side*, and the Church is not imaged positively in response to that need. Clearly, the old paradigm no longer has currency, but no new paradigm is yet in place. This is highlighted in Sheila O'Connor's linked stories collected in *Tokens of Grace* (1990).

A CHURCH FOR THE CHILDREN

Tokens of Grace identifies a specific need for Church presence in the modern world and simultaneously depicts a Catholicism unable to meet that need. The narrative recounts a divorce and the dissolution of a family, focusing on the experience of the eldest child, ten-year-old Callie. Both parents are absorbed in the trauma of separation, so it is Callie who attempts to be both mother and father to her two younger sisters. Physically separated from her adored father who took the children to Mass each week, Callie's own religious observance is strongly colored by her desire to preserve her father's presence in the family and meet her own need for parental guidance.

However, the Church not only does nothing to assist the struggling child, the vignettes O'Connor offers reveal an institution that is, as Sister Otile would say, "a shrine to its own woodwork." Preconciliar modes reign. The parish priest, Father Fitzpatrick, dotes on Callie's younger sister Ryan because the child's extraordinary memory provides him with the opportunity to display her proficiency in reciting lengthy prayers. But when Ryan is awarded a small statue of Mary for reading the most books in first grade, parochial provincialism rears its head. The first-grade teacher, Sister Angela, accedes to the demand of a parent who insists Ryan cannot have read more books than her own daughter. After all, she can vouch for her daughter's accomplishment but it is not so with Ryan's family: "Does she [Ryan] have any proof? Isn't it only her mother at home and isn't she always working?"[8] The nun capitulates and asks Ryan to return the award without regard for the child's feelings—or the ethics of the situation.

The Church that might be expected to be sympathetic to the plight of a child from a single-parent family, reinforces the prejudices of its members. Indeed, it shares those prejudices, as is evident when Callie takes piano lessons from Sister Anne Eugene who, responding to the child's modern improvisation, warns, "A girl from your background can't afford to indulge in rock and roll. I'm sure it wouldn't take much to push you off a cliff. Piano will give you purity" (pp. 93–94). Callie wisely quits piano.

Callie's Confirmation day finds her resplendent in symbolically pristine clothing, recalling Mary Gordon's comment that at the heart of Catholicism is "a combination of the esthetic ideal and the ethical ideal."[9] Yet, in the final vignette in this collection, we see the alternative aspect of the Church that has pervaded this narrative. The Church is not only insensitive to the plight of these children, it is, ultimately, dysfunctional. In "The Blessing," Father Fitzpatrick comes to bless the girls' apartment (at Ryan's insistence), and it is obvious to the reader that the jaded, whiskey-imbibing priest will not be a paternal image for these resourceful and intelligent children much longer. Although they receive his blessing with eyelids "clenched like fists, the rapture of children trusting a magician" (p. 122), the leitmotif of this section is Father Fitzpatrick's tippling. In the contrast between the struggling children's need for guidance and support and the Church's inability to respond appropriately, O'Connor highlights the failure of contemporary Catholicism at the parish level.

If Callie matures according to her promise in this narrative, she will be a Camille MacNamara, an ethically self-reliant woman whose Catholicism belongs to her childhood. In two of her novels, Valerie Sayers similarly depicts a need for the sacramental presence of the Church in the modern world and Catholicism's inability to enact that presence effectively.

FAITH LOST/FAITH REGAINED

Sayers' first novel *Due East* (1987), which takes its name from the fictional South Carolina coastal town in which it is set, is the story of a most unlikely pregnant teenager, Mary Faith Rapple, and her determination to keep her expected child. But Mary Faith's pregnancy, though central to the plot, is symptomatic of a broader issue, for *Due East* is a story of the loss of innocence in more than sexual terms.

Mary Faith's pregnancy is unexpected among the inhabitants of Due East because at fifteen she does not date (does not even *talk* to boys, says her shocked father). She is an outstanding student. Her school's first state winner in a Latin competition and notably proficient at math, Mary Faith helps tutor the adult high school equivalency evening classes. Nevertheless, she deliberately plans to seduce a boy and become pregnant. Though she offers no explanation for this decision to radically alter her life and sacrifice her chance for the college scholarships her guidance counselor is already predicting, it is not too difficult for the reader to understand.

An only child, when Mary Faith was twelve years old she watched her mother die horribly of uterine cancer. Left alone with her loving but undemonstrative father, the girl has no support to help her deal with her tremendous sense of loss and guilt. The mother's name was Faith, a name she adopted when she was "born again," and the failure of the combined prayers of mother and daughter to spare Faith results in Mary Faith's "loss of Faith"—in both parental and religious terms. Her pregnancy is a desperate and instinctive attempt to affirm life and achieve a measure of self-definition.

Blind to the complex emotions that motivated this pregnancy, Mary

Faith's relatives think only pragmatically and urge her to have an abortion. At fifteen, without any real power to resist, she plans to run away to find a Catholic home for unwed mothers, confident the nuns will enable her to bear her child. Her father interrupts these plans but, impressed with her determination to keep her child, he acquiesces and agrees to support both daughter and grandchild. To celebrate their reconciliation, Jesse Rapple asks his daughter to accompany him to services at their Baptist Church the following Sunday. Mary Faith agrees, and in the ensuing chapter Sayers creates a powerful scene presenting the tension between the claims of religion and the nature of faith.

The subject of the minister's sermon is the obligation of sinners to the community. If the sinner refuses to repent and be reconciled, he reasons, Christians have the duty to confront the sinner, offering forgiveness but not condoning the sin. Like the prodigal son, the sinner must recognize his or her responsibility to seek forgiveness. This theme, carefully nuanced, possibly could be presented in the spirit of Jesus, but in this very small congregation with the minister himself staring at the visibly pregnant teenager, it is difficult to imagine this as other than self-righteous Phariseeism. The reader, already well acquainted with Mary Faith's inner life and aware of the psychological complexity involved in this pregnancy, recognizes that "sin" is not a helpful category in this situation and applauds Mary Faith's parting line, "I do *not* beg your forgiveness," as she walks out before the sermon is completed.[10]

Ultimately, Mary Faith will suffer more from Catholics. She begins a relationship with the teacher in charge of the program in which she tutors, Stephen Dugan, a married, lapsed Catholic. As the novel develops, Mary Faith becomes increasingly involved with Stephen, but his visiting sister warns the pregnant teenager not to lose her heart to Stephen Dugan because Catholic that he is, however lapsed, he will never leave his wife. That prophecy is fulfilled almost five years later when, in Sayers' subsequent novel, Stephen finally decides to remain with his wife, and can only say, "I'm sorry" to the young mother he has been involved with for five years because he has some "remnants of conscience" and Mary Faith can offer him no absolution.[11]

In this second novel, *How I Got Him Back* (1989), Sayers continues Mary Faith's story but focuses attention on the small Catholic community in Due East. In continuing the distinction between faith and religion begun in the earlier book, Sayers indicates that the current crisis in Catholicism is a result of the conflation of faith and religion in the old paradigm ("The Faith" as the central focus) that results in a tendency to use religion to mask the failure to achieve mature faith.

Using the fictional Catholic community of Our Lady of Perpetual Help, Sayers explores the complex relationships Catholics have with their changing Church. Becky Perdue, a wife and mother recently abandoned by her husband, is an apparently active member of her parish community. But in the course of the narrative she reveals that she lost faith in God long ago during her mother's illness when her image of God was challenged. She decided:

> I had worshipped a God who gave and took back the gift of reason with utter indifference. I put away my rosary beads, and I quit the Church. (p. 162)

To raise her children, she returns to religious observance but not to faith. When her husband leaves her, she feels a betrayal similar to her initial loss of faith because

> I believed him when he said—with the same clear-eyed look he wore to recite the Credo—that a man picked a wife for life. (p. 176)

Becky's attitude toward her husband has been similar to her notion of God—someone who would care for her and protect her with no responsibility on her part to effect a mutuality. Initially, Becky is simply motivated by social convention and Catholic discipline to preserve her marriage and "get him back." But as she reflects on the past, she discovers the absence of a true relationship in her marriage. Six months later, when Jack decides to return, Becky chooses divorce and an attempt at life for herself.

The contrast between the independent Becky at the end of the novel and Marygail Dugan who actually saves her marriage provides Sayers' most telling comment. Marygail Dugan, determined to get her husband back, capitalizes on Stephen's sense of guilt and uses assorted drugs to induce a psychosis that necessitates her hospitalization. By evoking Stephen's latent guilt, Marygail elicits a commitment from him. Both Dugans use the marriage as an excuse to avoid responsibility—Marygail avoids being a mature adult, and Stephen avoids dealing with his responsibility for five years of promises to Mary Faith Rapple. Far from devaluing marriage, Sayers points to the way a legal contract can provide a haven for the immature.

This is reinforced in Sayers' use of the ladies of Our Lady of Perpetual Help Altar Guild as a type of Greek chorus that comments on the action and characters in the novel but is not a part of it, a technique that emphasizes the fact that participation in organized religion can separate adherents from life rather than engage them in it. If Mary Faith Rapple asserts faith in life through the birth of her son Jesse, Becky Perdue's response is to rely on her own self and begin an independent life. Both women, however, receive no support from their religious affiliation. In Due East, religion has lost its power to foster faith.

Sayers has written that her title *How I Got Him Back* must be understood with both a lower case and a capital for "him."[12] Thus, in spite of Becky's mistaken notion that faith exists exclusively in a denominational context, her effort to achieve personal identity, her commitment to faith in herself, should be understood as an act of faith in a religious sense as well. She is beginning the journey charted by the novelists in Chapter 8.

However, the Church does not facilitate the journey for any of the characters in Sayers' fiction. Institutional structures predominate, and those people allied with the institution express decidedly un-Christian sentiments in *How I Got Him Back*. In the first pages of the novel, the Altar Guild ladies discuss Becky Perdue's abandonment, and one member argues: "She can make him pay. She doesn't have to give him a divorce. She's a Catholic!" But another woman counters, "Sugar lamb, we are living in the 1980s. What good does that do her?" (p. 5) While the assumption that the indissolubility of marriage has any currency in the modern world is challenged, the larger significance of the first comment is unremarked by the other characters. Apparently it is natural for them to think of Church discipline in terms of its coercive power. In this fiction, Catholicism is a legalistic presence that has lost its spiritual vitality.

Ostensibly a modern parish, Our Lady of Perpetual Help of Due East, South Carolina operates according to preconciliar norms and values. The classic Catholic application of rule and law to human experience predominates. In *Due East*, Mary Faith Rapple identifies the problem when she tries to locate a Catholic home for unwed mothers but decides against asking Father Berkeley for help:

He had kind, light eyes, and I knew if I called him asking where I could go he'd call me *sweetheart* or *sugar* and try to find out who I was. Next thing I knew, he'd be talking to my father and driving me to the home himself. He'd feel sorry for me and ask me to address the Due East Right to Life Committee and his heart would break if I told him I didn't believe in God and didn't mind who else had an abortion. (p. 60)

Pregnant in an effort at affirmation and self-definition, Mary Faith does not want to be merely an unwed mother, still less a witness against abortion. The classical paradigm, fueled by the Scholastic tendency to label and categorize, is unacceptable in the modern world. Sayers contrasts Mary Faith's opinion of Father Berkeley's beneficent orthodoxy with her ideal haven:

> No, what I needed was nuns, some tough cookies with a maternity center for girls who weren't praying when they said *Jesus Christ*. The sisters would talk to me about religion, but they'd know beforehand I wasn't going to buy it, and they'd see I had good books to read and they'd make all the mothers-to-be turn out the lights at ten o'clock. (p. 60)

Although she does not run a maternity center, Sister Otile Ryan of Gordon's *The Other Side* is one of the tough cookies Mary Faith describes. She is more concerned with achieving an ideal within the real world than in applying an ideal to reality. And she is not averse to dismantling the institution as needed. Yet, as Gordon points out, the cost of Otile's liberalism is the disappearance of objective moral norms. One of the lessons of the Protestant experience in confronting modernity has been that in the search for an openness to human experience, there is a danger of sliding into what ethicists term the "vast wasteland of relativism," so Gordon's depiction of Sister Otile is an exceedingly acute observation.[13]

One of the important lessons of literature is that authorial intention is less significant than achieved purpose. And Sayers' fiction reminds us that we must look beyond intentionality to achieved purpose in religion as well as literature. For all his benevolence, Sayers' Father Berkeley represents the "dead world" of Catholicism. Thus, although *How I Got Him Back* ends with a chapter called "The Beginning," as the members of Our Lady of Perpetual Help Altar Guild assemble at the site of their new church building, that title has ironic implications. The site has been chosen by the pastor against the wishes of the parishioners, and although the women complain, it is clear that they willingly preserve this paternalistic system:

> "He got *his* way. Having us all drive out to the ends of the earth."
> "Oh, men always clap their hands and have us snap to attention. That's the way of the world, honey." They giggled again, and swung their car doors shut so that Father could have the site to himself. (p. 300)

In the giggling, middle-aged handmaids of Our Lady of Perpetual Help parish, Sayers hints at another aspect of contemporary Catholicism, the unhealthy relationships that are nurtured in the soil of religion.

This aspect of modern Catholicism is devastatingly presented in the title story of Starkey Flythe, Jr.'s award-winning collection, *Lent: The Slow Fast* (1990). The entire collection is about relationships—healthy and unhealthy—and Flythe's title refers to the difficulty in letting go of unhealthy attachments. The dominance of priests like Sayers' Father Berkeley is more explicitly sexual in Flythe's story of a young Catholic woman who feeds her parish and her priest, ultimately depriving her husband and her children.

FEEDING THE SHEPHERD

The short story, "Lent: The Slow Fast" recounts the tale of Jo Ellen, a young Catholic housewife and gourmet cook, whose culinary talents are tapped by the parish priest, Peter, ostensibly to help the new parishioner become part of parish life. Soon Peter is gaining weight and Jo Ellen's family is feeling neglected, as there seem to be more and more occasions when Jo Ellen's elegant meals are needed at the parish. Although on one occasion Peter remarks to her, "You know you cross the most intimate boundaries when you offer food to people?" he seems totally oblivious to the fact that he is indeed challenging her husband in a subtly manipulative manner.

Flythe indicates this in the retrospective arrangement of the story and its primary setting. The narrative opens on Easter morning with Jo Ellen and her husband enjoying a peaceful morning in bed with the children off comparing Easter candy with their friends. She has recently terminated her endless cooking duties at the parish, taking the opportunity of Peter's hospitalization (too much rich food having aggravated his diverticulosis) to avoid dealing with the priest's entreaties. As the story opens, Peter calls, asking for the promised Easter morning breakfast for the choir (and the priest), and Jo Ellen is conscious of both husband beside her and priest on the phone, although "only the ravenousness of the two men made any sound."[14] During the entire story, Jo Ellen is thinking about past events while lying in bed with her husband and talking to the priest on the phone. Thus, the central conflict of the story, the male competition to possess Jo Ellen, is blatantly indicated in the physical setting of the narrative.

In this apparently simple story of priest and parishioner, Flythe extends his meaning beyond the individual priest and parishioner to indicate the difficulty with contemporary Catholicism. The reference to the priest exclusively as "Peter" throughout the story suggests the trendy contemporary American clergy who disdain titles, the Biblical leader of the apostles, and the Chair of Peter occupied by the apostle's successor, representative of the Church as a whole. The story's feeding metaphor similarly evokes the Scriptural parallel of Jesus' feeding the multitude in the gospels, as well as the table fellowship he instituted at the Last Supper and the sacrifice of his body that it foreshadowed. Thus, Flythe suggests the irony in the fact that the touchstone of the Eucharistic life for Christians, Jesus' table fellowship, has been distorted in the modern parish to a passive consumption of the goods of a provider—with the concomitant exploitation of the provider.

In the story, the intimacy of the feeding metaphor and its clear sexual connotation is reflected in Peter's homily on the Biblical story of Jesus' feeding of the multitude. Peter focuses neither on the people fed nor on Jesus as provider but on the imagined mother of the small boy who shares his food, speculating about how lovingly she must have prepared her son's lunch. And while preaching,

> He looked right at Jo Ellen, going over the rows of parishioners whose Sundays (and Wednesdays and Thursdays) had been so pleasantly altered by her cooking. She tingled with pride. (p. 5)

It is clear that the priest is satisfying more than one appetite in his attachment to Jo Ellen, even if the overweight Peter has consciously sublimated his sexual feelings. And it is equally clear that Peter (in all the ecclesial associations of that name) can have no viable spiritual presence until he comes to terms with the subtle psychological and social forces that motivate him—until he can be faithful to the New Testament feeding metaphor rather than misreading the Scripture to accord with his own unacknowledged feelings.

While Flythe suggests that the Church, in attempting to enter the modern world, has lost touch with its roots, Alfred Alcorn illustrates that problem more fully in his second novel, *Vestments* (1988). Alcorn locates the problem in Catholicism's abandonment of the vertical dimension of life in its anxiety to affirm the horizontal. His earlier novel, *The Pull of the Earth*, was set in the preconciliar 1950's and had emphasized the difficulty in the supernaturalism of the old paradigm. In *Vestments*, Alcorn ironically highlights the absence of the supernatural in postconciliar Catholicism. His narrative depicts the impoverishment of the Church in the modern world but simultaneously shows the persistent action of grace.

HEAVENLY ATTIRE

Vestments is both a realistic novel and a parable, and it provides an acute perception of what has been lost at the cultural level in the wake of the revolutionary changes in Catholicism. The novel's central character, Sebastian Taggart, is a young Bostonian on the fast track who is waiting for his aunt's death to supply him with money to support an extravagant lifestyle that he desires to make increasingly extravagant. His aunt, who raised him, had always wished he would become a priest. In the confusion of her final illness, she imagines he *is* a priest, and one day she castigates him for not wearing his collar.

Fearing that she may decide to disinherit him if she learns the truth, Sebastian tries to insure his inheritance by dressing as a priest when he visits her. At the last moment, he leaves his scarf and overcoat on, vaguely reluctant to go through with the impersonation, but he also realizes that something strange has begun to happen to him. Dressed as a priest, he feels somewhat more peaceful, almost benevolent. Soon he is wearing clerical clothes more often, just to acquire the sense of peace the garments seem to impart.

Eventually Sebastian dissolves the relationship with his girlfriend, leaving the luxury apartment they share for a bleak room where he begins to read St. Augustine, work at a local shelter for homeless men, and try to develop a life of prayer. He confides in Sister Vincia, the head of the nursing home in which his aunt resides, and she directs him to local Jesuits for advice on his decision to enter the seminary and study for the priesthood.

During the interview, Sebastian is startled by the priest's asking, "What do you think precipitated this urge you have to join the priesthood?" Not wanting to admit this vocation stems from his having walked around wearing a Roman collar, Sebastian offers the fine example he has had in Sister Vincia and Father Donnellen, the chaplain at the nursing home, and Brother Ron, who runs the shelter he works at as the inspiration for him. So the priest asks, "Why don't you become a social worker?" And it is here that Alcorn connects the impersonation with the essence.

Sebastian Taggart, unable to explain rationally how he sees his vocation as different from that of a social worker, blurts out, "I like the externals."[15] To clarify his answer for the puzzled priest, Sebastian explains, "The rituals, the vestments, especially the garments of the Mass." Oh, the priest responds, "Of course they're not what they used to be" (p. 235). There is an authorial irony in the priest's response, for the "vestments" of the novel's title refer to the emphasis on the transcendent, which Alcorn sees as missing in the contemporary Church. In *The Other Side*, Gordon's Sister Otile dismantles the institution for human need, but Alcorn's fiction reminds us that in reducing the excessive focus on supernaturalism, we must beware of eliminating the supernatural altogether.

Returning to his bleak room, Sebastian draws on his memory of traditional ascetic practices and devotes himself to the development of sanctity. When his aunt finally dies, he is not disappointed at the small amount of his inheritance because it is enough to finance his seminary education. The problem is that in spite of all the good feelings the collar has engendered, Sebastian does not actually have faith, and all his efforts at prayer, fasting, spiritual reading, and good works do not seem to be producing any faith.

Finally, the strain of the effort is too much, and Sebastian goes on a binge. When he shows up at the shelter intoxicated, he is banned from the premises. Almost utterly destroyed by the failure of his dreams of sanctity, Sebastian awakens the next morning to an experience of God's presence, the glorious fulfillment of his hoped for faith.

It is in his use of the clothing metaphor in *Vestments* that Alcorn's fullest meaning is conveyed. The parallel with Thomas Carlyle's nineteenth-century narrative *Sartor Resartus* is inescapable. In *Sartor Resartus* (literally, "the tailor-re-tailored"), Carlyle develops the "clothes philosophy" to highlight the difference between appearance and reality. The appearance of people is obviously strongly affected by their clothing (as we are well aware of today with the injunction to dress for success), but Carlyle extends the comparison, identifying institutions as the "clothes" of the reality they represent. Like clothes that can be worn out or go out of fashion and no longer convey the desired image, institutions can deteriorate and fail to be an appropriate referent. In both cases, re-tailoring is needed.

In Alcorn's use of Carlyle's metaphor, it is the institution's abandonment of its vestments that is the problem. In the novel, clothing is efficacious of the reality; wearing the clerical collar initiates Sebastian's quest for God. The clothing rather than the person "heralds the word of God and elicits the response of faith."[16] But the Church, in this novel, has abandoned its traditional clothing too readily. The externals that the Boston priest dismisses are the sacramentals that facilitate the action of grace in Sebastian's life.

It is easier to change clothes than to change patterns of thinking, this novel reminds us, and in the process of renewal following the Second Vatican Council, the Church in America enthusiastically changed clothes without regard for the fact that different attire signified a different referent. In changing signifiers, Catholicism unwittingly diminished the central meaning of Church as symbolic of the Transcendent Presence in our midst.

Sebastian's only explanation for why he wants to be a priest rather than a social worker centers on the vestments, the signifier of a sacramental identity. Without that dimension the nondenominational humanistic faith of Dan and Camille in *The Other Side* becomes the norm, the orphaned children of *Tokens of Grace* remain unparented, and the Eucharistic images of the gospels become parish soup kitchens exploiting female cooks, as in "Lent: A Slow Fast." Alcorn's novel shows that God continues to act in the world, but Catholicism must re-tailor itself to be faithful to His presence.

NOTES

1. Langdon Gilkey, *Catholicism Confronts Modernity* (New York: The Seabury Press, 1975), p. 15. This is also central to Richard John Neuhaus, *The Catholic Moment: The Paradox of the Church in the Postmodern World* (San Francisco: Harper and Row, 1987), see especially p. ix.

2. Gilkey, p. 30.

3. Ibid., p. 16.

4. Mary Gordon, *The Other Side* (New York: Viking, 1989), p. 346.

5. See especially William Zinsser, ed., *Spiritual Quests: The Art and Craft of Religious Writing* (Boston: Houghton Mifflin Company, 1988), pp. 27–53; and Peter Occhiogrosso, ed., *Once a Catholic* (Boston: Houghton Mifflin Company, 1987), pp. 65–78.

6. Mary Gordon, "A Moral Choice," *The Atlantic* (April 1990), pp. 78, 80–84.

7. Jay Dolan, *The American Catholic Experience* (New York: Doubleday and Company, Inc., 1985), pp. 160–62. The entire chapter, "The Parish and the People" (pp. 158–94), is relevant to this point and is the source of the information in the remainder of my paragraph.

8. Sheila O'Connor, *Tokens of Grace* (Minneapolis: Milkweed Editions, 1990), p. 56.

9. Quoted in Occhiogrosso, p. 74.

10. Valerie Sayers, *Due East* (New York: Berkley Books, 1988), p. 138.

11. Valerie Sayers, *How I Got Him Back* (New York: Doubleday and Company, Inc., 1989), p. 297.

12. Valerie Sayers, "When the Catholic Novelist Portrays the Church," *CCICA Annual 1990* (vol. 9, Catholic Writers), 30.

13 James M. Gustafson, *Protestant and Roman Catholic Ethics: Prospects for Rapprochement* (Chicago and London: University of Chicago Press, 1978), p. 33. Gustafson's second chapter, pp. 30–59, is especially instructive.

14. Starkey Flythe, Jr., *Lent: The Slow Fast* (Iowa City: University of Iowa Press, 1990), p. 6.

15. Alfred Alcorn, *Vestments* (Boston: Houghton Mifflin Company, 1988), p. 234.

16. Avery Dulles, *The Reshaping of Catholicism: Current Challenges in the Theology of Church* (San Francisco: Harper and Row, 1988), p. 149. Dulles' phrase, referring to the Church's responsibility in the world, is a particularly apt description of the effect of wearing clerical clothing on Sebastian, reinforcing Alcorn's emblematic use of clothing as the physical expression of the institution.

10

Conclusion: Vision of a Changing Church

... so he who wishes to see a Vision, a perfect Whole,
Must see it in its Minute Particulars, Organized.

William Blake

Despite the need to offer a conclusion to this study, it is important to note that the modern spirit is wary of closure. And the quintessential modern literary form, the novel, dwells in "the spontaneity of the inconclusive present," its authors drawn to everything that is not yet completed.[1] Unfortunately, Richard John Neuhaus has noted that within contemporary Catholicism the tendency to premature closure, a vestige of the pre-conciliar era, is still strong.

> And it makes little difference whether it is the old triumphalism of the exclusive salvific mission of the Roman Catholic church or the new triumphalism of the Church equated with revolutionary praxis, psychological fulfillment, or some other human project.[2]

While Neuhaus is writing of competing theological ideologies, the fiction of Catholic experience records a similar tendency to attempt to achieve closure. From this perspective the conservatism of Ralph McInerny who longs for a valorized past is as wrongheaded as the passionate intensity of novelists who promulgate the Sentimental Love Ethic as the ideal of postconciliar Catholicism. Their concern for closure is premature and at odds with the spirit of the novel as a literary genre.

By now it should be apparent to both theologians and historians that the most difficult aspect of paradigm change is the intellectual challenge. It is not easy to envision reality in a new way, but that is very much the task facing Catholicism today. As has been frequently observed throughout this study, Thomas Kuhn insists that a new paradigm is not rationally deduced but imaginatively conceived, so, as Archbishop Rembert Weakland has commented, "We are living at a time in which we must re-imagine the Catholic Church."[3]

What is significant is not that the process of re-imagining Catholicism *can* be documented in contemporary fiction but that the process of change in Catholicism is *best* documented in this fiction. Raymond Williams succinctly identifies the cultural importance of literature in terms that are especially applicable to the current situation of Catholicism in the United States:

> The most interesting and difficult part of any cultural analysis, in complex societies, is that which seeks to grasp the hegemonic in its active and formative but also its transformational processes. Works of art, by their substantial and general character, are often especially important as sources of this complex evidence.[4]

Contemporary fiction of Catholic experience is expressive of the unique situation of the Church in the United States at this particular historical moment and, while interesting in its minute particulars, forms an important vision of cultural change when those particulars are organized. This fiction documents a significant cultural shift in Catholicism, serving as a barometer of that shift, and it provides insight into the transformational processes at work in contemporary Catholic culture in the United States.

From the evidence of fiction, postconciliar Catholicism seems mired in the residual ethos of the old paradigm while unable to effectively envision the emergent culture of the new. The differences between these two paradigms can be appreciated by locating the Scriptural texts they prioritize. Traditional Catholicism derived meaning from Matthew 16:18–19:

> And so I say to you, you are Peter, and upon this rock I will build my church, and the gates of the netherworld shall not prevail against it. I will give you the keys to the kingdom of heaven. Whatever you bind on earth shall be bound in heaven; and whatever you loose on earth shall be loosed in heaven.

This legitimizes a Church that controls salvation, a Church in which The Faith is the only faith to consider, and a Church in which the priest is such a sacred person that he must be a male (the dominant gender), purified by perpetual celibacy. An institution that is investing its energies in preserving that model of priesthood is clearly still operating from the residual ethos of Matthew 16:18–19, regardless of the proclamations of the Second Vatican Council.

For it has become obvious during the past twenty-five years that the Council was not a circumscribed event so much as the inauguration of a new era for Catholicism. Ironically, the fiction in this study most faithful to the transformational processes of this changing Church are usually those that are most readily dismissed. The clamor against visions of experience like Christopher Durang's *Sister Mary Ignatius Tells It All* is based primarily on an allegiance to the residual culture of American Catholicism and its icons of innocence. But reductive charges of anti-Catholicism also derive from the literary provincialism that is the heritage of that culture and impedes appreciation of this literature. Such provincialism stems from a classical ideology that regards didacticism as the primary end of literature, so fiction that fails to bolster the dominant ethos is inevitably condemned.

Another vestige of the preconciliar paradigm is the tendency toward closure, so it is not surprising that the outrage at Durang's play among Catholics is balanced by the wide readership of Andrew Greeley's sentimentalized novels of an idealized, "new" Catholicism. The preference for didacticism in art characteristic of preconciliar Catholicism is susceptible to the lure of the thesis-ridden fiction of passionate intensity. And Greeley's idealized Church of the Ryan clan is comforting to those whose secure haven in Mother Church has been disturbed by the paradigm shift in progress.

The fiction in this study that avoids premature closure is not only closer to the ideal of the modern spirit, it most reliably registers the transformational processes in contemporary Catholicism. In addition to the various visions presented in the preceding chapters, this fiction also offers a dominant vision of the current Catholic moment in three separate but interrelated movements. The first movement is a clear critique of the residual ethos of the preconciliar Church, an ethos that impedes the envisioning of a new paradigm for Catholicism. This critique is a shared vision among writers in Chapters, 2, 6, and 9. A common denominator in the fiction of Walker Percy, J. F. Powers, John Gregory Dunne, Alfred Alcorn, Philip Deaver, and Starkey Flythe, Jr. is an image of the Church as a dysfunctional institution manned by priests mired in the paternalism of the past. In this fiction, there seems to be a common belief that the Church entered the modern world too naively and has lost its ground of being. As Percy's Lancelot admonishes, "Now you're part of the age. You've the same fleas as the dogs you've lain down with."[5]

Ironically, the paternalism that marks Powers' Joe Hackett has been handed down to the younger priests in Deaver's "Silent Retreats" and Flythe's "Lent: The Slow Fast." Despite the appearance of engaging modernity, Catholicism is imaged as clinging to the most negative aspects of the preconciliar Church. Joe Hackett's clericalism in Powers' *Wheat That Springeth Green* seems to reflect an attempt to retain the outward forms of the past to disguise his decayed inner spiritual life. Joe's personal dilemma is indicated by the author as a microcosm of the institutional dilemma. The industrial park Church of Powers' novel reflects a loss of spiritual presence that Alcorn also images in *Vestments*. The vestments that assist in the conversion of Sebastian Taggart in Alcorn's novel are symbolic of the spiritual dimension of life, which seems to have vanished in renewal. Both novels end with their protagonists' personal conversion to gospel values, but no realistic novel in this study offers a vision of institutional presence commensurate with that type of personal renewal.

Both Greeley and Eugene Kennedy have, of course, prophesied the decline of institutional Catholicism, and this first movement in the vision of the contemporary Church in fiction seem to confirm their perspective. However, their exaltation of Catholic individualism seems naive in light of the fiction in this book. Christianity is at its core a communal religion. Sebastian Taggart must leave his isolated room following his experience of faith; he must find some social context for his spiritual life. Similarly, *Wheat That Springeth Green* ends with Joe Hackett's departure for a parish that he hopes will enable him to live a priestly life more faithful to his ideals. The concept of "church" is integral to Christianity.

Of course, it is possible that the individualized Catholicism that Greeley and Kennedy laud will result in the formation of smaller communities of committed Christians unaffiliated with the declining institution, thereby developing a new model of church more consonant with modernity. However, the fiction of Andre Dubus and David Plante serves as a significant indicator of the fact that unbridled individualism results in an idiosyncratic Catholicism that has little relation to the Church of history and tradition.

At the same time, the lessons of history indicate that the overriding spirit of individualism in America must be accounted for in any new model of church for Catholicism. Thus, the fiction of personal spiritual journey, the second movement in this vision of contemporary Catholicism, is so significant. It provides a new locus of meaning for the experience of church in modern life, offering a perspective that is consonant with contemporary theological method.

Instead of the triumphalism of Matthew 16, postconciliar Catholic theology locates the source of meaning within the human, an incarnational vision reflected in Luke 17:20–21:

> Asked by the Pharisees when the kingdom of God would come, he said in reply, "The coming of the kingdom of God cannot be observed, and no one will announce, 'Look, here it is,' or, 'There it is.' For behold, the kingdom of God is among you."

This perspective refuses to identify the Kingdom with any specific denomination and highlights the importance of vision in identifying the kingdom of God. The vision of contemporary American fiction indicates that institutional Catholicism is slow to adopt the Lukan perspective. In A. G. Mojtabai's *Ordinary Time*, Father Gilvary frequently mutters the line "The Kingdom of God is among you," as though to convince himself of a reality he cannot see enfleshed in the world, and in the fiction of Catholic experience, Father Gilvary is not alone in the attempt to locate the kingdom of God in the natural world.

The singular journey Paul Theroux records in *My Secret History* is affirmed in the prophetic vision of spiritual quest in Chapter 8. The spiritual quest evidenced in this fiction is aptly described by Walter Murphy's Pope in his 1979 best-seller, *Vicar of Christ*:

> People aren't rejecting religion or God so much as they're looking for new answers that fit new problems. The old catechism's approach doesn't help. These people are yearning, not rejecting.[6]

This fiction forms the second significant movement in the threefold vision of contemporary fiction. It offers a model of spiritual development that should be the preamble to any new model of church. For postconciliar theology emphasizes that it is not the arbitrary imposition of rule and law but the experience of the People of God in light of the gospel message that should serve as a guide in life. Such a viewpoint challenges the Church, for it asks that the experience of people be the focus of ministry. Thus, the critique of continued clericalism, part of the first movement in this vision, derives from an implicit understanding of the importance of the individual spiritual journey as the focus of ministry.

The challenge to contemporary Catholicism is most clear in the fiction of Chapter 9, which completes the vision of contemporary fiction. This third movement depicts a dysfunctional modern Church unable to minister to those engaged in personal spiritual journey (indeed, often unable to even identify those people). In this fiction, Catholicism is hampered by the prevalence of the residual culture, usually manifest in patriarchal attitudes that leave the Church "a shrine to its own woodwork," as Mary Gordon's Sister Otile comments in *The Other Side*. Paradigmatic of this movement is Valerie Sayers' fictional parish of Our Lady of Perpetual Help in Due East, South Carolina. Here the pastor, ministering according to his formation in the preconciliar Church, is well-meaning but ineffectual, and parish life is imaged in the ladies of the Altar Guild, a group devoted to decor and gossip. Ironically, in Sheila O'Connor's *Tokens of Grace*, the contemporary Church, operating according to the preconciliar ethos of triumphalism, cannot even minister to the child-protagonists who might welcome the security of paternalism. For the preconciliar model is elitist, protecting itself from the loss of innocence that might result from affirming the children of divorce.

Another aspect of this third movement is provided in fiction that images a Church that has entered the modern world and thereby lost spiritual significance. The industrial park of *Wheat That Springeth Green* is paralleled in the corporate agenda of Father Gilvary's diocese in *Ordinary Time*. The elderly priest's impending blindness, symbolic of his inability to "see" the kingdom of God in any viable social context in this novel, reflects a vision of a spiritually impotent Church paralleled in Alcorn's *Vestments*. The discarded garments of a past age initiate Sebastian Taggart's spiritual journey, rather than any viable institutional presence.

At the end of *Virgins*, an adult Peg Morrison reflects on her adolescence in the preconciliar Church and comments that "the Church we knew . . . was the last gasp of another age, the remnants of an immigrant religion of mysteries and miracles, saints and visions. It would be swept away by winds that had already begun to stir."[7] The problem is that Peg is both right and wrong, as the fiction in this study shows. New eras do not begin so neatly, and the remnants of an immigrant religion remain, perhaps not in the newly modernized church buildings, but certainly in the hearts and minds of those who cling to the preconciliar paradigm for meaning. And some perhaps cling to that paradigm because the Church has been unable to imaginatively appropriate any viable new paradigm, as the fiction suggests.

In an essay written at the beginning of the last decade, the noted ecclesiologist Avery Dulles argued that many problems faced by Catholicism in relation to its disaffected members could be solved if a viable model of Church could be found. He asserted:

If we could fashion an inspiring and realistic image of the Church, we might be able to act confidently, and in such a way that our self-understanding would be reinforced by feedback from others.[8]

Sadly, contemporary fiction does not offer such an "inspiring and realistic image of the Church." Fiction, grounded in realism, presents no positive images of Church in contemporary society. Postconciliar best-sellers that offer a progressive vision of Catholicism have been works like Murphy's *Vicar of Christ* or Greeley's *The Cardinal Sins*, fiction redolent with romance rather than realism.

Ironically, although the predominance of the Sentimental Love Ethic in Greeley's fiction reflects the reaction (nay, overreaction) to authoritarian religion, Greeley's novels offer an inspiring—if unrealistic—image of the Church of the emergent culture. As Leslie Fiedler has commented, there is an "unwitting duplicity" in the best-seller that "confuses the wish with the fact, and presents the dreams of its readers as an account of real actions in the real world."[9] Thus, Greeley recreates the "old neighborhood" of the Immigrant Church for his readers, a classic wish-fulfillment fantasy. His mythic Ryan clan and their family priest, Blackie, are an interesting mixture of the residual culture of Catholicism blended with American individualism—Catholicism "going my way," with an emphasis on the personal possessive pronoun.

The acute sociologist in novelist Greeley has identified the Church that Catholics in the United States would embrace—a strong and loving local community headed by wise and compassionate leaders who respect individuality, the type of group Valerie Sayers' Mary Faith Rapple seeks. This would be, in effect, an extension of the table-fellowship inaugurated by Jesus. And the need for such an element of spiritual fellowship in human life is particularly apparent in the fiction of Paul Theroux, Larry Woiwode, Mary Gordon, A. J. Mojtabai, and Sheila O'Connor.

The novels in Chapters 6 and 9 that offer a critique of the postconciliar Church indicate that this fellowship is not being experienced at the present time; it exists solely in romance fiction. At the risk of offering a conclusion, it seems obvious that the challenge to Catholicism, articulated by Father Dulles more than a decade ago, is reflected in the title of his essay collection; for its people of faith, Catholicism needs to fashion a Church to believe in.

To end this study with Joycean circularity rather than linear closure, I return to Jeanne Schinto's short story "Before Sewing One Must Cut." Words from a crucial letter that the narrator reads in that story serve as a fitting admonition for Catholicism from its fiction: "You must accept who you are and what has happened to you."[10] It is to be hoped that the Church will learn to appreciate the message of fiction as an especially powerful source for achieving that self-understanding.

NOTES

1. M. M. Bakhtin, *The Dialogic Imagination*, trans. Caryl Emerson; ed. and trans., Michael Holquist. (Austin: University of Texas Press, 1981), p. 27.

2. Richard John Neuhaus, *The Catholic Moment: The Paradox of the Church in the Postmodern World* (San Francisco: Harper and Row, 1987), p. 45.

3. Cited by Eugene Kennedy, *Re-imaging American Catholicism* (New York: Vintage Books, 1985), p. 19.

4. Raymond Williams, *Marxism and Literature* (Oxford and New York: Oxford University Press, 1977), pp. 113–14.

5. Walker Percy, *Lancelot* (New York: Farrar, Straus and Giroux, 1977), p. 157.

6. Walter F. Murphy, *The Vicar of Christ* (New York: Ballantine Books, 1979), p. 256.

7. Caryl Rivers, *Virgins* (New York: Pocket Books, 1984), p. 274.

8. Avery Dulles, S.J., *A Church to Believe In* (New York: Crossroad, 1980), p. 3.

9. Leslie Fiedler, *Love and Death in the American Novel* (New York: Stein and Day, 1966), p. 95.

10. Jeanne Schinto, *Shadow Bands* (Princeton: Ontario Review Press, 1988), p. 55.

Bibliography

PRIMARY SOURCES (FICTION)

Alcorn, Alfred. *The Pull of the Earth*. Boston: Houghton Mifflin Company, 1985.
———. *Vestments*. Boston: Houghton Mifflin Company, 1988.
Benard, Robert. *A Catholic Education*. New York: Holt, Rinehart and Winston, 1982.
Bonanno, Margaret Wander. *Ember Days*. New York: Seaview Books, 1980.
Byrne, Robert. *Once a Catholic*. New York: Pinnacle Books, 1970 (originally published under the title *Memories of a Non-Jewish Childhood*).
Cahill, Susan. *Earth Angels: Portraits from Childhood and Youth*. 1976. Reprint. Harrington Park, New Jersey: Ampersand Associates, 1988.
Carroll, James. *Madonna Red*. 1976. Reprint. New York: Golden Apple, 1984.
———. *Prince of Peace*. Boston: Little, Brown and Company, 1984.
Chace, Susan. *Intimacy*. New York: Random House, 1989.
Chesterton, G. K. *The Father Brown Omnibus*. New York: Dodd Mead and Company, 1961.
Cullinan, Elizabeth. *House of Gold*. Boston: Houghton Mifflin Company, 1970.
Deaver, Philip F. *Silent Retreats*. Athens, Georgia and London: University of Georgia Press, 1988.
Drucker, Peter F. *The Temptation To Do Good*. New York: Harper & Row, 1984.
Dubus, Andre. *The Last Worthless Evening*. Boston: David R. Godine, 1986.
———. *Selected Stories*. Boston: David R. Godine, 1988.
———. *The Times Are Never So Bad*. Boston: David R. Godine, 1983.
———. *Voices from the Moon*. Boston: David R. Godine, 1984.
Dunne, John Gregory. *The Red White and Blue*. New York: Simon and Schuster, 1987.
———. *True Confessions*. New York: E. P. Dutton, 1977.
Durang. Christopher. *Sister Mary Ignatius Explains It All For You/The Actor's Nightmare*. New York: Nelson Doubleday, Inc., 1981.
Flythe, Starkey, Jr. *Lent: The Slow Fast*. Iowa City: University of Iowa Press, 1990.

Gernes, Sonia. *The Way to St. Ives*. New York: Charles Scribner's Sons, 1982.

Gordon, Mary. *The Company of Women*. New York: Ballantine Books, 1980.

———. *Final Payments*. New York: Random House, 1978.

———. *Men and Angels*. New York: Random House, 1985.

———. *The Other Side*. New York: Viking, 1980.

Greeley, Andrew M. *All About Women*. New York: Tor Books, 1990.

———. *Angel Fire*. New York: Warner Books, 1988.

———. *Angels of September*. New York: Warner Books, 1986.

———. *Ascent Into Hell*. New York: Warner Books, 1983.

———. *The Cardinal Sins*. New York: Warner Books, 1981.

———. *Happy Are The Clean of Heart*. New York: Warner Books, 1986.

———. *Happy Are The Meek*. New York: Warner Books, 1985.

———. *Happy Are Those Who Thirst for Justice*. New York: Warner Books, 1987.

———. *Lord of the Dance*. New York: Warner Books, 1984.

———. *Patience of a Saint*. New York: Warner Books, 1987.

———. *Rite of Spring*. New York: Warner Books, 1987.

———. *St. Valentine's Night*. New York: Warner Books, 1989.

———. *Thy Brother's Wife*. New York: Warner Books, 1982.

———. *Virgin and Martyr*. New York: Warner Books, 1985.

Hassler, John. *A Green Journey*. New York: William Morrow and Company, 1985.

———. *North of Hope*. New York: Ballantine Books, 1990.

Kavanaugh, James. *The Celibates*. New York: Harper and Row, 1985.

Kennedy, Eugene. *Father's Day*. New York: Pocket Books, 1981.

———. *Fixes*. New York: Doubleday and Company, Inc., 1989.

Kienzle, William. *Assault With Intent*. New York: Ballantine Books, 1982.

———. *Deadline for a Critic*. Kansas City and New York: Andrews, McMeel and Parker, 1987.

———. *Deathbed*. Kansas City and New York: Andrews, McMeel and Parker, 1986.

———. *Death Wears a Red Hat*. New York: Bantam Books, 1980.

———. *Eminence*. Kansas City and New York: Andrews, McMeel and Parker, 1989.

———. *Kill and Tell*. Kansas City and New York: Andrews, McMeel and Parker, 1984.

———. *Marked for Murder*. New York: Ballantine Books, 1989.

———. *Masquerade*. New York: Andrews, McMeel and Parker, 1990.

———. *Mind Over Murder*. New York: Bantam Books, 1981.

———. *The Rosary Murders*. New York: Bantam Books, 1979.

———. *Shadow of Death*. New York: Ballantine Books, 1983.

Lawrence, Kathleen Rockwell. *Maud Gone*. New York: Atheneum, 1986.

Maitland, Sara. *Virgin Territory*. New York: Beaufort Books, 1984.

Martin, Malachi. *The Final Conclave*. New York: Stein and Day, 1978.

Martin, Valerie. *A Recent Martyr*. Boston: Houghton Mifflin Company, 1987.

McHale, Tom. *Farragan's Retreat*. New York: The Viking Press, 1971.

———. *Principato*. New York: The Viking Press, 1969.

———. *School Spirit*. New York: Doubleday and Company, Inc., 1976.

McInerny, Ralph. *Abracadaver*. New York: St. Martin's Press, 1990.

———. *The Basket Case*. New York: St. Martin's Press, 1987.

———. *Bishop as Pawn*. New York: The Vanguard Press, 1978.

———. *Cause and Effect*. New York: Atheneum, 1987.

———. *Connolly's Life*. New York: Atheneum, 1983.

———. *Gate of Heaven*. New York: Harper and Row, 1975.

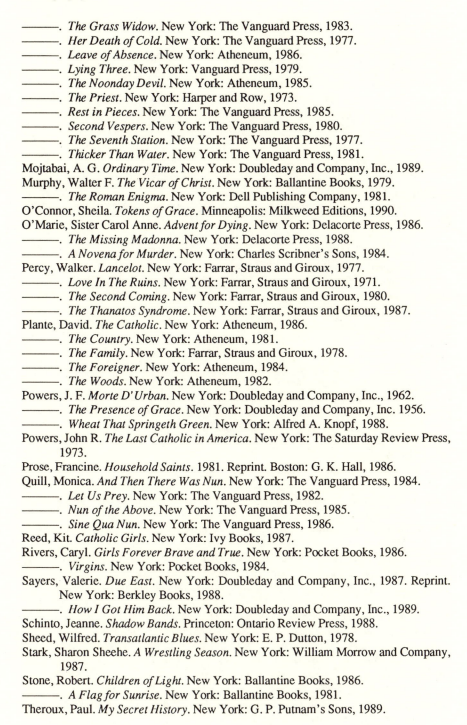
————. *The Grass Widow*. New York: The Vanguard Press, 1983.
————. *Her Death of Cold*. New York: The Vanguard Press, 1977.
————. *Leave of Absence*. New York: Atheneum, 1986.
————. *Lying Three*. New York: Vanguard Press, 1979.
————. *The Noonday Devil*. New York: Atheneum, 1985.
————. *The Priest*. New York: Harper and Row, 1973.
————. *Rest in Pieces*. New York: The Vanguard Press, 1985.
————. *Second Vespers*. New York: The Vanguard Press, 1980.
————. *The Seventh Station*. New York: The Vanguard Press, 1977.
————. *Thicker Than Water*. New York: The Vanguard Press, 1981.
Mojtabai, A. G. *Ordinary Time*. New York: Doubleday and Company, Inc., 1989.
Murphy, Walter F. *The Vicar of Christ*. New York: Ballantine Books, 1979.
————. *The Roman Enigma*. New York: Dell Publishing Company, 1981.
O'Connor, Sheila. *Tokens of Grace*. Minneapolis: Milkweed Editions, 1990.
O'Marie, Sister Carol Anne. *Advent for Dying*. New York: Delacorte Press, 1986.
————. *The Missing Madonna*. New York: Delacorte Press, 1988.
————. *A Novena for Murder*. New York: Charles Scribner's Sons, 1984.
Percy, Walker. *Lancelot*. New York: Farrar, Straus and Giroux, 1977.
————. *Love In The Ruins*. New York: Farrar, Straus and Giroux, 1971.
————. *The Second Coming*. New York: Farrar, Straus and Giroux, 1980.
————. *The Thanatos Syndrome*. New York: Farrar, Straus and Giroux, 1987.
Plante, David. *The Catholic*. New York: Atheneum, 1986.
————. *The Country*. New York: Atheneum, 1981.
————. *The Family*. New York: Farrar, Straus and Giroux, 1978.
————. *The Foreigner*. New York: Atheneum, 1984.
————. *The Woods*. New York: Atheneum, 1982.
Powers, J. F. *Morte D'Urban*. New York: Doubleday and Company, Inc., 1962.
————. *The Presence of Grace*. New York: Doubleday and Company, Inc. 1956.
————. *Wheat That Springeth Green*. New York: Alfred A. Knopf, 1988.
Powers, John R. *The Last Catholic in America*. New York: The Saturday Review Press, 1973.
Prose, Francine. *Household Saints*. 1981. Reprint. Boston: G. K. Hall, 1986.
Quill, Monica. *And Then There Was Nun*. New York: The Vanguard Press, 1984.
————. *Let Us Prey*. New York: The Vanguard Press, 1982.
————. *Nun of the Above*. New York: The Vanguard Press, 1985.
————. *Sine Qua Nun*. New York: The Vanguard Press, 1986.
Reed, Kit. *Catholic Girls*. New York: Ivy Books, 1987.
Rivers, Caryl. *Girls Forever Brave and True*. New York: Pocket Books, 1986.
————. *Virgins*. New York: Pocket Books, 1984.
Sayers, Valerie. *Due East*. New York: Doubleday and Company, Inc., 1987. Reprint. New York: Berkley Books, 1988.
————. *How I Got Him Back*. New York: Doubleday and Company, Inc., 1989.
Schinto, Jeanne. *Shadow Bands*. Princeton: Ontario Review Press, 1988.
Sheed, Wilfred. *Transatlantic Blues*. New York: E. P. Dutton, 1978.
Stark, Sharon Sheehe. *A Wrestling Season*. New York: William Morrow and Company, 1987.
Stone, Robert. *Children of Light*. New York: Ballantine Books, 1986.
————. *A Flag for Sunrise*. New York: Ballantine Books, 1981.
Theroux, Paul. *My Secret History*. New York: G. P. Putnam's Sons, 1989.

Toole, John Kennedy. *A Confederacy of Dunces*. Baton Rouge and London: Louisiana State University Press, 1980.
Warren, Patricia Nell. *The Fancy Dancer*. New York: Bantam Books, 1977.
West, Morris. *The Clowns of God*. New York: Bantam Books, 1981.
———. *Lazarus*. New York: St. Martin's Press, 1990.
———. *The Shoes of the Fisherman*. 1963. Reprint. New York: Pocket Books, 1974.
Woiwode, Larry. *Beyond the Bedroom Wall: A Family Album*. New York: Penguin, 1975.
———. *Born Brothers*. New York: Farrar, Straus and Giroux, 1988.

SELECTED SOURCES (NONFICTION)

Bakhtin, M. M. *The Dialogic Imagination*. Edited by Michael Holquist; Translated by Caryl Emerson and Michael Holquist. Austin: University of Texas Press, 1981.
Bausch, William J. *Storytelling: Imagination and Faith*. Mystic, Connecticut: Twenty-Third Publications, 1984.
Bellah, Robert N., et al. *Habits of the Heart: Individualism and Commitment in American Life*. New York: Harper and Row Perennial Library, 1985.
Booth, Wayne. *The Rhetoric of Fiction*. Chicago: University of Chicago Press, 1961.
Daly, Mary. *Beyond God the Father: Toward a Philosophy of Women's Liberation*. Boston: Beacon Press, 1973.
Dolan, Jay. *The American Catholic Experience*. New York: Doubleday and Company, Inc., 1985.
Dulles, Avery, S.J. *A Church to Believe In*. New York: Crossroad Books, 1980.
———. *The Reshaping of Catholicism: Current Challenges in the Theology of Church*. San Francisco: Harper and Row, 1968.
Fiedler, Leslie. *Love and Death in the American Novel*. New York: Stein and Day, 1966.
Fowler, James W. *Stages of Faith: The Psychology of Human Development and the Quest for Meaning*. San Francisco: Harper and Row, 1981.
Frye, Northrop. *Anatomy of Criticism*. Princeton, New Jersey: Princeton University Press, 1957.
———. *Fables of Identity: Studies in Poetic Mythology*. New York: Harcourt, Brace and World, 1963.
Gaughan, Norbert F. *Troubled Catholics: The Lessons of Discontent*. Chicago: The Thomas More Press, 1988.
Gilkey, Langdon. *Catholicism Confronts Modernity*. New York: The Seabury Press, 1975.
Gilligan, Carol. *In a Different Voice: Psychological Theory and Women's Development*. Cambridge and London: Harvard University Press, 1982.
Greeley, Andrew. *Come Blow Your Mind With Me*. New York: Doubleday and Company, Inc., 1971.
———. *The Communal Catholic*. New York: The Seabury Press, 1976.
———. *Confessions of a Parish Priest*. New York: Pocket Books, 1987.
———. *Religion: A Secular Theory*. New York: The Free Press, 1982.
———. *The Religious Imagination*. New York: Sadlier, 1981.
Greeley, Andrew, and Durkin, Mary Greeley. *How To Save the Catholic Church*. New York: Viking, 1984.
Gunn, Giles. *The Culture of Criticism and the Criticism of Culture*. New York and Oxford: Oxford University Press, 1987.

Gustafson, James M. *Protestant and Roman Catholic Ethics: Prospects for Rapprochement.* Chicago and London: University of Chicago Press, 1978.

Halsey, William. *The Survival of American Innocence: Catholicism in an Era of Disillusionment, 1920–1940.* Notre Dame: University of Notre Dame Press, 1980.

Hennesey, James, S.J. *American Catholics: A History of the Roman Catholic Community in the United States.* New York and Oxford: Oxford University Press, 1981.

Herberg, Will. *Protestant–Catholic–Jew: An Essay in American Religious Sociology.* New York: Anchor Books, 1960.

Kavanaugh, James. *A Modern Priest Looks At His Outdated Church.* New York: Trident Press, 1967.

Keane, Philip S., S.S. *Christian Ethics and Imagination.* New York and Ramsey: Paulist Press, 1984.

Kearney, Richard. *The Wake of Imagination: Toward a Postmodern Culture.* Minneapolis: University of Minnesota Press, 1988.

Kellogg, Gene. *The Vital Tradition: The Catholic Novel in a Period of Convergence.* Chicago: Loyola University Press, 1970.

Kennedy, Eugene. *Comfort My People: The Pastoral Presence of the Church.* New York: Sheed and Ward, 1968.

———. *The Now and Future Church.* New York: Doubleday and Company, Inc., 1984.

———. *Tomorrow's Catholics/Yesterday's Church: The Two Cultures of American Catholicism.* New York: Harper and Row, 1988.

Kermode, Frank. *The Art of Telling: Essays on Fiction.* Cambridge: Harvard University Press, 1983.

Kolbenschlag, Madonna. *Kiss Sleeping Beauty Good-Bye: Breaking the Spell of Feminine Myths and Models.* New York: Doubleday and Company, Inc., 1979.

Kuhn, Thomas. *The Structure of Scientific Revolutions.* Chicago: University of Chicago Press, 1970.

Kung, Hans. *Theology for the Third Millennium.* Translated by Peter Heinegg. New York: Doubleday and Company, Inc., 1988.

Lears, Jackson. *No Place for Grace: Antimodernism and the Transformation of American Culture, 1880–1920.* New York: Pantheon, 1981.

Maitland, Sara. *A Map of the New Country: Women and Christianity.* London: Routledge and Kegan Paul, 1983.

Messbarger, Paul R. *Fiction with a Parochial Purpose: Social Uses of American Catholic Literature, 1884–1900.* Boston: Boston University Press, 1971.

Neuhaus, Richard John. *The Catholic Moment: The Paradox of the Church in the Postmodern World.* San Francisco: Harper and Row, 1987.

Novak, Michael. *A New Generation: American and Catholic.* New York: Herder and Herder, 1964.

Occhiogrosso, Peter, ed. *Once a Catholic.* Boston: Houghton Mifflin Company, 1987.

O'Connor, Flannery. *Mystery and Manners.* Edited by Sally and Robert Fitzgerald. New York: Farrar, Straus and Giroux, 1969.

Rank, Hugh D. "The Image of The Priest in American Catholic Fiction, 1945–65." Ph.D. diss., University of Notre Dame, 1969.

Scholes, Robert and Kellogg, Robert. *The Nature of Narrative.* New York: Oxford University Press, 1966.

Shafer, Ingrid. *Eros and the Womanliness of God.* Chicago: Loyola University Press, 1986.

———, ed. *The Incarnate Imagination.* Bowling Green, Ohio: Popular Press, 1988.

Shea, John. *Stories of Faith*. Chicago: The Thomas More Press, 1980.

Sheed, Wilfred. *Frank and Maisie: A Memoir With Parents*. New York: Simon and Schuster, 1985.

Sparr, Arnold J. "From Self-Congratulation to Self-Criticism: Main Currents in American Catholic Fiction, 1900–1960." *U.S. Catholic Historian* 6 (Spring/Summer 1987): 213–30.

Spencer, William David. *Mysterium and Mystery: The Clerical Crime Novel*. Ann Arbor and London: UMI Research Press, 1989.

Tillich, Paul. *A History of Christian Thought*. Edited by Carl E. Braaten. New York: Simon and Schuster, 1968.

Tracy, David. *The Analogical Imagination*. New York: Crossroad Publishing Company, 1981.

Weber, Max. *The Sociology of Religion*. Translated by Ephraim Fischoff. Boston: Beacon Press, 1963.

Wiggins, James B., ed. *Religion As Story*. New York: Harper and Row, 1975.

Williams, Raymond. *Marxism and Literature*. Oxford and New York: Oxford University Press, 1977.

Wills, Gary. *Bare Ruined Choirs*. New York: Doubleday and Company, Inc., 1972.

———. "Catholic Faith and Fiction," *New York Times Book Review* (January 16, 1972), 1.

Winks, Robin W. *Detective Fiction: A Collection of Critical Essays*. Englewood Cliffs, N.J.: Prentice-Hall, Inc., 1980.

Zinsser, William, ed. *Spiritual Quests: The Art and Craft of Religious Writing*. Boston: Houghton Mifflin Company, 1988.

Index

The Actor's Nightmare (Durang), 30–31
Advent for Dying (O'Marie), 80, 81
Alcorn, Alfred, 123–25, 129, 200–203, 207, 208
Angel Fire (Greeley), 59
Angels of September (Greeley), 89
Ascent Into Hell (Greeley), 63
Assault With Intent (Kienzle), 83
Auden, W. H., 73, 128

Bakhtin, M. M., 19, 67 n.9
Baltimore Catechism, 3, 5, 29, 126
Bare Ruined Choirs (Wills), 23 n.8
Be Not Angry (Michelfelder), 49, 50, 52, 53
"Before Sewing One Must Cut" (Schinto), 1, 165–66, 212
Bellah, Robert N., 141, 142
"The Belles of St. Mary's" (Schinto), 113
The Bells of St. Mary's, 3
Benard, Robert, 125–27, 129, 155
Berger, Joseph, 143
Beyond the Bedroom Wall: A Family Album (Woiwode), 156
Biographia Literaria, 10
Bonanno, Margaret Wander, 164
Booth, Wayne, 50

Born Brothers (Woiwode), 156
Byrne, Robert, 142

Cahill, Susan, 127–28, 129, 164
Campbell, Joseph, 13
The Cardinal (Robinson), 47, 48, 50, 66, 122
The Cardinal Sins (Greeley), 19, 48, 58, 59, 62, 65, 122, 123
Carlyle, Thomas, 202
Carroll, James, 54–57, 65, 69 n.34, 87, 128, 135, 136, 162, 163
The Catholic (Plante), 145–47
A Catholic Education (Benard), 125–27, 128, 154, 155
Catholic Girls (Reed), 109–12
Catholicism: aspects of the preconciliar era, 2–4, 6, 14; authority in, 5, 83, 142, 155; and literature, 17–21; liturgical change in, 8, 12–15, 24 n.31; nostalgia for the Golden Age of, 76, 78–79, 95, 102; "on one's own terms," 142–44; triumphalism in, 19, 25 n.52. *See also* Immigrant Church
The Celibates (Kavanaugh), 50–52, 53
Chace, Susan, 156–57
de Chardin, Teilhard, 169, 173
Chesterton, G. K., 72, 76, 81, 90

Children of Light (Stone), 159 n.26
The Clowns of God (West), 137–38
Coleridge, Samuel Taylor, 10, 11
The Company of Women (Gordon), 165, 169, 173–75, 178, 191
A Confederacy of Dunces (Toole), 21, 22
Confessions of a Parish Priest (Greeley), 57, 59, 89
Connolly's Life (McInerny), 98–101, 102, 103, 115
The Country (Plante), 145
Critique of Pure Reason (Kant), 10
Cullinan, Elizabeth, 120–22, 124, 129

Daly, Mary, 164
Death Wears a Red Hat (Kienzle), 84
Deathbed (Kienzle), 83, 87
"Death's at Sea" (Dubus), 149
Deaver, Philip F., 20, 35–37, 43, 163, 207, 208
Detective fiction: Catholicism in, 71–91; development of, 71–73; narrative mode of, 73
Dowling, Father, 71, 74–78, 79, 82, 90, 91 n.19, 92 n.38, 95, 98, 99
Drucker, Peter F., 133–35
Dubus, Andre, 145, 147–51, 157, 163, 208
Due East (Sayers), 194–95, 197–98
Dulles, Avery, S.J., 43, 210, 211
Dunne, John Gregory, 19, 37–39, 43, 74, 137, 207
Durang, Christopher, 28–31, 33, 126, 207

Earth Angels (Cahill), 127–28, 164
Ellis, John Tracy, 7, 14
Ember Days (Bonanno), 164
Eminence (Kienzle), 84
Eros and the Womanliness of God (Shafer), 68 n.19

Faith: imagination and, 12, 16; stages of development, 15–16
The Family (Plante), 145
The Fancy Dancer (Warren), 53, 125
Farragan's Retreat (McHale), 19, 31–33

Father's Day (Kennedy), 103–105, 122
"A Father's Story" (Dubus), 149–50
Fiction. *See* Novel
Fiedler, Leslie, 60, 66, 211
The Final Conclave (Martin), 136–37
Final Payments (Gordon), 20, 169–71, 179
Fixes (Kennedy), 106, 139
A Flag for Sunrise (Stone), 159, n.26
Flythe, Starkey, Jr., 199–200, 207, 208
Fowler, James, 9, 12, 15, 144, 157, 168, 173
Frankenstein (Shelley), 11

Gate of Heaven (McInerny), 97, 133, 135
Gaughan, Bishop Norbert F., 19–20, 43
Gernes, Sonia, 169, 171–72
Gilkey, Langdon, 22, 142, 144, 189, 190
Gilligan, Carol, 163, 169, 173
Girls Forever Brave and True (Rivers), 112–15, 144
Gordon, Mary, 8, 163, 165, 169–71, 173–75, 178–80, 185, 189, 190–92, 193, 198, 210, 211
Greeley, Andrew, 14, 19, 39, 43, 47–48, 50, 57–67, 68 n.19, 69 n.34, 82, 88–90, 101, 107–8, 122, 128, 142, 162, 207, 208, 210
A Green Journey (Hassler), 108–109
Growing Up Female (White), 166

Habits of the Heart: Individualism and Commitment in American Life (Bellah et al.), 141
Halsey, William, 2, 27
Happy Are the Clean of Heart (Greeley), 63–64, 90
Happy Are the Meek (Greeley), 61–62, 63, 88, 90
Happy Are Those Who Thirst for Justice (Greeley), 61, 90
Hassler, Jon, 106–109, 111
Her Death of Cold (McInerny), 71, 74
Herberg, Will, 8
House of Gold (Cullinan), 120–22, 124
Household Saints (Prose), 180–83, 185
How I Got Him Back (Sayers), 195–97, 198

How To Save the Catholic Church (Greeley and Durkin), 142

Imagination: in forming ideas and influencing behavior, 67; and liturgical change, 13–14; in preconciliar Catholicism, 7, 12; throughout history, 9–12
Immigrant Church, 2, 3, 7, 103–105, 112, 122, 124, 134, 139, 155, 192, 210, 211
Individualism: in the culture of the United States, 52, 72, 141; among postconciliar Catholics, 142, 151, 208, 211
Innocence: characteristic of preconciliar Catholicism, 2, 3, 4, 8, 48, 73, 74, 171; postconciliar longing for, 20–21, 66, 73, 76, 78
Intimacy (Chace), 156–57

John XXIII, Pope, 13, 137
Joyce, James, 18, 130, 154

Kant, Emmanuel, 10
Kavanaugh, James, 50–52, 53, 54, 56, 65, 69 n.34, 87, 128
Kennedy, Eugene, 13, 36, 103–6, 111, 114, 116, 120, 122, 139, 142, 143, 208
Kienzle, William X., 82–88, 90, 128
Kill and Tell (Kienzle), 82, 83, 92 n.38
"Killings" (Dubus), 151
Kiss Sleeping Beauty Good-Bye (Kolbenschlag), 168–69
Kolbenschlag, Madonna, 168–69
Kuhn, Thomas, 5, 12, 162, 205
Küng, Hans, 165

Lancelot (Percy), 19
The Last Catholic in America (Powers), 44 n.7
The Last Worthless Evening (Dubus), 149
Lawrence, Kathleen Rockwell, 164
Lazarus (West), 138
Leave of Absence (McInerny), 98, 101–2, 115, 122

Lent: The Slow Fast (Flythe), 199–200, 203, 208
Lord of the Dance (Greeley), 61, 63, 64
Love and Death in the American Novel (Fiedler), 60
Love in the Ruins (Percy), 40

Madonna Red (Carroll), 55–56
Maitland, Sara, 163, 166–68
Marked for Murder (Kienzle), 83
Martin, Malachi, 136–37, 138
Martin, Valerie, 175–76
Maud Gone (Lawrence), 164
McHale, Tom, 19, 31–35, 37, 43, 76
McInerny, Ralph, 74–79, 80, 82, 86, 91, 95–103, 107, 111, 120, 122, 133, 135, 139, 148, 205. *See also* Quill, Monica
Men and Angels (Gordon), 169, 178–80, 185, 191
Michelfelder, William, 49, 50
Mind Over Murder (Kienzle), 83, 85, 86
The Missing Madonna (O'Marie), 81
A Modern Priest Looks At His Outdated Church (Kavanaugh), 50
Mojtabai, A. G., 183–86, 209, 211
Morte D'Urban (Powers), 4, 48, 129–30
Murphy, Walter F., 135–36, 163, 209, 211
My Secret History (Theroux), 152, 153–56, 161, 209

Narrative, theological importance of, 16. *See also* Novel
Neuhaus, Richard John, 189, 205
The Noonday Devil (McInerny), 139
North of Hope (Hassler), 106–8
Novel: development of the genre, 17–18; preconciliar Catholic form of, 17, 18–19, 48, 49; romance in, 48. *See also* Narrative
A Novena for Murder (O'Marie), 79, 80, 81
The Now and Future Church (Kennedy), 105

Occhiogrosso, Peter, 29
O'Connor, Flannery, 12, 15
O'Connor, Sheila, 192–94, 210, 211

O'Malley, Father Chuck, 3, 4, 23 n.8, 106
O'Marie, Sister Carol Anne, 79–81, 86, 91, 164
Once a Catholic (Byrne), 142
Once A Catholic (Occhiogrosso), 29
Ordinary Time (Mojtabai), 183–86, 209, 210
The Other Side (Gordon), 190–92, 198, 202, 203, 210

Paradigm shift, 5, 12, 21–22, 162, 189, 205, 210
Patience of a Saint (Greeley), 89
Percy, Walker, 19, 21, 39–43, 74, 111, 162, 163, 207, 208
Plante, David, 145–47, 148, 151, 157, 163, 208
A Portrait of the Artist as a Young Man (Joyce), 18, 154
Powers, J. F., 4, 48, 54, 129–33, 137, 207, 208
Powers, John R., 29, 44 n.7
"The Presence of Grace" (Powers), 4
"The Pretty Girl" (Dubus), 149, 151
The Priest (McInerny), 95–97, 98, 101
Priests: as authors, 49, 52, 82, 108, 128; as depicted in fiction, 47–57, 71, 73, 74–79, 82–90
Prince of Peace (Carroll), 54–57
Principato (McHale), 19, 31–33
Prose, Francine, 180–83, 185
The Pull of the Earth (Alcorn), 123–25, 200
Puritanism, decline of, 49, 60

Quill, Monica, 78. *See also* McInerny, Ralph
Quindlen, Anna, 113

A Recent Martyr (Martin), 175–76, 178, 183
Red White and Blue (Dunne), 38–39
Reed, Kit, 109–11, 114, 116, 144, 162, 164
Religion: A Secular Theory (Greeley), 67
The Religious Imagination (Greeley), 67
Rite of Spring (Greeley), 89

Rivers, Caryl, 112–16
Robinson, Henry Morton, 47, 48, 50, 66, 122
The Roman Enigma (Murphy), 136
The Rosary Murders (Kienzle), 82, 86

Sacerdotal school, 49, 52, 82, 108, 128
St. Valentine's Night (Greeley), 59
Sartor Resartus, 202
Sayers, Valerie, 194–99, 210, 211
Schinto, Jeanne, 1, 113, 165–66, 212
School Spirit (McHale), 34
Scorsese, Martin, 29, 44 n.6
The Second Coming (Percy), 42
Second Vatican Council. *See* Vatican II
Selected Stories (Dubus), 149
Sentimental Love Ethic, 49–50, 52, 53, 54, 60, 65, 71, 74, 77, 86, 87, 88, 90, 113, 138, 149, 205, 211
Shafer, Ingrid, 68 n.19
Shea, John, 16, 57
Sheed, Frank, 6
Sheed, Wilfred, 37, 74
Sheed & Ward, 6
Sheen, Bishop Fulton J., 4
Shelley, Mary, 11
The Shoes of the Fisherman (West), 137, 138, 139
Silent Retreats (Deaver), 20, 35–37, 208
Sister Mary Ignatius Explains It All For You (Durang), 28–31, 126, 207
"Sorrowful Mysteries" (Dubus), 149
Stages of Faith: The Psychology of Human Development and the Quest for Meaning (Fowler), 9, 12, 15
Stark, Sharon Sheehe, 176–77
Stone, Robert, 159 n.26
The Structure of Scientific Revolutions (Kuhn), 5, 12

The Temptation To Do Good (Drucker), 133–35
The Thanatos Syndrome (Percy), 40–41, 43, 162
Theroux, Paul, 152, 153–56, 157, 161, 162, 164, 209, 211
Thy Brother's Wife (Greeley), 65–66
Tillich, Paul, 152–53, 155, 161, 164, 166, 169, 173

Tokens of Grace (O'Connor), 192–94, 203, 210
Tomorrow's Catholics/Yesterday's Church: The Two Cultures of American Catholicism (Kennedy), 116
Toole, John Kennedy, 21
Tracy, David, 16, 57, 60
Transatlantic Blues (Sheed), 37
True Confessions (Dunne), 19, 38–39

Vatican I, 4, 5
Vatican II, 9, 12, 13, 14, 19, 24 n.31, 43, 48, 66, 73, 119, 124, 133, 141, 192, 202, 207
Vestments (Alcorn), 200–202, 208, 210
The Vicar of Christ (Murphy), 135–36, 209, 210
Virgin and Martyr (Greeley), 63, 64, 88, 89
Virgin Territory (Maitland), 166–68, 169

Virgins (Rivers), 112–15, 144, 210
Voices from the Moon (Dubus), 148–49

Warren, Patricia Nell, 53, 56, 125
The Way to St. Ives (Gernes), 169, 171–73
Weakland, Archbishop Rembert, 206
Weber, Max, 7
West, Morris, 137–38
Wheat That Springeth Green (Powers), 129, 130–33, 208, 210
White, Barbara, 166
Williams, Raymond, 206
Wills, Garry, 23 n.8, 24 n.31
Woiwode, Larry, 152, 156–57, 161, 162, 211
Woman's Movement, 73, 157, 163, 164, 165
The Woods (Plante), 145
A Wrestling Season (Stark), 176–77, 178

About the Author

ANITA GANDOLFO is Associate Professor of English at West Virginia University. She is the author of several articles and co-editor of *The Letters of Lewis Carroll to the House of Macmillan* (1987).